EMPLOYED MOTHERS AND THEIR CHILDREN

REFERENCE BOOKS
ON FAMILY ISSUES
(VOL. 17)

GARLAND REFERENCE LIBRARY
OF SOCIAL SCIENCE
(VOL. 475)

Reference Books
On Family Issues

1. Resources for Early Childhood: *An Annotated Bibliography and Guide for Educators, Librarians, Health Care Professionals, and Parents*, Hannah Nuba Scheffler, General Editor

2. Problems of Early Childhood: *An Annotated Bibliography and Guide* , by Elisabeth S. Hirsch

3. Children and Divorce: *An Annotated Bibliography and Guide*, by Evelyn B. Hausslein

4. Stepfamilies: *A Guide to the Sources and Resources*, by Ellen J. Gruber

5. Experiencing Adolescents: *A Sourcebook for Parents, Teachers, and Teens*, by Richard M. Lerner and Nancy L. Galambos

6. Sex Guides: *Books and Films About Sexuality for Young Adults*, by Patty Campbell

7. Infancy: *A Guide to Research and Resources*, by Hannah Nuba-Scheffler, Deborah Lovitky Sheiman, and Kathleen Pullan Watkins

8. Postpartum Depression: *A Research Guide and International Bibliography*, by Laurence Kruckman and Chris Asmann-Finch

9. Childbirth: *An Annotated Bibliography and Guide*, by Rosemary Cline Diulio

10. Adoption: *An Annotated Bibliography and Guide*, by Lois Ruskai Melina

11. Parent-Child Attachment: *A Guide to Research*, by Kathleen Pullan Watkins

12. Resources for Middle Childhood: *A Source Book*, by Deborah Lovitky Sheiman and Maureen Slonim

13. Children and Adjustment to Divorce: *An Annotated Bibliography*, by Mary M. Nofsinger

14. One-Parent Children, The Growing Minority: *A Research Guide*, by Mary Noel Gouke and Arline McClarty Rollins

15. Child Abuse and Neglect: *An Information and Reference Guide* , by Timothy J. Iverson and Marilyn Segal

16. Adolescent Pregnancy and Parenthood: *An Annotated Guide*, by Ann Creighton-Zollar

17. Employed Mothers and Their Children, by Jacqueline V. Lerner and Nancy L. Galambos

EMPLOYED MOTHERS AND THEIR CHILDREN

Jacqueline V. Lerner
Nancy L. Galambos

GARLAND PUBLISHING, INC. • NEW YORK & LONDON
1991

Library of Congress Cataloging-in-Publication Data

Lerner, Jacqueline V.
    Employed mothers and their children / Jacqueline V. Lerner, Nancy
L. Galambos.
    p. cm. — (Reference books on family issues ; vol. 17)\ m
(Garland reference library of social science ; vol. 475)
    Includes bibliographical references and index.
    ISBN 0-8240-6344-9
    1. Working mothers—United States. 2. Children of working
mothers—United States. 3. Work and family—United States.
I. Galambos, Nancy L. II. Title. III. Series: Reference books on
family issues ; v. 17. IV. Series: Garland reference library of
social science ; v. 475.
HQ759.48.L47   1991
306.874'3—dc20   90–25897
                                                           CIP

Printed on acid-free, 250-year-life paper
Manufactured in the United States of America

To our children . . .

Justin Samuel Lerner
Blair Elizabeth Lerner
Jarrett Maxwell Lerner

and

Gillian Emily Dixon

CONTENTS

Foreword

Balancing Work and Family Life: Why Should It Be So Hard?

Sandra Scarr

In 1969 I wrote a letter to *Science* protesting the unfair treatment of academic mothers, who were expected to work full-time and to be fully responsible for their children's care and welfare.

> Once a female professor has decided to demonstrate her dedication by male rules, the larger community which judges her children's well-being may undermine her in capricious ways. Schools schedule mothers' meetings during teaching hours; the guidance counselor decides that a child with a full employed mother needs "special" attention; ordinary school and neighborhood "scrapes" that her children experience are attributed to mother's neglect. The professional mother is vulnerable because in the eyes of many she is not doing the best for her children. (p. 1260)

At that time, I wanted to work half time and still be considered to be on a serious academic track (as opposed to being on the "Mommy Track," as was suggested for mothers as an alternative to a real career in the late 1980s). My three young children could have used more unhurried attention. And I certainly could have enjoyed life more without the overwhelming pressures of a full-time academic position and a very young family. But it was not to be, unless I was willing to be an ancillary teacher without a serious future in academic psychology.

My problem with balancing work and family life was typical of the problems of most young parents in the United States. More than 20 years later, the same problems have not been solved, even though more than twice as many families are headed by a fully-employed parent or parents. In our society, the problem of work and family responsibilities is framed wrong.

Unlike most of the rest of the world, parents in the United States are saddled with all of the responsibilities of both earning the living for and giving direct care to their offspring. To us, this situation seems "normal," because we are wedded to a highly individualistic ideology about children and families. Each family (especially father) is charged with providing sufficient income for its children's upbringing. Each family (especially mother) must also provide sufficient home management and child care to assure the children's normal development. The dual responsibilities of work and family life, when unsupported by the larger community, is a staggering burden for parents of young children today (Scarr, Phillips, & McCartney, 1989; 1990).

In fact, few other parents in the world are so burdened with the combination of work and family responsibilities. In many parts of the world, extended family members relieve some of the parents' burdens of income production and childrearing. In most industrialized countries, the tax base is used to support parental (maternal) leaves to help parents of very young children to care for their babies, primarily because good infant care is very expensive to provide, and it is cheaper to pay mothers to stay at home with their babies. And community taxes support child care while parents work, thereby insuring that parents do not have to support the full cost of quality care for the next generation.[1]

Individualism and Community Responsibility

Children are the next generation for all of us, regardless of who their parents are. This truism was brought home to middle-aged Americans recently by the calculation of the number of workers who will be available to support their social security benefits when they retire over the next 20 years. Retirees at the end of this century will be supported by only 3 workers (instead of the 5 to 7 workers of the past), and one of those three workers will be a minority, whose

---

[1]In Europe, parents support between 6 and 15 percent of the cost of their children's care, the majority being supported by the tax base. In Canada, parents support 60 to 70 percent of child care costs. In the United States, parents support more than 90 percent of the cost of their children's care.

educational achievements and work skills are currently at risk. This economic lesson reminds mainstream Americans that they have a stake in the educational and occupational competencies of minority and disadvantaged children.

Why should self-interest have to be invoked to compel advantaged members of the society to feel *any* responsibility for disadvantaged children? If those children are the future of our society, why does not everyone recognize that fact, without direct reference to individual self-interest? *Because the United States is the most individualistic society of any modern nation.* In other nations, the larger community assumes some responsibility for the care and support of all young children. Parents are given family allowances to help support children; mothers (and sometimes fathers) are given time off from their jobs to care for infants; and child care is a publicly-supported service for employed parents.

In the United States, public education for children from five (or six) to eighteen years is funded by the larger community, because the battle for community responsibility for education was fought on the economic ground of industries' and businesses' need for a literate and disciplined labor force for skilled work and white-collar jobs. In the nineteenth century and before, education of children was solely a family responsibility. Schools were privately funded for the children of economically advantaged families. Early in this century, most states passed legislation that supported free education through secondary school. Compulsory schooling to age sixteen was considered essential to prepare young people for productive labor, and the community accepted this responsibility. Recently, public education to age eighteen has become the desired norm, at community expense.

Higher education, on the other hand, is still largely a family responsibility, to the near-bankruptcy of many middle-income families. Despite last century's victories in the establishment of public universities and land grant colleges that could make higher education accessible to "everyone," the rising costs of higher education now exceed the economic grasp of large segments of today's population. There is little momentum at the present time to reverse this inequality of opportunity, perhaps, because higher education is seen as largely an economic benefit to the educated individual, for which that individual should pay.

The battle for community responsibility for younger children is now being fought on the same ground as public education for children and adolescents. Everyone must appreciate the fact that the care and normal development of all children are of great importance to all members of the society, even if they are considered only with the success of the workforce that will support their own retirement benefits. Although it is seldom said, the economic and social interests of all members of the society depend on having an educable and socialized population of young children, who can become successful students in the universal public educational system.

The Future

And so, working families today are caught in the battle of community versus individual family responsibility for the support and care of infants and young children. It is unlikely that our national values of individual family responsibility for children will be changed by imploring citizens to become more altruistic toward helpless children whose families cannot or will not assume responsibility for their care and nurturance. But it is likely that economic changes will compel our nation to change its practices in the direction of community responsibility for the support and care of infants and young children whose parents are needed in the labor force.

As European nations realized after World War II, women are needed in the labor force. In fact, if women left the labor force in large numbers, the economy would collapse. The United States would look like East Germany after the exodus of millions of workers to the West. If industries and businesses are to recruit women into the labor force during their child-bearing years, provisions will have to be made for time off to bear and nurse infants without jeopardizing either their incomes or their return to their jobs. If mothers are to return to the work place, child care will have to be made available for their children. The logic is so simple, and well accepted in Europe, yet in the United States these ideas seem revolutionary to many.

Because of changes in the composition of the United States population--we are in an aging nation--and changes in the labor force--there are too few male workers for the jobs to be filled--community-supported steps will have to be taken to assure the labor force enough new workers. The major problem is that there are too few traditional, white male workers to recruit into the labor force in the next 20 years (and thereafter). New labor force entrants will be predominantly women of child-bearing age, whose needs for job-guaranteed, paid parental leaves and child care are obvious, and minority males, whose individual families have often been unable to provide adequately for their care and education. Thus, economic interests will guarantee national attention to the support and care of infants and young children, as long as their mothers are likely to be the best-qualified new workers available. The solution will be uniquely American: Employers, rather than elected officials, will spearhead the future of child care and family support in the United States.

What we need is a larger sense of community responsibility for children, whoever their parents are. If their parents are to be members of the labor force, the future looks bright, for economic reasons, if not for humane ones. Even if their parents are not productive workers, now or ever, their children are part of our future. I hope we will cherish them enough to take moral and social responsibility for all the children of our nation.

In this volume, the authors survey the many problems of employed parents and their children. Documenting problems by sound research and pointing to the future solutions is a valuable contribution to the psychological literature. I urge concerned readers to urge political action on behalf of American families and children.

Bibliography

Scarr, S. (1969). Letter. *Science, 170,* 1260.

Scarr, S., Phillips, D., & McCartney, K. (1989). Working mothers and their families. *American Psychologist, 11,* 1402-1409.

Scarr, S., Phillips, D., & McCartney, K. (1990). Facts, fantasies, and the future of child care in the United States. *Psychological Science, 1*(1), 26-35.

Employed Mothers and
Their Children

Employed Mothers and Their Children: A View of The Issues[1]

Jacqueline V. Lerner and Nancy L. Galambos

The dramatic increase in maternal employment during the last decades has led mothers, fathers, caregivers, scientists, and policymakers to be concerned about the consequences that a mother's work life and work conditions have on children. This increase has also been associated with changes in family roles, forms of child care, and attitudes toward employed mothers. Infants, preschoolers, school-aged children, and adolescents of the 1990s are experiencing the challenges, opportunities, and problems associated with life in families where the mother is a wage earner. Along with the benefits of mother's employment, the management of work and family may place stresses on families, and the solutions are rarely simple (Scarr, 1984).

Fortunately, there has been a burgeoning of research by child and family developmentalists directed toward a common goal: To provide empirical data to enlighten scientists, social policymakers, and citizens about the influence that mothers' work has on children and families. The chapters in this volume present important ideas derived from this body of research and cover issues relevant from infancy through adolescence.

When mothers work outside the home, alternative care for their children is sought. Increasingly, this search involves the placement of infants into day care settings. In Chapter 2, Ross Thompson discusses the controversy surrounding the effects of infant day care on socioemotional development. He presents a careful evaluation of the factual status of infant day care effects. Thompson's major conclusion is that the research evidence is insufficiently clear

---

[1]Jacqueline V. Lerner's work on this chapter was supported in part by NICHD Grant HD23229 to Richard M. and Jacqueline V. Lerner. We would like to express our extreme gratitude to Bobbi Jo Bennett and Teri Charmbury for their help in the preparation of this book.

1

to link early, extended day care to problematic attachment behaviors or to negative psychosocial functioning. Therefore, we cannot always be confident about the accuracy of any broad generalizations regarding effects of infant day care. Researchers and formulators of policy must conduct more thorough and specific investigations of the influences of day care experiences, that is, studies must be conducted to understand how specific structural and/or functional features of the day care experience influence selected aspects of infants immediate and long-term psychosocial development. Thompson has already begun such a program of scholarship by developing new measures of parent-child interaction, ones that are better suited to the experiences of children in day care. Through multimethod strategies we may be better equipped to sort out the ambiguities that have plagued this area of inquiry.

One argument frequently made against mothers returning to work during their child's infancy is that in the long run it may have negative consequences on the infant's cognitive development. In Chapter 3, Lindsay Chase-Lansdale, Robert Michael, and Sonalde Desai use data from the National Longitudinal Survey of Youth (NLSY) to evaluate what is known about the influence of mothers' work on the cognitive development of infants. Specifically, these researchers were interested in the timing and intensity of mothers' employment. A key conclusion pertains to diversity: The influences of mothers' employment patterns on infant cognitive development are not consistent across race, social class, and gender. From the information presented by Thompson in Chapter 2 and by Chase-Lansdale, et al. in Chapter 3, we may conclude that it is necessary to formulate quite differentiated questions for research, intervention, and policy: What sorts of day care experiences influence which particular facets of cognitive development among what sorts of children (e.g., children of what age, sex, race, economic class, regional, and religious characteristics)? Simply, then, both Chapters 2 and 3 lead us to view as unadvisable the formulation of conclusions about day care effects and/or cognitive developmental patterns which do not incorporate a thorough concern with individual differences.

Indeed, when both parents are employed changes can and do occur in the home environment. For example, the income of the family may increase and this may alter various aspects of the home setting. Dual employment may enhance the resources available to purchase basic material goods and luxury items; in turn, dual employment may decrease parental availability to children and, almost always, requires a more tightly scheduled, routinized household. In Chapter 4, Adele Gottfried discusses some of these resource issues confronting children and families wherein both parents work outside the home. The influence of such a home environment on child development is illustrated by presenting data from an eight-year longitudinal study. Gottfried concludes that children develop similarly whether or not their mothers are employed. However, such variables as providing stimulating materials at home, reading to the child, holding high aspirations for the child, father involvement, and a warm family interaction style influence the child's development in positive ways.

Concerns about the influence of maternal employment on children shift somewhat in focus for adolescents. For example, issues such as occupational and educational choices, the mother as a vocational role model, effects of self-care, maternal availability and supervision, and increased maturity demands on adolescents become important during this period (Lerner & Hess, 1988). Chapters 5, 6, and 7 focus on some of these issues. In Chapter 5, Maryse Richards and Elena Duckett review how maternal employment may affect aspects of the adolescent's family relationships and psychosocial functioning. For example, they note that the increasing independence at this age makes maternal employment a much different experience for the adolescent and his or her mother than for the younger child. For instance, since adolescents spend most of their waking hours in school or in peer-related activities, demands on their mothers' time is lessened. Richards and Duckett review the impact of maternal employment on adolescent functioning for the early, middle, and late adolescent periods. Their major conclusion is one that is shared by many others in this field--that maternal employment per se does not affect adolescent functioning. Rather, it is the quality of guidance, family interaction, and social support that are influential to the adolescent's adjustment. As a consequence, these contextual variables merit greater research attention.

In Chapter 6, Nancy Galambos and Jennifer Maggs discuss some specific concomitants of children in self-care--those children not supervised by an adult after school. Because many children spend some portion of their day in self-care, the need for research on this topic is essential. Galambos and Maggs review the existing research and conclude that the context of self-care is an important variable to examine, that is, where, with whom, and in what setting the child is spending out-of-school time. In addition, they present results from their study of self-care children and suggest that self-care children who spend their time in the company of friends might have more opportunity for engaging in problematic behaviors.

In Chapter 7, Todd Bartko and Susan McHale detail a phenomena that has become relevant to adolescents in dual-earner families--that of their participation in household labor. Dual-earner parents tend to expect more household work participation from their children than do single-earner parents, and these increased maturity demands might affect children's functioning. By examining household task performance, Bartko and McHale are able to appraise differences between families in the extent to which demands for help are placed on children. In turn, they evaluate the potential consequences of children's different experiences. In general, these authors conclude that there are gender and earner-status differences in how involved children are in household tasks. Nevertheless, the ways in which this involvement may affect child development is a more complex question. For example, the meaning of children's work in their family, as well as the congruence between the tasks that they and their parents perform are important domains to examine.

Although the focus of this volume is on the implications of mothers' employment, it is useful to include a chapter on a neglected topic in the employment literature, that of the influences of fathers' employment on children. In Chapter 8, Julian Barling discusses the literature in this area. Whereas much research examines the link between mothers' work and family life, the fathers' employment is equally important. After all, the child's experiences are determined by the activities of mothers and fathers. Barling explores the issues of occupational choice and ordinary versus extraordinary job-related absences and how each influences child development. He concludes

that the process of influence functioning here is one in which the
father's job-related experiences affect the quality of father-child
interactions, and father-child interactions, in turn, influence the child's
behavior. In Chapter 9, Alan Hawkins and Ann Crouter discuss the
issues surrounding the dual-earner marriage and present some of the
benefits and liabilities experienced by these couples. They note that
today's dual-earner couples must balance work and family roles, a
challenge which is complicated by the fact that many of these couples
did not have models from which to learn how to successfully manage
multiple roles. As a result, researchers in this area are faced with the
challenge of exploring a largely new domain of scholarship in order
to provide guidance for today's dual-earner couples. The discussion
by Hawkins and Crouter focuses on two important aspects of
dual-earner life: The allocation of domestic labor and the challenge
of coordinating two jobs while finding the time for marital
companionship. Given that societal expectations regarding the
various roles of parent, spouse, and employee are changing rapidly,
these alterations influence the nature of dual-earner family life. As
such, Hawkins and Crouter emphasize the need to prepare young
people for the challenges of contemporary marriage through social
institutions.

Finally, many researchers have argued and have provided
data to show that the link between maternal employment and child
development is not a direct one (Hoffman, 1979). In Chapter 10,
Martha Zaslow, Beth Rabinovich, and Joan Suwalsky detail the
intervening factors, or moderating variables, that seem to influence
the relationship between maternal employment and child
development. Zaslow et al. discuss the variables that help to explain
the circumstances through which maternal employment is related to
child outcomes. These variables include child characteristics (e.g.,
involving gender, age, and temperament), family characteristics (e.g.,
socioeconomic status and culture, maternal role satisfaction, and
father involvement), and characteristics such as mother's employment
circumstances and quality of child care. They examine also
preexisting group differences between families where the mother is
employed and those in which she is not. Zaslow et al. conclude that
the focus of current research is on the circumstances and underlying
processes that give rise to child and family outcomes. Given the

available evidence the authors argue that differences in child outcomes are most closely linked to gender, maternal role satisfaction, and quality of child care. These conclusions present social scientists, employers, and policymakers with a "window" on the sorts of information they need to optimize the lives of children.

This volume also contains a Foreword and an Afterword written by two of the most eminent scholars in maternal employment research, Sandra Scarr and Lois Hoffman. Their contributions underscore the interrelation of the policy and the research issues that are involved in the understanding of employed mothers and their children. Together, their ideas highlight the several issues of scholarship and intervention which remain to be addressed in further attempts to elucidate and enhance the lives of employed women and their families.

In addition to presenting information on research concerning employed mothers and their families, this volume can serve as a source book for parents, pediatricians, and others who would like to know where to turn for information helping them and others deal practically with the problems of being an employed parent. The chapters include an "Annotated Bibliography" which provides a brief description of relevant reference materials. In addition, in most chapters there is a "Sources of Help" section that provides names and addresses of professional organizations and centers, and of other resources for working parents.

In sum, this volume attempts to communicate research findings regarding the links between parental work, families, and child development. We have presented and examined many of the conceptual and important empirical issues that have been brought to the fore in an attempt to understand the complicated lives of today's families. Our hope is that the information and perspectives included in this book will be a basis for advances in research and for more appropriate discussions of policy in this area. We hope as well that parents and the children they rear will be aided in the attempt to integrate the world of work and the world of the family.

Bibliography

Hoffman, L. W. (1984). Maternal employment and the young child. In M. Perlmutter (Ed.), *Parent-child interaction, Minnesota Symposium Series* (Vol. 17, pp. 101-127). Hillsdale, NJ: Erlbaum.

Lerner, J. V., & Hess, L. E. (1988). Maternal employment influences on early adolescent development. In M. E. Levine & E. R. McArarney (Eds.), *Early Adolescent Transitions* (pp. 69-78). Lexington, MA: D.C. Heath & Co.

Scarr, S. (1984). *Mother care, other care.* New York: Basic Books.

Infant Day Care:
Concerns, Controversies, Choices

Ross A. Thompson

The current debate over infant day care crystallizes the tensions that exist between our perceptions of the needs of young children and existing social realities. Infants have traditionally been regarded as malleable and vulnerable, requiring special care so that a foundation for healthy psychological development is firmly established. Thus we have reason to be most concerned about the care they receive. The view that parents can optimally provide this care derives from many sources, including the views of many developmental experts, conservative social philosophy, and the legacy of late nineteenth-century Romanticism. However, the dual-earner family has become normative in the social and economic climate of the last two decades, and the increasing reliance on day care is additionally fostered by the needs of growing cohorts of single parents and adolescent mothers. Yet parents from all these groups are likely to feel ambivalent about leaving their babies in day care. Added to this calculus is the fact that the availability of good quality infant day care is undermined by its high cost (relative to other forms of child care) and underregulation (Young & Zigler, 1986). Perhaps for these reasons, infant day care remains one of the thorniest dilemmas facing social policymakers, practitioners, developmental researchers, and the parents of young children.

Fortunately, students of socioemotional development have devoted considerable attention to the effects of early day care experience on infants and young children, both because of its practical importance as well as to further our understanding of early attachments and social development. Unfortunately, researchers have disagreed strenuously among themselves concerning the interpretation of research results and their practical implications. Their debates--aired publicly as well as in scientific forums--have not only been confusing to parents but also to policymakers who have sought to include scientific data in their ongoing discussions of child care regulation and support. Meanwhile, practitioners who provide infant day care services have received mixed signals concerning the conditions that will make day care a development-enhancing experience for young children.

The purpose of this chapter is to summarize and critically evaluate the arguments underlying this scientific debate and to clarify what we do--and do not--know about the effects of day care on infants. The focus is on the consequences of day care experience for the mother-infant attachment relationship because this has been of greatest popular and scientific concern, and the ways that existing research has been interpreted will be discussed as well as findings from our own laboratory. In doing so, the goal is to advance the policymaking debate by clarifying the contributions of developmental research to this issue, and thus the implications of this research for the dilemma of infant day care will be considered in a concluding comment.

Early Day Care and Attachment

The initial studies of the developmental consequences of day care experience focused on preschoolers, who constitute the largest cohort of children in out-of-home care centers. In general, reviewers of this research have concluded that day care experience poses no risks to healthy socioemotional, personality, and cognitive development, and for some children (such as those from disadvantaged backgrounds) day care experience may enhance their intellectual achievements (see Belsky & Steinberg, 1978; Belsky, Steinberg, & Walker, 1982; Clarke-Stewart & Fein, 1983; Etaugh, 1980; Lamb & Sternberg, in press; Rutter, 1981). On the whole, it appears that it is not experience in day care *per se* but rather its quality--indexed by the ratio of caregivers to children, training and turnover of staff, availability of developmentally-appropriate activities, and related dimensions--that predicts its effects on preschool children. These conclusions have not only been reassuring to parents but also provide reasonably clear guidelines by which qualitative differences between day care settings can be appraised and evaluated.

Consequently, researchers turned their attention to the effects of day care on infants and obtained a more mixed pattern of results. They discovered that the attachments an infant naturally develops with day care staff do not diminish the intensity of the attachment to the mother. The *quality* of infant-mother attachment, however, may be affected by day-care experience. In an early study by Blanchard and Main (1979), for example, one- to two-year-olds in day care exhibited some avoidance of their mothers, although this was attributed to the transitional effects of the onset of day care experience. Nevertheless, early findings such as these (see also Vaughn, Gove, & Egeland, 1980 and Fraiberg, 1977) raised concerns.

These concerns increased dramatically in 1986 with the publication of a research review entitled "Infant Day Care: A Cause for Concern?" by Jay Belsky (1986), a developmental psychologist at the Pennsylvania State University. Belsky had previously written authoritative reviews of day care research and had testified on this topic before Congress on behalf of the American Psychological Association, so his concerns about infant day care attracted immediate attention. Belsky's research review (subsequently elaborated in 1988) led him to three conclusions concerning the consequences of infant day care. First, based on recent studies (including his own), Belsky concluded that *extended* day care experience (i.e., more than 20 hours weekly) beginning *early* in life (i.e., within the first year) constitutes a "risk factor" for the development of insecure infant-parent attachments. Summarizing across the relevant investigations, Belsky (1988) estimated that 41 percent of the infants with early and extended day care experience became insecurely attached, compared with 26 percent in comparison groups without this experience. (In her own review of these and other studies, Clarke-Stewart [1988, 1989] concluded that the difference between the two groups is narrower--37 percent vs. 29 percent--but still a statistically significant difference.) Second, Belsky (1986, 1988) argued that current research findings indicate also that early day care experience contributes to the development of heightened aggressiveness and noncompliance in preschoolers (contrary to the conclusions of other reviews noted above). According to Belsky, such a finding is "strikingly consistent" with the formulations of attachment theory, which emphasizes that insecure attachments in infancy have a formative and deleterious effect on later personality development. Thus the insecurity engendered by early, extended day care experience may have long-term consequences leading to maladaptive social behavior in the preschool years. Third, Belsky noted that the effects of early and extended day care experience may be moderated, to some extent, by the quality and stability of child care, child characteristics (e.g., gender, temperament), and attributes of the mother and the family as a whole.

Belsky's (1986, 1988) provocative conclusions attracted considerable attention. One reason is that his conclusions accord with many people's intuitive, commonsense concerns about the effects of day care experience in infancy, as well as the worries of young parents. It is reasonable, in other words, to expect that the daily experience of separation from mother at a day care center would tax a young baby's coping capacities and threaten the child's developing sense of trust in the parent, with insecurity in their attachment relationship the result. In addition, Belsky's arguments appeared in highly visible popular as well as professional forums and were portrayed in stark terms (e.g., "Is Day Care Bad for Babies?" in *Time* magazine, June 22, 1987). In the context of ongoing Congressional consideration of child care and parental leave legislation, these arguments were immediately enlisted into the public policy debate. Finally, Belsky's authority as a recognized and respected developmental researcher with expertise in day care issues added credence to his views.

Belsky's conclusions provoked an immediate response from diverse audiences. In the issue immediately following the one in which his concerns initially were published, a group of prominent day care researchers wrote a rebuttal entitled "Selective Review of Infant Day Care Research: A Cause for Concern!" (Phillips, McCartney, Scarr, & Howes, 1987). They argued that Belsky's review was incomplete and misinterpretive, leading to conclusions that were premature at best but misleading at worst. Shortly afterward, the National Center for Clinical Infant Programs (in whose periodical, *Zero to Three,* Belsky's research review had first appeared) organized a convention of prominent infant day care researchers and developmental experts to seek concensus on the state of existing knowledge and future research needs concerning the effects of day care. Members of this "summit meeting" agreed only that high quality infant day care does not threaten healthy socioemotional development and on the need for improved child-care options for young families, and they outlined a comprehensive (and ambitious) research agenda (NCCIP, 1988; Szanton, 1989). Following this, the National Institute for Child Health and Human Development (NICHD) issued a call for cooperative research proposals based on this agenda that would involve a consortium of day care researchers conducting coordinated projects at independent sites to yield stronger, more comprehensive, and better generalizable findings concerning day care effects on infants. These projects are currently in progress. The NICHD initiative was timely because Belsky's concerns had already found their way into Congressional debate on the Act for Better Child Care, a comprehensive child care plan strongly supported by many child advocates.

It is rare to find academic debate concerning policy issues provoking such an immediate response from policymakers, but Belsky's concerns touched a nerve in both advocates and opponents of early day care. It is thus reasonable to ask: What is the strength of the evidence underlying his concerns?

Infant Day Care and Attachment Theory

In one sense, the strong reaction to Belsky's research review is surprising given that many of his conclusions were not new. Researchers had long known that infants with substantial out-of-home caregiving experience tend to maintain greater distance from their mothers and sometimes behave avoidantly (e.g., Clarke-Stewart & Fein, 1983; but see McCartney & Phillips, 1988 for a different view). They have also been aware that day care experience is associated with a broader range of negative (as well as positive) social behaviors in preschoolers (e.g., Etaugh, 1980; Rutter, 1981). Not surprisingly, these findings have been interpreted in a variety of ways.

What *was* new and significant in Belsky's review was his effort to link these findings developmentally and to interpret their meaning in light of attachment theory (Ainsworth, Blehar, Waters, & Wall, 1978; Bowlby, 1969). Attachment theory confers special meaning to these day care studies in at least two ways. First, by portraying the avoidant behavior of some day care infants as indicating an insecure infant-mother bond, attachment theory galvanizes concern about the detrimental effects of day care experience. A one-year-old who moves away from the mother, after all, can easily be regarded as precociously independent or even developmentally advanced (cf. Clarke-Stewart, 1988), but few can feel sanguine if this behavior is viewed as reflecting an insecurely-avoidant attachment relationship. Second, by postulating a theoretical link between insecure attachment in infancy and antisocial behavior in the preschool years, attachment theory heightens concerns about the effects of early day care by underscoring its long-term deleterious consequences. This is consistent not only with theoretical models of the formative effects of early experiences, but with popular notions also (e.g., "as the twig is bent . . .").

Attachment theory also influenced Belsky's review of the infant day care research by guiding his selection of the methodological tools for assessing its effects on infant-mother attachment. The studies that are the focus of his review each used the Strange Situation, a 21-minute laboratory procedure that has become the standard assessment of attachment security in infancy (see Ainsworth et al., 1978; Lamb, Thompson, Gardner, & Charnov, 1985). It is designed to heighten the baby's need for the mother on the assumption that this is when the security of attachment is most clearly revealed, and thus the procedure includes brief (3-minute) episodes during which an unfamiliar adult plays with the child and other episodes in which the mother is absent. Researchers devote particular attention to the episodes in which mother and baby are reunited because the child's behavior then is thought to be most revealing of her trust in this relationship. Primarily on this basis, infants are deemed either securely attached or are instead assigned to one of three insecurely-attached classifications: insecure-avoidant, insecure-resistant, or insecure-disorganized. The heightened insecurity observed among infants with early, extended day care experience is primarily due to a higher proportion of infants deemed insecure-avoidant, who reunite with mothers by either greeting them in a delayed, subdued, or distinctly avoidant fashion or by mingling ignoring or avoidant behavior with their positive reunion greetings.

The Strange Situation is not the only available method for assessing the effects of day care experience on infant-parent relationships, of course, and there are advantages and disadvantages in researchers' reliance on a single, standard assessment procedure in studies of infant-mother attachment, especially when the effects of day care experience are considered. On one hand, this permits rare methodological consistency across diverse studies, enabling reviewers like Belsky to critically compare results using the same procedure with different samples. Indeed, reviewers can even combine results across studies to derive more confident conclusions from the aggregate sample, as Belsky (1988) has done.

On the other hand, reliance on a single procedure is risky if the procedure is subject to biasing influences that can contribute to misleading conclusions. The baby's prior experiences with separations or strangers, for example, could influence his Strange Situation behavior, especially if the baby's experiential history is markedly different from the experience of babies for whom the procedure was designed. The Strange Situation was originally designed to provide a moderately stressful experience (thus incrementing the baby's need for the mother) for middle-class infants who were nearly exclusively home reared (only two mothers worked part time in the original sample; see Ainsworth & Bell, 1969). Most one-year-olds with this background have had some experience with brief separations and unfamiliar adults but nevertheless find these experiences somewhat stressful. Cross-cultural studies using the Strange Situation have found, however, that when infants have had very little prior experience with separation from mother (as in Japan) or with strangers (as on traditional Israeli Kibbutzim), they are markedly distressed by the Strange Situation episodes and show high rates of insecure attachment as a consequence (see Lamb et al., 1985, for a review). Most commentators have concluded, moreover, that the apparent insecurity derives from the unsuitability of the Strange Situation as an assessment for infants from these backgrounds. In other words, when the child's experiential history departs significantly from the typical experiences of most home-reared American infants, their Strange Situation behavior may not mean the same thing, and this procedure may not provide a valid assessment of the security of attachment.

This reasoning may apply also to comparisons of the Strange Situation behavior of day care and exclusively home-reared infants. Infants with early and extended day care experience differ from exclusively home-reared infants in precisely those ways that cross-cultural researchers find significant: they have much greater prior experience with strangers, and regularly witness mother's departure. To be sure, these recurring experiences could be insecurity-inducing and contribute to avoidant attachments. But alternatively, the avoidant behavior of day care infants may index their familiarity with these experiences in the laboratory, and their avoidance may reflect less immediate need for the mother's support while they are playing. It will be difficult to determine which of these alternative interpretations is correct until developmentalists complete further research assessing the meaning of the Strange Situation behavior of infants with substantial day care experience. Current efforts to defend the use of the Strange Situation in efforts to determine the effects of day care rely extensively on internal analyses of existing small-sample studies that do not provide clear conclusions concerning the interpretation of Strange Situation behavior (cf. Belsky, in press). Clearly, more extensive research is needed; our own initial efforts in this direction are reported later in this chapter.

Evaluating the Research Evidence

There are other reasons for regarding critically the proposed links between early, extended day care experience, insecure attachment, and social maladaptation in the preschool years.

Varieties of Avoidance. As suggested above, behaviors reflecting insecurity--including avoidance--may not always index an insecure attachment. Infants may act avoidantly because they are unstressed by the Strange Situation procedure, or because of child-rearing practices that foster independence, or because of the infant's preferred style of social interaction (e.g., using distal rather than proximal interactive modes), or because of an insecure attachment. At present, however, it is difficult to distinguish the various bases of avoidance within this procedure because of the limited number of predictive studies with infants from diverse rearing and experiential backgrounds. It is noteworthy, however, that even many infants who are deemed securely attached in the Strange Situation exhibit avoidant behavior, differing from insecurely-attached infants primarily in its diminished intensity and persistence. It thus remains to be discovered whether infants with early, extensive day care experience manifest a secure attachment using a different behavioral repertoire in the Strange Situation compared with exclusively home-reared infants and whether maintaining distance from the caregiver is part of that repertoire.

Magnitude of Influence. Although the proportions of insecurely-attached infants in day care and exclusively home-reared samples are sufficiently different to be statistically significant, the difference is not large (a difference of 15 percent according to Belsky [1988]; 8 percent according to Clarke-Stewart [1988; 1989]). Furthermore, the rate of insecurity in day care samples is also not strikingly different from that of other normative estimates.[1] Summarizing attachment studies from around the world, for example, van IJzendoorn and Kroonenberg (1988) reported that an average of 35 percent of infants were deemed insecurely attached, compared with 37 percent to 42 percent in samples with early, extensive day care experience. Moreover, when one reviewer compared the patterns of attachment found in several studies of infant day care (Barglow, Vaughn, & Molitor, 1987; Belsky & Rovine, 1988) with the normative attachment patterns identified by the originators of the Strange Situation procedure (Ainsworth et al., 1978), no significant differences were detected (Thompson, 1988). The same was true when data from a pooled aggregate of day care studies surveyed by Belsky were compared with these normative attachment patterns. Thus while infants with substantial day care experience show a somewhat higher tendency toward avoidant attachment, this difference is not substantial enough to mark their overall pattern of attachments as significantly different from the norm (see also McCartney & Phillips, 1988).

In view of the fact that the large majority of infants in day care are securely attached, it seems inappropriate to regard early,

---

[1]These estimates are based on samples, however, which may have included some infants with day care experience.

extended day care experience as a "risk factor"[2] for the development of insecure attachment. (Indeed, if day care experience is such a risk, these data attest to the remarkable resiliency of infants in such settings [cf. Richters & Zahn-Waxler, 1988].) In fact, day care is associated with only a relatively minor increment in the likelihood of an insecure attachment developing between mother and baby--an increment which, as argued later, should not figure prominently in the public policy debate concerning infant day care.

Confounding Differences. Families who enroll their infants in day care differ in many ways, of course, from those who rear infants exclusively at home. In addition to the use of out-of-home care, they differ also in the domestic roles and responsibilities of each parent, the opportunities and contexts for parent-infant interaction, the juggling of domestic and employment responsibilities by parents, maternal feelings and attitudes about her role, and a variety of other ways. Each of these could influence the infant's Strange Situation behavior through patterns of care at home that are independent of the infant's experiences in day care (as Belsky [1986, 1988] has noted). As a consequence, the "effects" of early, extended day care experience may derive instead from the other ways that these families differ from those who rear their children exclusively at home.

Indeed, these family influences provide a good beginning for examining the various kinds of avoidant behavior exhibited by day care infants in the Strange Situation. If Gamble and Zigler (1986) are correct in hypothesizing that early day care experience has negative consequences for attachment only in the context of other stressors on the baby, then parental job demands, marital conflict, time pressures, and other family stressors may--in tandem with the

---

[2]The term "risk factor" carries various connotative meanings. In studies of developmental psychopathology, for example, it denotes a meaningful increment in the probability of a maladaptive developmental outcome, even though most persons experiencing this risk may develop normally (Sroufe, 1988). Even though this use of the term "risk factor" may be criticized when day care studies are summarized, the term is even less appropriate in light of popular connotations of the term as deterministic and highly probable of psychosocial difficulty. This is one example of how misunderstandings may arise when researchers use terms in popular forums that carry variant scientific and popular meanings (Thompson, 1989).

demands of early, extended day care experience--heighten the probability of insecure-avoidant attachments in the dual-earner family. Conversely, when these stressors are minimal, the demands of day care experience are not as significant, and avoidant behavior in the Strange Situation may have alternative origins. At present, however, developmental theorists lack the research findings necessary for clarifying the interactive influences of day care experience, quality of home care, and other family processes on the security of infant-parent attachment. When these findings are obtained, varieties of avoidance in the Strange Situation may become clearer.

Later Psychosocial Development. One reason that Belsky's review raised such concern is his argument that early, extended day care experience has not only immediate but also long-term consequences. That is, in concluding from a review of research that preschoolers enrolled early in day care exhibit heightened aggressiveness and noncompliance, Belsky noted that such a finding is consistent with other research indicating that secure or insecure attachments in infancy foreshadow later differences in social and personality functioning. In his portrayal, therefore, early and extended day care experience heightens the risk of insecure attachment in infancy *and* later social maladaptation in the preschool years.

There are several reasons for concluding that this argument may be overstated. First, research findings do not support the view that infantile attachments have such a formative influence on later personality functioning. In our own review of this research (Lamb et al., 1985; Thompson, in press; Thompson & Lamb, 1986), we concluded that when early attachment foreshadowed later social and personality development, it was primarily because children experienced consistent caregiving influences that fostered either healthy or problematic social behavior at each age. Some children experienced early sensitive care that led to a secure attachment and, over time, the same sensitive parental care fostered prosocial, empathic responding in children as preschoolers. Other children experienced less helpful, responsive care that may have contributed to an insecure attachment in infancy and, later, to problematic social behavior as preschoolers. In short, we concluded that it is primarily the quality and consistency of care over time that predicts psychosocial development not the formative influence of a secure or insecure attachment in infancy. And when caregiving conditions change, attachment does not predict later sociopersonality functioning very well. Contemporary caregiving influences are more important than early influences, it seems, in shaping a young child's personality (Thompson, in press).

Since infants in day care are especially likely to experience changes in their conditions of care over time (e.g., transitions to new caregivers or new care arrangements, turnovers of substitute caregivers, etc.), predicting their psychosocial development as preschoolers on the basis of attachment security would appear to be especially difficult, based on the analysis above. And, indeed, a careful review of the research evidence indicates that the link between day care experience and later aggression/noncompliance is not a reliable one; many of these negative behaviors diminish and disappear over time, and there are important associations between later behavior and the *quality* of care the child experiences (Belsky, 1988; Clarke-Stewart, 1988; Clarke-Stewart & Fein, 1983; Lamb & Sternberg, in press; Rutter, 1981). This makes sense if we assume that preschoolers' behavior is affected not only by early experiences of care (leading to a secure or insecure attachment) but primarily by subsequent caregiving experiences that may maintain or change these early influences.

Finally, it should be noted that compared with exclusively home-reared children, preschoolers in day care exhibit heightened *prosocial* as well as antisocial behavior, including higher scores on indices of sociability and social competence (Belsky, 1988; Clarke-Stewart, 1988; Gamble & Zigler, 1986; Phillips et al., 1987; Rutter, 1981). In other words, experience in day care equips preschoolers with a broader repertoire of social skills that can be enlisted for either friendly sociability or dominant assertiveness. This should not be surprising, given that day care experience provides a valuable arena for the development of a versatile social repertoire in young children. It seems unfair, however, to attribute only aggressive, noncompliant behavior to the effects of an early insecure attachment in day care children and not to likewise regard their later prosocial behavior as its consequence also. The latter association is, of course, inconsistent with theoretical expectations, but it maintains better fidelity to the empirical picture.

Conclusion. Although there is value to the efforts of scientists to draw collegial attention to emerging research findings that challenge current assumptions, considerable caution is necessary when this occurs in the context of a highly visible public policy debate. Caution is necessary because avowedly preliminary conclusions from research are likely to become prematurely enlisted into the debate and provide a false perception of scientific authority for one argument or another. This can harm both science and policymaking: the latter because it potentially skews the debate in inappropriate ways, the former because scientific credibility is undermined when poorly-substantiated conclusions assume such influence (cf. Gardner, Scherer, & Tester, 1989).

Although the preceding review of research suggests that concerns about the deleterious effects of early, extended day care experience on attachment and later psychosocial functioning are probably unfounded, it is also important to acknowledge that the evidence is insufficiently clear to warrant *any* confident conclusions about the effects of infant day care. In other words, those who conclude that existing research provides no basis for concern would be as guilty of reaching premature conclusions from this evidence as those who argue that infant day care is a cause for concern. In addition to the research reviewed earlier, we are wise to think carefully and cautiously about the effects of infant care because of the limitations experienced by many young families in the cost of care they can afford, the generally high turnover of child care workers, widespread social perceptions that caring for young children is essentially "unskilled" labor, and the very limited regulatory standards and enforcement processes used to ensure minimal health and safety requirements. In fact, however, there is also much that we do *not* know concerning its developmental consequences. We do not know clearly, for example, how the effects of early, extended day care experience are qualified by the interaction of family influences, child characteristics, and the nature of out-of-home care. We have few insights for interpreting the meaning of the Strange Situation behavior of day care infants, and the need for alternative (ecologically as well as developmentally) appropriate attachment assessments is paramount. We also need better studies of the ecology of the day care environment and its immediate and long-term effects on infants. In short, a considerable research agenda remains (see Weinraub, Jaeger, & Hoffman, 1988, for a good example of the kind of research that is needed).

In concluding, however, that researchers do not yet have the evidence to offer substantive conclusions concerning infant day care and attachment--and that this scientific debate has been prematurely enlisted into public policy discussions--I am not arguing that researchers have nothing to contribute to policy questions concerning infant day care. One conclusion that derives considerable support from existing research is that the *quality* of day care has a considerable impact on infants' developmental outcomes (e.g., Lamb & Sternberg, in press; McCartney, Scarr, Phillips, Grajek, & Schwarz, 1982; NCCIP, 1988; Rutter, 1981): infants thrive in settings that are safe and provide age-appropriate toys and activities, include well-trained, sensitive caregivers with a favorable adult-child ratio and provide stability of staff, settings, and peers (see Howes, 1983). Thus, in a manner similar to findings from studies with preschoolers, the influence of qualitative variations in infant day care settings is much greater than the impact of the out-of-home care experience *per se*, and this has significant implications for policy efforts to ensure good quality care for infants and young children.

This leaves unresolved, however, the question of how day care affects the developing infant-mother attachment bond. Progress in addressing this question will likely occur as researchers develop more sensitive methodological tools for appraising parent-child relationships in relation to the ecology of infant day care. The next section reports some preliminary efforts completed recently in our own lab.

Reunion Behavior in Day Care

Although there are reasons for questioning whether the Strange Situation behavior of infants with day care experience can be interpreted comparably to exclusively home-reared babies, the overall strategy of the Strange Situation may nevertheless remain informative. When infants are moderately stressed in the context of separation from their caregivers, reunion behavior may sensitively index the expectations and emotions associated with a secure or insecure parent-child relationship. This is likely to be true also of children with day care experience, and my students and I have sought to apply this view in studying the naturally-occurring reunions between parents and children at day care.

There are several reasons that reunion behavior in day care may be a potentially useful index of the parent-child relationship. The end-of-day reunion is an important transition in the child's daily experience and forms the bridge between the day care and home environments. Consequently, children's reunion greetings may reflect their affective responses to this transition and their expectations of what will occur at home. Positive greetings may reflect pleasure at the parent's return, an eagerness to go home, and confidence confirmed that the parent would return for them. On the other hand, more negative reunions may reflect a different set of expectations: reluctance to return home, uncertainty about the parent's responsiveness or helpfulness, or anger, distress, or anxiety at having to leave day care. Moreover, we have found that the quality of parent-child reunions at day care is determined primarily by the child's behavior because parents usually arrive in a "responsive mode," waiting to act on signals from the child (see also Blurton-Jones & Leach, 1972). Finally, at the end of the day young children are usually tired, somewhat hungry, and have been apart from parents for a considerable duration, and their reunion greetings may thus index their needs and expectations for the parent's support under mildly stressful circumstances. For these reasons, day care reunions may usefully index variations in parent-child relationships for children with substantial day care experience.

However, several questions must be addressed in assessing the sensitivity and usefulness of children's reunion responses in day care. One concerns their reliability. Many factors militate against the likelihood that reunion responses index consistent features of parent-child interaction. Children's reunion behavior in day care is

likely to be affected, for example, by transient situational influences--
such as whether the child was engaged in a favorite activity at the
time of the parent's arrival--as well as by short-term moods and other
influences. Because existing studies of reunion behavior in day care
seldom assessed reunions on more than one occasion, the first goal
of our research was to determine whether children's reunion
responses were, in fact, consistent over time. Demonstrating that
they are consistent would not substantiate their validity as indices of
parent-child relationships, but it would add credence to this view.
Our second goal was to identify the range and variability of the
reunion responses of children in day care. Because earlier studies of
reunions in day care tended to assess a rather limited range of
reunion greetings (based primarily on laboratory studies of parent-
infant attachment), we began our research with extensive naturalistic
observations at day care as well as conversations with day care
practitioners to tap the more diverse reunion repertoire exhibited by
children with substantial day care experience (suggested also by the
findings of Blurton-Jones and Leach [1972] and Field, Gewirtz, Cohn,
Garcia, Greenberg, & Collins [1984]). Third, and finally, we have
also sought to understand whether these reunion greetings are
systematically associated with other measures of the parent-child
relationship, to provide preliminary validity data concerning their use
in studies of the effects of day care experience.

We began our research with studies of young preschoolers
(i.e., two-and-one-half to four years old) before studying infants
because of the greater complexity and sophistication of the older
child's reunion behavior. In our first study (Sheldon, Thompson, &
Earl, 1985), 22 preschoolers were observed at the end of the day on
six occasions over a seven-week period. Their reunion responses
were appraised using a measure entailing 15 mutually-exclusive
categories of behavioral responses varying in their affective tone (see
Table 1). We focused on the child's *initial* reunion response (i.e., the
first response to the parent after the child was aware of the parent's
arrival) because this behavior was most likely to index the child's
initial reactions and expectations when the parent's arrival was most
salient and before parental or teacher reactions occurred, and these
responses could be rated reliably by highly-trained observers.

TABLE 1
Preschool Reunion Behavior Measure

Category name	Symbol	Behavioral description
I Acting out	AO	Child uses negative attention-getting devices, such as hitting other children, disobeying school rules, etc.
II Resistant 1 Passive	RP	Child exhibits delayed compliance, with little eye contact or physical or verbal contact with the parent.
2 Active	RA	Verbal or physical abuse directed at the parent, such as temper tantrums, crying, "I don't want to go!"
III Active avoidant	AA	Child runs away, hides, avoids reunion with parent.
IV Extortion	EX	Child seeks bribery in return for co-operation (e.g. taking the center's toy, "What will you give me?" etc.).
V Regression	RG	Child displays developmentally regressed behavior (e.g. wets pants, "can't walk", goes limp, can't do self-help skills such as tying shoes or putting on coat).
VI Passive avoidant	PA	Child ignores parent's entrance and greeting, but may make brief eye contact.
VII Clinging	CL	Child hangs on tightly to parent's leg, arm, etc. without positive facial expression.
VIII Hurried departure	HD	Child attempts by physical or verbal means to rush the parent out of the center.
IX Delayed departure	DD	Child makes a non-negative request of the parent for time to complete an activity.
X Showing off	SO	Child displays positive attention-getting behaviors, such as demonstrating physical talents, showing parent what he or she has made, etc.
XI Distal greeting	DG	Child makes eye contact and offers a brief verbal greeting, but offers no physical contact or approach.
XII Involves parent	IP	Child involves parent in an interactive activity such as a game.

TABLE 1

(Continued)

Category name	Symbol	Behavioral description
XIII Proximal greeting		
1 With close physical contact	PP	Child approaches parent to hug or kiss; picked up or asks to be picked up.
2 Without close physical contact	PG	Same as above, except that physical contact is limited (e.g. hand-holding).

Source: E. L. Sheldon, R. A. Thompson, & G. B. Earl (1985). Preschoolers' reunion responses in day care. *Journal of Social and Personal Relationships*. Copyright © 1989 by Sage Publications. Reprinted by permission.

We discovered that these young preschoolers were highly consistent in their reunion responses over this seven-week period: on this 15-category measure, they showed the same behavior on three of six observations on average. Considering the range of behaviors exhibited by a child during any particular reunion episode, this degree of consistency in initial greeting is impressive. Moreover, when response categories were clustered by their underlying emotional tone (positive, neutral, or negative), children showed the same response 72 percent of the time. Thus variability in specific reunion behaviors may nevertheless reflect a consistent emotional tone toward the parent. There were no differences in the quality or consistency of reunion responses according to the child's gender or whether mother or father retrieved them. On the whole, the large majority of these reunion greetings were either positive (50 percent) or ambivalent/neutral (21 percent) in emotional tone, and only 29 percent of children's reunion responses were clearly negative in quality. Thus young preschoolers do not seem to exhibit considerable avoidance or insecurity in their greetings to parents at the end of the day: most are glad to see their parents.

In a follow-up study (Sheldon, 1986) these findings were replicated and extended. Forty-eight young preschoolers were observed at day care on six occasions over a seven-week period, and again they showed significant consistency in their specific reunion behavior and underlying affective tone. In addition, parents and children were observed in an interactive laboratory session on one occasion during this period to independently assess aspects of the parent-child relationship. The laboratory procedure was designed to index everyday social situations varying in structure, demands, and stress for parent and child, and included episodes of free play, a parental teaching task, a frustrating "barrier box" task in which children could enlist parental help, and a joint clean-up task. Observational measures of the child's social and emotional reactions to the parent were derived from videotapes of this session, and our analyses indicated that they were moderately associated with the child's characteristic reunion response in day care. That is, especially when we compared children whose day care reunions were either most negative or most positive, children behaved in the laboratory in a manner that was comparable to their behavior in day care when reuniting with the parent. Children whose reunions were affectively most negative tended to respond to the parent in the laboratory with more negative, resistant behavior compared to children most characterized by emotionally positive reunion responses. These findings thus provided modest support for the view that the everyday reunion responses of children in day care may reflect broader aspects of the parent-child relationship.

In our most recent work we have studied 30 one- to two-year-old infants during their naturally-occurring reunions with parents at day care (Corkill, Sternitzke, & Thompson, 1990). During weekly observations over a six-week period, detailed five-point ratings of the baby's emotional response, facial expression, speed of approach, eye contact, and verbal behavior were conducted on each occasion. There were no significant changes on any of these measures across the six observations and infants received the same score between 60 percent and 70 percent of the time on each measure, contributing to our emerging picture of significant consistency in infants' reunion behavior over time. Moreover, there was a modest association between these reunion behaviors and children's Strange Situation behavior suggesting--consistent with the earlier studies--that the affective quality of day care reunion behavior is also reflected in the laboratory, and we are currently examining this association in greater detail.

Taken together, these research results provide encouragement for the development of new measures of parent-child interaction that are better-suited to the normative ecology and experiences of children in day care. Such measures--to be used convergently with more conventional attachment indices in a multimethod strategy--promise to index aspects of parent-child interaction that are most salient to children in day care settings (just as the Strange Situation was designed in light of the typical experiences of home-reared, middle-class children), and should bring us closer to elucidating the effects of early, extended day care experience on infant-parent attachment. Until then, however, developmental researchers still face the thorny question of how they can best inform public policymaking concerning infant day care, and thus we turn to a concluding consideration of policy implications of the research in this area.

Infant Day Care Research and Public Policy

This discussion has focused on the relationship between public values and concerns about infant day care, the scientific debate concerning its effects, and the dilemmas of legal policymakers (as well as of practitioners and parents) because of their significant, and catalytic, mutual influences. Day care researchers cannot help but be influenced, for example, by cultural values concerning infant care as well as by their own child-rearing choices as they seek to inform the policymaking discussion. This complex relationship raises important questions about how developmental researchers can, and should, contribute to the broader policy debate on issues related to their research: When can researchers offer *authoritative* recommendations, and when must they acknowledge their ignorance (and their biases)? With respect to the developmental effects of infant day care, this question is further complicated by the heated quality of public discussions of day care which derives from the links between this issue and concerns about maternal and feminine roles, the perceived needs of children, and the economics of the family. Opponents of infant day care commonly characterize themselves as defenders of children's interests, while those advocating public support of day care services regard themselves as advocates for women and the family.

As Lindblom and Cohen (1979) have pointed out, the degree to which social research is perceived as authoritative by policymakers depends on several features of its relationship to social values and public problems. On one hand, research findings reach an appreciative public audience when they confirm (rather than contradict) deeply-held, commonsense views of human behavior and add scientific credibility to them. With respect to the debate over infant day care, developmental researchers who argue that the effects of early day care are either negative or negligible will be regarded as authoritative by different parties to this debate. This creates problems for the accurate dissemination of research findings, partly because existing studies do not reliably lend themselves to such simple, straightforward conclusions. As suggested earlier, for example, early day care experience may be detrimental when it occurs in tandem with other family stressors on the child but not otherwise. Because popular audiences are not interested in more complex portrayals of research findings, however, researchers are tempted to simplify their conclusions to reach this popular (and appreciative) audience. On the other hand, Lindblom and Cohen note that the perceived authority of social research depends also on its capacity to provide thoughtful perspectives on public problems that can lead toward insightful solutions. When research findings clarify rather than obfuscate policy alternatives, Lindblom and Cohen argue that they become "usable knowledge" to the public and its policymakers.

What "usable knowledge" has emerged out of the scientific debate concerning infant day care that can assume an authoritative role in the public debate? On one hand, neither Belsky nor his critics would advocate restrictions on the availability of infant day care services because the research evidence is too weak and the disutility of such a recommendation too great to support this view. On the other hand, there exists considerable consensus among researchers concerning the characteristics of good quality infant day care and its developmental benefits, as noted earlier. Concerted advocacy efforts to promote the widespread availability--and affordability--of good quality infant day care would seem to be a worthwhile effort by developmental researchers and other child advocates.

Unfortunately, current advocacy efforts are not sufficiently well-informed by policymaking considerations to successfully transform these research insights into "usable knowledge." Beyond vague recommendations that policies concerning paid (or unpaid) parental leave following the baby's birth be enacted, or that federal or state governments enforce quality standards in infant day care centers, or that alternative care options should be fostered by government efforts, developmental researchers have provided few ideas that clarify feasible policy alternatives deriving from developmental research in this area. Although the importance of fostering optimal early development is self-evident to most child advocates, the translation of this admirable goal into day care policy recommendations requires tackling thorny issues of public values and policy alternatives. For example, although more than half the mothers of infants are in the labor force (Szanton, 1989), a very small minority of their offspring are in day care centers. By contrast, the large majority of their babies receive care in family homes with babysitters, relatives, friends or neighbors (Belsky, 1986). Perhaps this can explain why improving the quality of infant day care does not appear to enjoy the widespread public support that would translate into broad policy initiatives: many families do not perceive a pressing need, and those that do commonly experience this need for a relatively short period. Furthermore, the enforcement of quality standards for infant day care centers would inevitably increase their cost, and because the cost of infant day care is already substantially higher than most other forms of child care, further cost increases are likely to affect the extent to which such services are used and are available in most communities. In a sense, mandated quality standards would benefit children but economically disadvantage single mothers, adolescent parents, and others in greatest need of affordable care for offspring. In view of their overtaxed budgets, federal and state governments are unlikely to assume a major role in subsidizing such care, especially in view of the absence of a traditional role for the state in early child care and the lack of popular concensus mandating such a role. Finally, when support for subsidized day care has emerged in policy discussions, it has usually been tied to other, overarching policy goals (e.g., encouraging welfare recipients to return to work; assisting the victims of parental maltreatment). But even in this context, financial support has been desperately inadequate to address the needs of eligible populations: even Head Start, a program for lower-income children that has enjoyed longstanding Congressional support, remains significantly underfunded.

In short, one important component of translating research insights concerning infant day care into "usable knowledge" is tackling difficult questions concerning the public values and policy options relating to day care regulation and funding (see also Phillips, 1983). Without this, policy recommendations based on research sound naive and ill-conceived and assume that an important government role is mandated in the absence of a careful analysis of why this should be so and what the state's intervention can reasonably accomplish.

Although enlisting government efforts to improve the normative quality of care for babies is a desirable goal, serious questions remain concerning the other interests and concerns that necessarily assume a role in the policymaking debate and that may mandate consideration of other alternatives. Despite the obvious advantages of government regulation and funding, for example, greater progress in fostering the availability of good quality infant care may derive from employer- and community-based efforts, perhaps enlisting an older generation of Americans. Developmental researchers can contribute to clarifying these alternative options by designing and evaluating demonstration programs, applying basic research insights to these ideas and, perhaps most of all, thinking carefully and critically about the complex calculus of values and interests that are necessarily involved in the formulation of child and family policy.

Sources of Help

The National Association for the Education of Young Children (NAEYC; 1834 Connecticut Ave. NW, Washington, DC 20009) is a nonprofit professional organization committed to improving the quality of services to young children. The membership (more than 70,000) includes family day care providers, day care center directors and employees, researchers, students, and parents, many of whom affiliate both with the national organization and also with local affiliates to advocate improvement in child-care services at both national and regional levels. The membership also participates in an annual conference and contributes to a monthly journal devoted to child-care concerns. NAEYC publishes a brochure entitled "How to Choose a Good Early Childhood Program" that provides helpful criteria for distinguishing high-quality child-care programs, and provides an information line offering referrals to local agencies, information about starting child-care services in businesses or elsewhere, and copies of NAEYC publications (call [800] 424-2460).

Annotated Bibliography

The following sources may provide further perspectives to the difficult and controversial question of the effects of infant day care.

Fein, G., & Fox, N. (Guest Editors). (1988). *Early Childhood Research Quarterly. Special Issue: Infant Day Care, 3 and 4* (Ablex Publishing Co.).
This pair of special issues (nos. 3 and 4 from Volume 3) provide a remarkably current and balanced portrayal of the scientific debate concerning research on the effects of infant day care. The first issue features an extended discussion by Belsky of his concerns, followed by four theoretical commentaries written by experts in the field. The second issue includes a variety of recent empirical studies of this topic that are good examples of much-needed future research.

Zero to Three (Bulletin of the National Center for Clinical Infant Programs), issues for September 1986, February 1987, June 1987, and December 1987 (published by the National Center for Clinical Infant Programs, 733 15th Street NW, Suite 912, Washington, DC 20005).
These issues feature the original essay by Belsky highlighting his concerns about infant day care, followed by thoughtful rejoinders by research and clinical experts in the field of infant mental health. Empirical disagreements as well as practical implications are considered.

Zigler, E. F., & Gordon, E. W. (Eds.). (1982). *Day Care: Scientific and social policy issues.* Boston, MA: Auburn House.
Although the volume has become somewhat dated, it nevertheless provides a comprehensive view of the day care debate, including concerns with infants. The contributors to this volume include developmental researchers, policy analysts, clinicians, practitioners, and policymakers, providing a diversity of perspectives and orientations that is rare in the literature on day care.

Bibliography

Ainsworth, M. D. S., & Bell, S. M. (1969). Some contemporary patterns of mother-infant interaction in the feeding situation. In A. Ambrose (Ed.), *Stimulation in early infancy* (pp. 133-163). London: Academic.

Ainsworth, M. D. S., Blehar, M. C., Waters, E., & Wall, S. (1978). *Patterns of attachment.* Hillsdale, NJ: Erlbaum.

Barglow, P., Vaughn, B. E., & Molitor, N. (1987). Effects of maternal absence due to employment on the quality of infant-mother attachment in a low-risk sample. *Child Development, 58,* 945-954.

Belsky, J. (1984). Two waves of day care research: Developmental effects and conditions of quality. In R. Ainslie (Ed.), *The child and the day care setting* (pp. 1-34). New York: Praeger.

Belsky, J. (1986). Infant day care: A cause for concern? *Zero to Three, 6,* 1-7.

Belsky, J. (1988). The effects of infant day care reconsidered. *Early Childhood Research Quarterly, 3,* 235-272.

Belsky, J. (in press). Infant-parent attachment and day care: In defense of the Strange Situation. In J. Lande, S. Scarr, & N. Gunzenhauser (Eds.), *Caring for Children: Challenge to America.* Hillsdale, NJ: Erlbaum.

Belsky, J., & Rovine, M. J. (1988). Nonmaternal care in the first year of life and the security of infant-parent attachment. *Child Development, 59,* 156-167.

Belsky, J., & Steinberg, L. D. (1978). The effects of day care: A critical review. *Child Development, 49,* 929-949.

Belsky, J., Steinberg, L. D., & Walker, A. (1982). The ecology of day care. In M. Lamb (Ed.), *Nontraditional families* (pp. 71-116). Hillsdale, NJ: Erlbaum.

Blanchard, M., & Main, M. (1979). Avoidance of the attachment figure and social-emotional adjustment in day-care infants. *Developmental Psychology, 15,* 445-446.

Blurton-Jones, N., & Leach, G. M. (1972). Behaviour of children and their mothers at separation and greeting. In N. Blurton-Jones (Ed.), *Ethological studies of child behaviour* (pp. 217-247). Cambridge: Cambridge University Press.

Bowlby, J. (1969). *Attachment and loss,* Vol. 1. *Attachment.* New York: Basic.

Clarke-Stewart, K. A. (1988). The effects of infant day care reconsidered. *Early Childhood Research Quarterly, 3,* 293-318.

Clarke-Stewart, K. A. (1989). Infant day care: Maligned or malignant? *American Psychologist, 44,* 266-273.

Clarke-Stewart, K., & Fein, G. G. (1983). Early childhood programs. In P. H. Mussen, M. M. Haith, & J. J. Campos (Eds.), *Handbook of child psychology, Vol. II. Infancy and developmental psychobiology* (pp. 917-999). New York: Wiley.

Corkill, A., Sternitzke, M., & Thompson, R. A. (1990). *Infants' reunion responses in day care: Reliability and external correlates.* Manuscript in preparation, University of Nebraska, Lincoln, NE.

Etaugh, C. (1980). Effects of nonmaternal care on children: Research evidence and popular views. *American Psychologist, 35,* 309-319.

Field, T., Gewirtz. J. L., Cohen, D., Garcia, R., Greenberg, R., & Collins, K. (1984). Leave-takings and reunions of infants, toddlers, preschoolers, and their parents. *Child Development, 55,* 628-635.

Fraiberg, S. (1977). *Every child's birthright: In defense of mothering.* New York: Basic.

Gamble, T. J., & Zigler, E. (1986). Effects of infant day care: Another look at the evidence. *American Journal of Orthopsychiatry, 56,* 26-42.

Gardner, W., Scherer, D., & Tester, M. (1989). Asserting scientific authority: Cognitive development and adolescent legal rights. *American Psychologist, 44,* 895-902.

Howes, C. (1983). Caregiver behavior in center and family day care. *Journal of Applied Developmental Psychology, 4,* 99-107.

Lamb, M. E., & Sternberg, K. J. (in press). Daycare. In H. Keller (Ed.), *Handbuch der Kleinkind forschung.* Heidelberg: Springer-Verlag.

Lamb, M. E., Thompson, R. A., Gardner, W. P., & Charnov, E. L. (1985). *Infant-mother attachment.* Hillsdale, NJ: Erlbaum.

Lindblom, C. E., & Cohen, D. K. (1979). *Usable knowledge: Social science and social problem solving.* New Haven: Yale University Press.

McCartney, K., & Phillips, D. (1988). Motherhood and child care. In B. Birns, & D. Hay (Eds.), *The different faces of motherhood* (pp. 157-183). New York: Plenum.

McCartney, K., Scarr, S., Phillips, D., Grajek, S., & Schwarz, J. C. (1982). Environment differences among day care centers and their effects on children's development. In E. F. Zigler, & E. W. Gordon (Eds.), *Day care: Scientific and social policy issues* (pp. 126-151). Boston, MA: Auburn House.

National Center for Clinical Infant Programs (NCCIP) (1988). *Infants, families, and child care: Toward a research agenda.* Washington, DC: NCCIP.

Phillips, D. (1984). Day care: Promoting collaboration between research and policymaking. *Journal of Applied Developmental Psychology, 5,* 91-113.

Phillips, D., McCartney, K., Scarr, S., & Howes, C. (1987). Selective review of infant day care research: A cause for concern! *Zero to Three, 7,* 18-21.

Richters, J. E., & Zahn-Waxler, C. (1988). The infant day care controversy: Current status and future directions. *Early Childhood Research Quarterly, 3,* 319-336.

Rutter, M. (1981). Social-emotional consequences of day care for preschool children. *American Journal of Orthopsychiatry, 51,* 4-28.

Sheldon, E. L. (1986). *Interrelationships between preschoolers' parent-directed behaviors in different settings.* Unpublished doctoral dissertation, University of Nebraska, Lincoln, NE.

Sheldon, E. L., Thompson, R. A., & Earl, G. B. (1985). Preschoolers' reunion responses in day care. *Journal of Social and Personal Relationships, 2,* 463-469.

Sroufe, L. A. (1988). A developmental perspective on day care. *Early Childhood Research Quarterly, 3,* 283-291.

Szanton, E. S. (1989). Day care for infants. *Division of Child, Youth, and Family Services Newsletter, 12,* 4-16.

Thompson, R. A. (in press). Construction and reconstruction of early attachments: Taking perspective on attachment theory and research. In D. P. Keating, & H. Rosen (Eds.), *Constructivist perspectives on atypical development and developmental psychopathology*. Hillsdale, NJ: Erlbaum.

Thompson, R. A. (1989, August). *Socioemotional development and social policy: A two-way street.* Invited McCandless Award address to the American Psychological Association, New Orleans, LA.

Thompson, R. A. (1988). The effects of infant day care through the prism of attachment theory: A critical appraisal. *Early Childhood Research Quarterly, 3,* 273-282.

Thompson, R. A., & Lamb, M. E. (1986). Infant-parent attachment: New directions for theory and research. In P. B. Baltes, D. L. Featherman, & R. M. Lerner (Eds.), *Life-span development and behavior* (Vol. 7, pp. 1-41). Hillsdale, NJ: Erlbaum.

van IJzendoorn, M. H., & Kroonenberg, P. M. (1988). Cross-cultural patterns of attachment: A meta-analysis of the Strange Situation. *Child Development, 59,* 147-156.

Vaughn, B., Gove, F. L., & Egeland, B. (1980). The relationship between out-of-home care and the quality of infant-mother attachment in an economically disadvantaged population. *Child Development, 51,* 1203-1214.

Weinraub, M., Jaeger, E., & Hoffman, L. (1988). Predicting infant outcomes in families of employed and nonemployed mothers. *Early Childhood Research Quarterly, 3,* 361-378.

Young, K. T., & Zigler, E. (1986). Infant and toddler day care: Regulations and policy implications. *American Journal of Orthopsychiatry, 56,* 43-55.

Maternal Employment During Infancy: An Analysis of "Children of the National Longitudinal Survey of Youth (NLSY)"[1]

P. Lindsay Chase-Lansdale,
Robert T. Michael, and Sonalde Desai

The dramatic rise in women's labor force participation involves very familiar statistics. The proportion of employed married women with children under age six increased from 18 percent in 1960 to 30 percent in 1970 to 45 percent in 1980, and by 1987, it was almost 57 percent (U.S. Bureau of the Census, 1988). Using Census data to make projections into the next decade, Hofferth and Phillips estimate that by 1995, 65 percent of young children will have a mother in the labor force, and this is likely to be an underestimate (Hofferth & Phillips, 1987; Scarr, Phillips, & McCartney, 1989).

The fastest growing subgroup of employed mothers are those with infants. In 1987, 51 percent of mothers whose youngest child was one year old or younger were in the labor force, up from 43 percent in 1982 and 32 percent in 1977. As is widely evident, women are not leaving their jobs after the births of their babies to resume employment when their children reach preschool or school age, as many have done in the past. Rather, they return to work soon after the births of their babies. This is reflected in recent Census Bureau statistics showing that of women with *first-born* infants under one year of age, 61 percent are employed.

The phenomenon of maternal employment during infancy and its consequences for child development is currently very much in the limelight--in the popular press, public policy debates, and the

[1]This research is supported by the William T. Grant Foundation and is gratefully acknowledged. This chapter is based on the research reported in Desai, S., Chase-Lansdale, P. L., & Michael, R. T. (1989). *Demography, 26,* 545-561. The authors wish to thank Jacqueline Lerner and Nancy Galambos for their thoughtful comments on an earlier draft.

research arena. Maternal employment during infancy has become a majority phenomenon, topping the 50 percent mark only within the last five years. Thus it is of enormous interest to the public, as witnessed by the extensive media coverage in the past several years. In the policy realm, there is also intense debate as to what the role of government should be (c.f., National Academy of Sciences' report on child care policy, Hayes, Palmer, & Zaslow, 1990). Regarding infant child care specifically, the issues are exacerbated because it is so costly and difficult to find adequate child care for this age group (Maynard, 1989). In 1988, 52 bills on child care were introduced in Congress, and for the first time, the Presidential candidates had specific platforms on child care policy. The current wave of welfare reform now in place, called the Family Support Act, specifies that young mothers receiving public assistance must stay in school or join the work force or job training when their children are preschoolers, thus necessitating child care. Furthermore, states now have the option of requiring this of mothers of infants as well. Such policy decisions have occurred in the absence of definitive research on maternal employment during children's infancy (Chase-Lansdale & Vinovskis, 1989).

In the scientific arena, there is considerable controversy over the impact of maternal employment during a baby's first year of life. The controversy has focused on the issue of mother-infant separation and whether the separation due to mother's full-time employment will harm the child's emotional ties or attachment relationships to mother and father (see Thompson, this volume). A number of recent studies with relatively small sample sizes have indicated that when the mother works full time outside the home during her child's infancy, there is a greater likelihood of insecure attachment by the child to the mother at one year of age. In particular, during the commonly used laboratory assessment of attachment behavior known as the "Strange Situation," infants of employed mothers are more likely to avoid their mothers during reunions, (e.g., Barglow, Vaughn, & Molitor, 1987; Schwartz, 1983). There is further indication from other studies (i.e., Belsky & Rovine, 1988; Chase-Lansdale & Owen, 1987) that this may be particularly true of boys, and that in the context of their mothers' early employment, boys are more likely to develop insecure attachment relationships to both mothers *and* fathers at one year of age. Currently no consensus exists as to whether the avoidant behavior characterizing insecure attachments (usually thought to be maladaptive) is in fact adaptive or useful to the child whose mother goes off to work each day. The behavior may, some argue, simply suggest that the child has become more independent (Clarke-Stewart, 1989). In addition, the quality of the alternate care--known to have significant effects on children (Phillips, 1987)--has not been examined in these particular studies finding negative effects. (See Thompson, this volume, for a fuller discussion of this issue).

Without observations of the babies in their child care settings and with their families at home, the reasons for these negative effects remain unclear. Furthermore, these studies pertain only to white middle class families, and there have been no long term follow-ups to see if the negative impact of maternal employment on infant attachment persists as such economically advantaged children grow older. These striking gaps in our research knowledge have fueled the controversy surrounding maternal employment in infancy and socioemotional development, with the result that lay people, policymakers, and researchers alike are questioning the reasons for these findings, their long term consequences, and the implications for families who are not middle class (Chase-Lansdale, 1989; Gamble & Zigler, 1985). (Fortunately, our knowledge will be significantly improved over the next five years as results along these lines are obtained from the NICHD Child Care Network Study of 1200 infants and their families.)

Surprisingly, the same controversy and concern that have arisen regarding early maternal employment and children's socioemotional development have *not* focused on cognitive development. In fact, one body of related literature has taken the opposite tack. Specifically, in order to demonstrate the efficacy of early intervention, efforts have been made to enroll economically disadvantaged infants in cognitively enriched and stimulating center-based programs as early in life as possible, and in some programs between 6 weeks and 3 months of age (c.f., Burchinal, Lee, & Ramey, 1989). Such early childhood intervention programs and research have had the goal of "breaking the cycle of poverty" (Zigler & Muenchow,

1984), by promoting cognitive growth in young children at risk for developmental delay.

This literature is not strictly within the purview of maternal employment research, since the focus is on the quality and effects of certain early childhood education programs, and not on mothers' employment *per se*. However, the research is relevant from the standpoint of asking about the impact of mother-infant separation on children's intellectual development. In the intervention literature, the importance of helping children who are at risk for developmental delay and school failure has been the driving force in implementing programs during infancy; any harmful consequences of mother-infant separation on emotional development have been considered secondary and indeed are not often measured in most of these studies (c.f., Baydar, Paikoff, & Brooks-Gunn, in press; Hayes, Palmer, & Zaslow, 1990). This particular body of research does show that well-designed early enrichment programs can significantly improve children's intellectual development and school achievement, irrespective of their separation from mothers during infancy (Brooks-Gunn, 1989; Burchinal et al., 1989; Clarke-Stewart & Fein, 1983; Lazar, Darlington, Murray, Royce, & Snipper, 1982; Ramey & Campbell, 1987). Considerable emphasis has been placed on the fact that these programs are special interventions with very high quality curricula; however, two studies have also shown that enrollment during infancy in child care centers normally available in the community (thus ranging in quality) may have a positive effect on toddlers' cognitive development (Burchinal et al., 1989; Golden, Rosenbluth, Grossi, Policare, Freeman, & Brownlee, 1978).

In contrast, the maternal employment literature has only very recently begun to explore the short and long term effects on cognitive outcomes of the timing of mothers' employment in infancy (see Gottfried, this volume). There is, however, a fairly large group of studies on older children indicating that maternal employment has negative consequences for intellectual development and school achievement for boys in middle class families, but not for girls in such families or children of either sex in low-income families (Bronfenbrenner & Crouter, 1982; Hoffman, 1980; Zaslow, 1987). There are a few exceptions to this general conclusion. For example,

Gold and Andres (1978) found no negative effects on adolescent children; Milne, Myers, Rosenthal, and Ginsberg (1986) found negative effects on school achievement for both boys and girls in elementary and high school (but see Heyns & Catsambis, 1986).

Against this backdrop of literature on older children, there are very few studies that specifically focus on mothers' employment histories beginning in their children's first year of life. Regarding short term effects, findings are mixed. In relatively small samples of white middle class infants, Pedersen, Cain, Zaslow, and Anderson (1982) and Hock (1980) found no differences between infants of employed and nonemployed mothers in cognitive development during the first year of life, as measured by the Bayley Scales of Infant Development. In contrast, Schacter (1981) and Cohen (1978) found higher Stanford Binet and Bayley scores (respectively) among toddlers of nonemployed mothers than toddlers of mothers who resumed employment during their children's infancy. The Cohen study, however, has been criticized due to the confounding of single parenthood and lower birthweight with mothers' employment status (Hoffman, 1984).

In terms of long term effects (7 to 8 years) on cognitive development of maternal employment during infancy, there are three studies along these lines, all with different methodologies and contexts. Two report positive outcomes of mothers' employment, one among an economically disadvantaged sample of black families in the southern United States (Cherry & Eaton, 1977), and the second among families from a range of income levels in Sweden (Andersson, 1989). The third study finds negative effects of mothers' early employment in a sample in Dallas, Texas (Vandell & Corasaniti, in press). Cherry and Eaton (1977) examined the impact of early work history on a large sample (200) of seven to eight year old children in low-income black families in Louisiana. Although the grouping of employed mothers did not distinguish between employment before or after the first year, the majority of employed mothers had been employed in their children's infancy. Children whose mothers were employed during the first three years of life were equivalent in cognitive test scores and grade performance to children of nonemployed mothers, and in some subgroups of employed mother-families (such as those with husbands present and small family sizes), children had more favorable outcomes (higher scores on the Illinois Test of Psycholinguistic Ability, higher grades in spelling, and better physical growth) than children of nonemployed mothers. The authors point out the general effect of low income on this sample (median IQ was 84) and demonstrate that certain family background characteristics were strongly related to cognitive development, specifically maternal education, number and spacing of children, and crowding in the household. Although it is stated in the presentation of results that these important predictors were controlled for when examining employment status effects, it is not clear how this was done.

Andersson (1989) examined the impact of early child care on 119 eight-year-olds' development in Sweden and found that children who entered child care before age one had higher scores on cognitive tests (verbal subscales of the WISC and nonverbal subscales of a Swedish test of cognitive abilities) than children who entered child care after age one or who remained at home with their mothers. In contrast, in a sample of 239 eight-year-olds, Vandell and Corasaniti (in press) found negative consequences of child care during the first year of life on children's performance on IQ tests and teachers' reports on children's work study skills. Each investigator from these latter two studies has offered strong cautions regarding the interpretations of their results. Andersson points out that the child care system in Sweden is publicly funded, widely accepted, and of very high quality, involving extensive teacher training. Consequently, the Swedish child care experience may mirror that of the cognitive enrichment programs used in intervention studies in the United States. (Unlike the U.S. intervention studies, however, Andersson did measure emotional adjustment and found positive outcomes in this domain as well related to early child care entry.) Vandell and Corasaniti caution that the quality of child care available in Dallas is very poor, and that child care standards in Texas are considered one of the lowest in the country. Inadequate child care, rather than timing, may be an important, unmeasured factor in the negative cognitive and socioemotional outcomes among the third graders whose mothers had resumed employment in infancy. In addition, as the authors point out, there is a confounding of maternal employment history with marital status changes, adding further uncertainty to the study's results.

As can be seen, the accumulation of scientific evidence regarding the effects of maternal employment during infancy is very thin. Even more significant, however, is an overriding limitation in the maternal employment literature, namely, difficulty in effectively capturing the complexity of the phenomenon of the mother's employment in research designs. Maternal employment is interwoven with other important family factors such as ethnicity, family structure, family income, mother's educational level and intellectual abilities, and family size. These factors need to be taken into consideration in research that attempts to sort out the influence of mother's employment (Kamerman & Hayes, 1982).

For example, maternal employment takes on a different meaning in the black culture than in the white culture, since black mothers have for many years had higher labor force participation rates and their employment is more widely accepted (Heyns, 1982; Washington, 1988). Similarly, maternal employment has different implications for single-mother families than for dual-wage-earner families, and different implications, as well, depending upon its timing before or after divorce (Hetherington, Cox, & Cox, 1982).

A second area of complexity is that mothers' labor force participation, and in particular their resumption of employment soon after the births of their babies, depends upon their own intellectual abilities and level of education. Studies show that women who return to employment soon after the birth of their infants are more likely to have higher levels of education, intellectual ability, and job training than women who do not return in the first year (Desai, Waite, & Leibowitz, 1989). These women feel that the opportunity costs of staying out of the work force are higher, or they are simply more capable of securing employment due to their higher abilities, and thus they are more likely to work soon after their babies are born. Some mothers resume employment early in their infants' lives because they need the income to support their baby while others return to work for very different reasons, and these financial differences can also affect the impact on the child of the mother's early reentry into the labor market.

A final area of complexity has to do with the relationship between a woman's labor force attachment and her fertility. Employed women are more likely to have fewer children and to space them more widely than non-employed mothers, and this spacing itself can benefit the child's development, increasing the material and psychological resources available to the child (Eggebeen, 1988). Thus, depending upon a variety of characteristics associated with employed and non-employed mother families, we might predict both positive and negative effects of early employment on children's development.

Taking this complexity into account has not typically been done in the traditional psychological studies of maternal employment, especially involving return during infancy. Fortunately, this is changing. In the past, psychologists have dealt with the complexity by narrowing the research focus to a few specific aspects of maternal employment, controlling for other possible confounding characteristics by not including families with such factors in the study. For example, a study might include only two-parent, white, middle-class families. This more narrow approach has been particularly characteristic of the studies focusing on early resumption of employment. As a result, we are left with a patchwork of different conclusions from disparate studies whose samples and methodologies cannot be readily integrated.

Our study has been designed to address many of these limitations. In particular, we are able to use a large, nationally representative sample of young mothers, from a newly available data set, "Children of the National Longitudinal Survey of Youth" (NLSY). We examine the impact of different maternal employment patterns, especially the impact of early return to work, on children's intellectual ability at age four, using a large sample of 503 children, with very broad variation in family background factors. We are thus able to take the complexity of factors associated with maternal employment into account, as smaller studies have not been able to do. In addition to these improvements, our study is also the first to involve a longer term prospective design, that is, data that are collected at progressive points in the children's lives, rather than relying upon retrospective accounts. The vast majority of studies in the maternal employment literature have obtained data on important family background predictors from previous years, drawing upon mothers' recollections during interviews during the same time period that the children are assessed. The "Children of the NLSY," consisting of interviews of the adults each year, thus enables us to construct a very accurate measure of mothers' employment histories during their children's first three years of life. This is a significant improvement in research design.

What follows is a description of this data set, its characteristics, our specific hypotheses, analytic framework, and empirical findings. The "Children of the NLSY" is actually the fifth in a series of surveys, funded by the Department of Labor, beginning in the mid-1960s. The survey series is called the NLS or the National Longitudinal Survey of Labor Market Experience. They are longitudinal surveys meaning that the respondents are interviewed year after year so that one can follow the careers, earnings and life events of these men and women. Two of the four surveys begun in the 60's are still being surveyed today, yielding about 25 years of information for analysts. The surveys have yielded in-depth knowledge of labor force participation in the United States, and have been used primarily by labor force economists and policymakers. The surveys have since become widely used by sociologists and demographers as well, and only recently have come to the attention of developmentalists (c.f., Baydar, Paikoff, & Brooks-Gunn, in press; Brooks-Gunn, Phelps, & Elder, in press; Chase-Lansdale, Mott, Brooks-Gunn, & Phillips, in press).

The NLSY or National Longitudinal Survey of Youth was begun in 1979, consisting of a nationally representative sample of men and women, ages fourteen to twenty-one. Also included is an oversampling of blacks, Hispanics, and economically disadvantaged white youth, resulting in a total sample of 12,686. Like the previous four NLS surveys, the NLSY has been directed each year by the Center for Human Resource Research at the Ohio State University; it has been fielded by NORC, National Opinion Research Center at University of Chicago. Extensive information each year since 1979 gives us a rich body of data on the past 10 years. The information covers marital history, income, participation in government programs, employment patterns, educational history, attitudes toward work and family, and some measures of psychological adjustment (see Baker & Mott [1989] and Center for Human Resource Research [1988] for more detail).

In the early 1980s, the Demographic and Behavioral Sciences Branch of the National Institute of Child Health and Human Development (NICHD) became involved in the design and funding of the NLSY, emphasizing the fact that the youth were of childbearing age. Thus, the sample became an important resource for studying childbearing and childrearing. Through the efforts of NICHD and a number of private foundations, including the Foundation for Child Development and the William T. Grant Foundation, an advisory board of child development scholars was formed to develop recommendations on how to assess the development of the children of the women in this longitudinal sample. In 1986 and again in 1988, both the cognitive and socioemotional development of over 5,000 children ranging in age from infancy to fifteen years were measured. This information on these children is now combined with the wide range of information collected each year about their mothers. For more information on the history of "Children of the NLSY," the measures used, and the strengths and limitations of the data set, see Chase-Lansdale, et al. (in press). Although the NLSY itself, i.e., the sample of 12,000 youth, is nationally representative, we draw attention to the fact that the sample of children is *not* nationally representative, and therefore results from our study do not apply to all children in the United States. Most of the children in the NLSY sample were born to adolescent and young adult women. Thus, the child sample is more socioeconomically disadvantaged than a nationally representative sample would be. We can, however, statistically adjust for this fact, and in our study we do so.

Our study asks, "What are the impacts of different patterns of maternal employment on intellectual ability as measured by PPVT scores?" (The PPVT--Peabody Picture Vocabulary Test--is a word knowledge test that correlates well with IQ and achievement test scores.) Our model is designed to test the effects of different employment patterns in the context of other very important family background variables. We are also able to disentangle various aspects of maternal employment itself so that the mother's work patterns are even more cleanly defined. For example, we separate out mothers' earnings, family size, and child spacing as separate influences on the four-year-old, all of which we anticipated to be positive components of maternal employment that would boost the child's PPVT scores--since mothers' higher earnings and fewer and more widely spaced children are likely to enhance the quality of the environment for the child. We control for other important factors likely to relate to the child's PPVT score: race, marital history, mothers' own verbal ability and education, and her age at the birth of the child.

The maternal employment variables of interest in our study are patterns reflecting the timing and intensity of mothers' employment. We use three variables. They indicate whether or not the mother was: (1) Continuously employed (employed all four years of child's life, beginning in the first year); (2) Intermittently employed (employed off and on during the four years, primarily in years 2, 3, and 4); or (3) Not employed at all during the child's four years. There are very few part-time employed women in this sample, so we could not test for full- and part-time differences. We start with these overall patterns and investigate their impact on the child's PPVT score at age four. Subsequently, we test the impact of the timing *per se* of the mother's employment. Although we can only speculate about the processes underlying these patterns, we see the patterns as representing different timing and intensity of mother-child separation during the child's life. We cannot say which of several processes may affect the child--it may be the separation *per se*, or the stress on the mother involved in combining work and childrearing roles, or the reduced quantity or quality of interaction at home at night or during weekends, or perhaps the quality of care in alternate care setting. Any or all of these processes may underlie the impact of the mother's work pattern on the child; we cannot distinguish among them specifically.

The final factor of complexity taken into account in our approach is that we test our model separately for boys and girls, since there is considerable evidence that boys are more likely to be negatively affected and girls more positively affected by maternal employment (Bronfenbrenner & Crouter, 1982; Hoffman, 1980; 1984). There is substantial evidence that boys are more likely to be susceptible to psychosocial stress than girls (Zaslow & Hayes, 1986), so if stress is an issue with maternal employment, it is important to analyze the effects separately by gender.

Sample

Our sample includes 503 four-year-olds, 253 boys, and 250 girls. We focus on this age group for two reasons: (a) there is a more even distribution of maternal age at birth than at other child ages; and (b) we did not want to examine the complex influence of school enrollment that would be necessary if older children were included.

Family background characteristics. There is a racial distribution of 73 percent white, 17 percent black, and 10 percent Hispanic, consonant with our emphasis that this is not a nationally representative sample. It is indeed an economically disadvantaged sample. The mean family income in 1986, not counting mother's earnings, is $14,998. Excluding the mother's own earnings, the family income ranges from zero to $46,458 among these 503 households. Out of a possible 4 years spent in poverty during the child's lifetime, the average length of time spent in poverty for these households was about two-thirds of one year. Splitting the sample near the mean income, we find that two-thirds of the sample (N=357) falls below the mean into the low-income group, with an average of $7,138 per family, excluding mother's income. The upper third (N=146), forming a middle income group, has a mean income of $27,548.

Regarding marital status, 60 percent of mothers were continuously married during the child's life, 16 percent were divorced after the child's birth, 15 percent were single mothers, either never married or divorced prior to the child's birth, and 9 percent married after the child's birth. The mean years of education completed by mothers was 11.59, and only the top 1 percent completed college. Mothers were approximately 21.4 years of age at the birth of this child, ranging in age from 16-25 years. Mothers' verbal ability, as measured by a word knowledge test that is part of the Armed Services Vocational Aptitude Battery, (ASVAB) indicated that they were, on average, a little less verbally able than the adult U.S. population as a whole. That fact is consonant with the characteristics of this sample, indicating a lower than average socioeconomic condition. Children had an average birth order of 1.55, i.e., they were predominantly first-born children. Thirty-five percent of the children had siblings closely spaced, and 12 percent had more distantly spaced siblings (more than a 3-year age difference).

Mothers' employment history. Mothers who were continuously employed all four years of the child's life, beginning with the first year, represent 41 percent of the sample (N = 181). Mothers' who were employed intermittently, off and on during the child's life, (primarily during years 2, 3, and 4) represent 41 percent of the sample (N = 217). The percentage of mothers not employed outside the home at anytime during the 4 years constituted the remaining 18 percent (N = 105) of the mothers. The reported annual average earnings of any continuously employed mothers was $10,510; intermittently employed mothers earned an average of $4,140.

Peabody Picture Vocabulary Test-Revised (PPVT-R). The PPVT-R is a brief assessment of word knowledge or receptive vocabulary (Dunn & Dunn, 1981). It has standardized scores, with a mean of 100 and standard deviation of 16. The score is often referred to as an IQ score but is not considered technically equivalent to the IQ score derived by full-fledged tests of multiple cognitive abilities, such as McCarthy Scales of Children's Abilities or the Wechsler Intelligence Scale for Children. It correlates strongly with these measures of IQ, however, and with other achievement test scores as well (Sattler, 1974). The test is given in an easel format. Four pictures per page are presented to the child, each page increasing in difficulty, and the child is asked to point to the picture that best represents the word said by the examiner. The pictures have recently been reworked for better racial and gender balance. The overall mean score in our sample of four-year-olds is 90, with a standard deviation of 20, again consonant with the disadvantaged nature of our sample.

Results

　　We used multiple regression analyses to examine the impact of different patterns of maternal employment, holding a variety of background factors constant. We will summarize the main findings here. For more detail, see Desai, Chase-Lansdale, & Michael (1989).

　　Effects of family background variables. The family background variables were related to PPVT scores in expected ways. First, there are strong effects of race. Both black and Hispanic boys and girls performed more poorly on PPVT than white children. Other studies have indicated lower performance by minority children on intellectual tests and have shown this to be due to poorer economic conditions (Lee, Brooks-Gunn, & Schnur, 1988). We find lower performance among minority children after controlling for income differences. It is possible that the PPVT is culturally biased (Sattler, 1974). The findings regarding Hispanic children should be interpreted with special caution because the PPVT-R was not administered in Spanish in our data, and a few of these Hispanic children may have performed better on a Spanish version, although this is a debatable point in the literature (Dunn, 1986; Hakuta, 1986). (None of the children, however, were noted by the interviewer as having difficulty understanding the English test battery.)

　　In terms of mothers' other characteristics, mothers' verbal ability predicted the children's verbal ability quite significantly, as did mothers' education level for girls but not for boys. These findings capture the influence of both genetic and environmental factors on children's intellectual development (Rutter, 1985). Age of mother was not related to the child's PPVT-R. This was not surprising since the literature suggests it is not age of mother *per se* that is related to poor outcomes for child but rather the lower socioeconomic conditions associated with teen parenthood (Furstenberg, Brooks-Gunn, & Chase-Lansdale, 1989). Because we are directly controlling for many of these economic conditions, we do not find a negative effect of mothers' age on the children's PPVT-R scores.

Neither family earnings, mothers' own earnings, nor marital history appeared to be related to the child's PPVT-R score. We expected to see an effect for income, and in fact, the simple correlation between income and PPVT-R is positive and quite strong, meaning that the higher the family income, the better the child's performance. In our regression models, however, other factors associated with income, e.g., mother's education and ability, pick up the positive relationship.

As expected, birth order was negatively related to the child's PPVT-R score, significantly so for girls, and almost so for boys. Child spacing was important as well: boys (but not girls) with more widely spaced siblings had higher PPVT-R scores. Other research has shown that the presence of younger siblings who are closely spaced has negative effects on children's intellectual development, so our results confirm this finding. The explanation for this is probably that close spacing decreases the parents' resources for the child, including their time, responsiveness, and financial resources (Stafford, 1987).

Effects of maternal employment patterns. In our first stage of analysis, we examined the impact of mothers' different employment patterns on the children's PPVT-R scores. With the various aspects of maternal employment teased apart (e.g., the dollar earnings, the timing of her return to work), and with other important family background factors controlled (e.g., race, marital history, family income, order and spacing of children, and mother's education and verbal ability), we found no effect of the different employment patterns. Taken collectively, the mother's employment pattern *per se* showed no relationship with the PPVT-R score for boys or for girls. Similarly, the timing of mothers' return to work (before or after the first year) did not have an effect on four-year-olds' PPVT-R scores.

However, we undertook a second stage of analyses, and it revealed adverse effects for certain subgroups of children. Our second stage of analysis grew out of two motivations. (1) Evidence in the literature suggests that maternal employment may have a sizable negative effect on boys' intellectual abilities and achievements, but only for middle class--not for lower class--boys. (2) Cornell

Professor Bronfenbrenner has theorized that in different social contexts (e.g., at different socioeconomic levels), the same phenomenon, (e.g., maternal employment) may operate very differently. Put in other words, Bronfenbrenner argues that in more favorable contexts, i.e., higher socioeconomic status, the influence of separation from the mother might make a big difference to the child's development, whereas, among lower socioeconomic families, other factors may be more essential, such as minimal economic security, day-to-day financial or social support (Bronfenbrenner, 1988). To explore Bronfenbrenner's hypothesis and to check the evidence on middle-class boys, we tested the effects of different patterns of maternal employment *within* each of two income groups. That is, we compared the effect of the mother being continuously employed versus never employed within the middle-class income group (where the mean income is $23,367) and separately within the low income group (where the mean income, excluding the mothers own income is $6,516). We tested intermittent employment versus never employed separately within the two income groups as well.

We found that among middle income families, when the mother was employed all four years of the child's life, the young boys had substantially lower PPVT-R scores--about 9 points lower. (This is more than half a standard deviation and is therefore considered a fairly large effect.) In contrast, intermittent employment by the mother (off and on, primarily in the second, third, and fourth years) showed no relationship to the children's PPVT-R scores. The negative relationship occurred only in middle income families, only for boys, and only for continuous employment.

We also tested the effects of timing of maternal employment more specifically, by examining the impact of mothers' return to work during the *first* year of the child's life. For boys in middle income families, there was a negative effect on mothers' return to work in the *first* year of life. In families where the mothers had returned to work in the first year, the boys' PPVT-R scores were about 7 points lower, a fairly sizable difference. Again, this relationship was not in evidence for girls nor for children in low income families. Middle income mothers who return quite soon after the birth of their child tend to have relatively high education and ability, and so we would, in general, expect their children to score high on the PPVT. Our findings suggest, however, that if the child is a boy, his test score is 7 to 9 points lower than we would otherwise expect, if his mother returned to work in her first year of life. Our finding of a negative effect of early return to employment by middle-class mothers of boys is consistent with other studies. We have also shown that there is no negative effect in low income families. This confirms hypotheses from several theories.

But what does this finding mean? It may mean that the daily absence of mothers in middle-class families represents a considerable loss of resources for their children (a loss in terms of responsiveness, verbal interactions, and a stimulating environment), and these are not replaced in the childcare setting, and furthermore, this loss is not compensated for by any advantages the mother's earnings bring. In contrast, for families living near the poverty level, the contribution of the mother's earnings to the family's economic security may more than offset these negative effects of maternal employment, or those negative effects may not be so great among the lower income families. On balance maternal employment in these poorer families is not a negative phenomenon and may well be positive.

But why is it that *boys* are negatively affected by early maternal employment while girls are not? A growing body of research indicates that parents believe that their daughters are more vulnerable emotionally than their sons, and that under stressful circumstances, parents believe boys do not need as much parental attention and responsiveness as girls do (Zaslow & Hayes, 1986). If maternal employment brings stress to the family, related to mother-child separation or to mothers' own feeling of stress, our findings suggest that parents protect their daughters from such stress but do not do so for sons. This hypothesis is supported by observational studies of middle class families, where parents in employed-mother families offered less caretaking, discipline, and stimulation to their sons than to their daughters, a pattern that was not true of nonemployed-mother families (Stuckey, McGhee, & Bell, 1982; Zaslow, M., Pedersen, F., Suwalsky, J., Cain, R., Anderson, B., & Fivel, M., 1985). The parents may compensate with their daughters but do not do so for their sons, believing there is less need. Another explanation is that boys are more irritating to middle class parents at the end of the workday, since boys' are usually more aggressive, and this tendency is often exacerbated in childcare settings. In an open-ended interview study by Bronfenbrenner, Alvarez, & Henderson (1984), the most favorable remarks and attitudes about their children were made by nonemployed mothers of sons, but the least favorable remarks were made by employed mothers of sons.

Finally, our results suggest that it is the early resumption of employment by mothers that is particularly strongly related to lower PPVT-R scores for their boys. Perhaps the mother-child separation, the stress on the mother, or the task overload due to employment in the first year leads to negative interactions with their boys, creating patterns that start a negative trajectory which continues over the four years. An alternative explanation is that adequate child care quality is particularly hard to find during infancy, and that boys are more vulnerable in these settings than girls. Unfortunately, data on the quality of child care are not available in our study, so we can only offer conjectures about the underlying reasons for the adverse relationship for boys.

Implications for Families

How should our results be interpreted? First, we remind the reader that the four-year-olds whom we have studied were born to relatively young women and our results cannot be generalized to four-year-olds born to women over about age twenty-four. Second, because the "Children of the NLSY" sample is comprised of these younger mothers, the sample is more economically disadvantaged than a nationally representative sample. Readers should keep in mind that our findings are most generalizable to this group. Yet, by dividing the sample into the upper one-third of family income versus the lower two-thirds, we have contrasted middle income families with low income families. Very few black and Hispanic families were included in the top third of middle income families. The negative impact of maternal employment on boys applies mostly to white boys in middle income families.

How do our results and those of others translate into everyday life for families? By addressing the complexity of maternal employment and its interrelatedness with other important characteristics of families, we have specified both positive and negative aspects of the phenomenon. As we discussed earlier, mothers who return to work early in the children's lives tend to be better educated and of higher intellectual ability, both of these qualities having positive implications for children's intellectual growth. Similarly, family sizes are smaller and children are spaced further apart, again factors that contribute to a home environment that is more stimulating due to mothers' ability to provide more individual attention to each child.

These factors thus portend well for families where mothers return to work early. However, given these positive predictors, we found an unexpected reduction in boys' PPVT-R scores by 9 points, in middle income families. If one thinks about adding all these influences together in an "additive" model that would capture the total effect (i.e., both positive and negative effects) of early maternal employment on the child, one might argue that the very beneficial qualities of these families, as detailed above, cancel out or at least compensate for the reduction in PPVT-R scores for this particular subgroup of boys. However, a more accurate interpretation is the following: these boys have everything going for them, and if their mothers had postponed the resumption of employment until the boys' second year of life, their scores would have been considerably higher.

We, however, would not presume to recommend maternal employment decisions based on this study, when such decisions are highly personal and reflect the particular circumstances, pressures, and goals of each family. Our finding *is* the result of a study with significantly improved methodology, and it does fit with the pattern identified in the maternal employment literature, that middle class boys' cognitive development and school achievement are vulnerable to maternal employment, and in particular, early maternal employment.

Although we have speculated in this chapter as to why this may be the case, the scientific literature does not have the necessary observational studies of family dynamics and child care environments to say with certainty what the reasons for the negative effects are. The possible processes that we have mentioned are specific patterns of interactions within employed mother families where parents do not provide enough stimulation and responsiveness to their sons but do to their daughters, and qualities of child care settings in infancy that may more negatively affect boys than girls.

Until we have research investigations exploring the actual experiences of children and families, we will not be able to say with confidence why the cognitive development of boys in middle income families seems to be negatively affected by mothers' early employment. Our findings should, however, along with other studies in the literature, heighten awareness on the part of parents and care providers that boys may need more attention, stimulation, soothing, and responsiveness than they are currently receiving when their mothers work outside the home.

Annotated Bibliography

Department of Health and Human Services (1980). *A Parent's Guide to Day Care.* Office of Human Development Services, Administration for Children, Youth, and Families, Day Care Division. DHHS Publication No. 80-30270. Washington, DC: Government Printing Office.
This short guide has been designed by child care experts to assist parents in deciding what is important for their children and their family when choosing child care. The guide provides a checklist and discussion of important aspects of quality to investigate for children of different ages, for various child care settings.

Flavell, J. (1977). *Cognitive development.* Englewood Cliffs, NJ: Prentice-Hall, Inc.
This volume is a classic overview of cognitive development by one of the leading psychologists in the field. The book, in paperback, provides a synthesis of children's cognition during infancy, childhood, and adolescence and is intended for a broad audience.

Segal, J., & Yahraes, H. (1979). *A child's journey: Forces that shape the lives of our young.* New York: McGraw-Hill.

This is a resource book for parents and professionals based upon research findings. The book "explains why children develop as they do and what we can and cannot do to shape the outcome of their journey" (Authors' preface). This book provides a context for thinking about the ways in which maternal employment may affect children.

Zaslow, M. (forthcoming). Midway through the second wave of day care research: Variations in quality and their implications for children. In S. Hofferth & D. Phillips (Eds.), *Journal of Social Issues.*

This article is a thoughtful, comprehensive review of what we know about the important dimensions of child care quality and how these affect children's development. Written in clear, nontechnical language, the chapter outlines the influence of the child care setting on children and also discusses the ways in which family and day care experiences can complement, contradict, or exacerbate one another.

Bibliography

Andersson, B-E. (1989). Effects of public day-care: A longitudinal study. *Child Development, 60,* 857-866.

Baker, P. C., & Mott, F. L. (1989). *NLSY Child Handbook.* Columbus: Center for Human Resource Research, Ohio State University.

Barglow, P., Vaughn, B., & Molitor, N. (1987). Effects of maternal absence due to employment on the quality of infant-mother attachment in a low-risk sample. *Child Development, 58,* 945-954.

Baydar, N., Paikoff, R., & Brooks-Gunn, J. (in press). Effects of childcare arrangements on cognitive and behavioral outcomes: Evidence from a national sample of 3-4 year olds. *Developmental Psychology.*

Belsky, J., and Rovine, M. J. (1988). Nonmaternal care in the first year of life and the security of infant-parent attachment. *Child Development, 59,* 157-167.

Bronfenbrenner, U. (1988). Interacting systems in human development research paradigms: Present and future. In N. Bolger, A. Caspi, G. Downey, & M. Moorehouse (Eds.), *Persons in context: Developmental processes (pp. 25-49).* New York: Cambridge University Press.

Bronfenbrenner, U., Alvarez, W. F., & Henderson, C. R. (1984). Working and watching: Maternal employment status and parent's perceptions of their three-year-old children. *Child Development, 55,* 1362-1378.

Bronfenbrenner, U., & Crouter, A. C. (1982). Work and family through time and space. In S. B. Kamerman & C. D. Hayes (Eds.), *Families that work: Children in a changing world* (pp. 39-83). Washington, DC: National Academy Press.

Brooks-Gunn, J. (1989, November). *Opportunities for change: Effects of intervention programs on mothers and children.* Paper presented at the National Forum on Children and the Family Support Act, Washington, DC.

Brooks-Gunn, J., Phelps, E., & Elder, G. (in press). Studying lives through time: Secondary data analyses in developmental psychology. *Developmental Psychology.*

Burchinal, M., Lee, M., & Ramey, C. (1989). Type of day-care and preschool intellectual development in disadvantaged children. *Child Development, 60,* 128-137.

Center for Human Resource Research. (1988). *NLS Handbook, 1988.* Columbus: The Ohio State University.

Chase-Lansdale, P. L. (1989). *The Day Care Controversy.* Paper presented at the conference, "Day Care: Who's minding our children?" Sponsored by the Texas Association for Infant Mental Health, May, Dallas.

Chase-Lansdale, P. L., Mott, F., Brooks-Gunn, J., & Phillips, D. A. (in press). Children of the NLSY: A unique research opportunity. *Developmental Psychology.*

Chase-Lansdale, P. L., & Owen, M. T. (1987). Maternal employment in a family context: Effects on infant-mother and infant-father attachments. *Child Development, 58,* 1505-1512.

Chase-Lansdale, P. L., & Vinovskis, M. A. (1989, November). *Whose responsibility? An historical analysis of the changing roles of mothers, fathers, and society in assuming responsibility for U.S. children.* Paper presented at the National Forum on Children and the Family Support Act, Washington, DC.

Cherry, F. F. and Eaton, E. G. (1977). Physical and cognitive development in children of low-income mothers working in the child's early years. *Child Development, 48,* 158-166.

Clark-Stewart, K. A., & Fein, G. (1983). Early childhood programs. In H. Haith & J. J. Campos (Eds.), *Infancy and Developmental Psychobiology* (Vol. 2, pp. 917-1000). New York: Wiley.

Clarke-Stewart, K. A. (1989). Infant day care: Maligned or Malignant? *American Psychologist, 44,* 266-273.

Cohen, S. E. (1978). Maternal employment and mother-child interaction. *Merrill-Palmer Quarterly, 24,* 189-197.

Desai, S., Waite, L., & Leibowitz, A. (1989). *Women's labor force participation before and after first birth: The effect of occupational characteristics and work commitment.* Paper presented at the annual meeting of the Population Association of America, Baltimore, MD.

Desai, S., Chase-Lansdale, P. L., & Michael, R. T. (1989). Mother or market: Effects of maternal employment on the intellectual ability of 4-year old children. *Demography, 26,* 545-561.

Dunn, L., & Dunn, L. (1981). *Peabody Picture Vocabulary Test Revised* (PPVT-R). Circle Pines, MN: American Guidance Service.

Dunn, L. (1986). *Bilingual Hispanic children on the U.S. mainland: A review of research on their cognitive, linguistic, and scholastic development.* AGS Research Monograph. Circle Pines, MN: American Guidance Service.

Eggebeen, D. J. (1988) Determinants of maternal employment for white preschool children: 1960-1980. *Journal of Marriage and the Family, 50,* 149-159.

Furstenberg, F. F., Jr., Brooks-Gunn, J., & Chase-Lansdale, P. L. (1989). Teenaged pregnancy and childbearing. *American Psychologist, 44,* 313-320.

Gamble, T. J., & Zigler, E. (1985). Effects of infant day care: Another look at the evidence. *American Journal of Orthopsychiatry, 56,* 26-40.

Gold, D., & Andres, D. (1978). Comparison of adolescent children with employed and nonemployed mothers. *Merrill-Palmer Quarterly, 24,* 243-254.

Golden, M., Rosenbluth, L., Grossi, M. T., Policare, H. J., Freeman, H., Jr., & Brownlee, E. M. (1978). *The New York City Infant Day Care Study.* New York: Medical and Health Research Association of New York City.

Hakuta, K. (1986). *Mirror of language: The debate on bilingualism.* New York: Basic Books.

Hayes, C., Palmer, J. & Zaslow, M. (1990). *Who cares for America's children: Child care for the 1990's.* Washington, DC: National Academy of Sciences.

Hetherington, E. M., Cox, M. & Cox, R. (1982). Effects of divorce on parents and children. In M. E. Lamb (Ed.), *Nontraditional Families: Parenting and Child Development,* (pp. 233-288). Hillsdale, NJ: Erlbaum.

Heyns, B., & Catsambis, S. (1986). Mother's employment and children's achievement: A critique. *Sociology of Education, 59,* 140-151.

Heyns, B. (1982). The influence of parents' work on children's school achievement. In S. B. Kamerman & C. D. Hayes (Eds.), *Families that work: Children in a changing world* (pp. 229-267). Washington, DC: National Academy Press.

Hock, E. (1980). Working and nonworking mothers and their infants: A comparative study of maternal caregiving characteristics and infant social behavior. *Merrill-Palmer Quarterly, 26,* 79-101.

Hofferth, S. L., & Phillips, D. H. (1987). Child care in the United States, 1970 to 1995. *Journal of Marriage and the Family, 49,* 559-571.

Hoffman, L. W. (1980). The effects of maternal employment on the academic studies and performance of school age children. *School Psychology Review, 9,* 319-335.

Hoffman, L. W. (1984). Maternal employment and the young child, In M. Perlmutter (Ed.), *Minnesota symposium in child psychology* (Vol. 17, pp. 101-127). Hillsdale, NJ: Erlbaum.

Kamerman, S. B., & Hayes, C. D. (Eds.). (1982). *Families that work: Children in a changing world.* Washington, DC: National Academy of Sciences Press.

Lazar, I., Darlington, R. B., Murray, H., Royce, J., & Snipper, A. (1982). Lasting effects of early education: A report from the Consortium for Lonigitudinal Studies. *Monographs of the Society of Research in Child Development, 47,* (Nos. 2-3, Serial No. 195).

Lee, V., Brooks-Gunn, J., & Schnur, E. (1988). Does Head Start Work? *Developmental Psychology, 24,* 210-222.

Maynard, R. A. (1989). *Child care, welfare programs, and federal policy.* Unpublished manuscript, Mathematica Policy Research.

Milne, A. M., Myers, D. E., Rosenthal, A. S., & Ginsberg, A. (1986). Single parents, working mothers, and the educational achievement of school children. *Sociology of Education, 59,* 125-139.

Pedersen, F. A., Cain, R. A., Zaslow, M. J., & Anderson, B. J. (1982). Variation in infant experience associated with alternative family roles. In L. Loasa and I. Sigel (Eds.), *Families as learning environments for children* (pp. 203-221). New York: Plenum.

Phillips, D. A. (Ed.). (1987). *Quality in child care: What does the research tell us?* Washington, DC: National Association for the Education of Young Children.

Ramey, C. T., & Campbell, F. (1987). The Carolina Abcedarian Project: An educational experiment concerning human malleability. In J. J. Gallagher, & C. T. Ramey (Eds.), *The malleability of children,* (pp. 127-139). Baltimore: Brooks.

Rutter, M. (1985). Family and school influences on cognitive development. *Journal of Child Psychology and Psychiatry, 26,* 683-704.

Sattler, J. M. (1974). *Assessment of children's intelligence.* Philadelphia: Saunders.

Schachter, F. F. (1981). Toddlers with employed mothers. *Child Development, 59,* 958-964.

Scarr, S., Phillips, D., & McCartney, K. (1989). Dilemmas of child care in the United States: Employed mothers and children at risk. *Canadian Psychology/Psychologie Canadienne, 30,* 126-138.

Schwartz, P. (1983). Length of day-care attendance and attachment behavior in eighteen-month-old infants. *Child Development, 54,* 1073-1078.

Stafford, F. P. (1987). Women's work, sibling competition, and children's school performance. *The American Economic Review, 77,* 972-80.

Stuckey, M. F., McGhee, P. E., & Bell, N. J. (1982). Parent-child interaction: The influence of maternal employment. *Developmental Psychology, 18,* 635-644.

U.S. Bureau of the Census (1988). Fertility of American Women: June 1987. *Current Population Reports,* Series P-20, No. 427, Washington, DC: US Government Printing Office.

Vandell, D. L., & Corasaniti, M. A. (in press). Child care and the Family: Complex contributors to child development. In K. McCartney (Ed.), *New Directions in Child Development Research.*

Washington, V. (1988). The Black mother in the United States: History, theory, research, and issues. In B. Birns & D. Hay (Eds.), *The different faces of motherhood* (pp. 185-214). New York: Plenum.

Zaslow, M., Pedersen, F., Suwalsky, J., Cain, R., Anderson, B., & Fivel, M. (1985). The early resumption of employment by mothers: Implications for parent-infant interaction. *Journal of Applied Developmental Psychology, 6,* 1-16.

Zaslow, M., & Hayes, C. D. (1986). Sex differences in children's response to psychosocial stress: Toward a cross-context analysis. In M. E. Lamb, A. Brown, & B. Rogoff (Eds.), *Advances in Developmental Psychology* (Vol. 4, pp. 287-335). Hillsdale, NJ: Erlbaum.

Zaslow, M. J. (1987). *Sex differences in children's response to maternal employment.* Paper presented at a symposium on Sex Differences in Children's Response to Psychosocial Stress, Woods Hole, Mass.

Zigler, E., & Muenchow, S. (1984). How to influence social policy affecting children and families. *American Psychologist, 39,* 415-420.

Maternal Employment in the Family Setting: Developmental and Environmental Issues[1]

Adele Eskeles Gottfried

Maternal employment has become the norm, and it is predicted that this trend will continue (Hayghe, 1982). Although maternal employment is not a new phenomenon, it continues to attract public and scientific attention, perhaps due to its pervasiveness. One of the most critical questions concerns the effect of mothers' employment on children's development (A. E. Gottfried, 1988).

This question cannot be answered in simple terms. Research indicates that a great deal of complexity typifies the relationship between maternal employment and children's development. Between maternal employment, on the one hand, and children's development, on the other, are a host of environmental, attitudinal, and workplace factors that mediate the impact of maternal employment (A. E. Gottfried & A. W. Gottfried, 1988a; Hoffman, 1989). It is the purpose of this chapter to focus on home environmental aspects of the family setting that are related to maternal employment and children's development.

Although earlier research made direct comparisons between employed vs. nonemployed mothers, this strategy was inadequate. When employed vs. nonemployed groups are directly compared there are numerous possible differences between the groups that are not necessarily due to maternal employment. The socioeconomic status (SES) of the groups may differ as well as the number of children in the home or the parents' marital status. Therefore, when children of

[1]Thanks to Allen W. Gottfried and Kay Bathurst for help in preparation of this chapter. This research was supported by grants from the Thrasher Research Fund, Spencer Foundation, and California State Universities at Fullerton and Northridge. Deepest appreciation is extended to the families who have participated in the longitudinal study.

employed and nonemployed mothers are directly compared without controlling for these factors, any differences which emerge may be due to these extraneous variables and not to maternal employment status per se (A. E. Gottfried & A. W. Gottfried, 1988a; A. E. Gottfried, A. W. Gottfried, & Bathurst, 1988; Hoffman, 1984). For example, when both parents work, higher income is likely to result, which in turn, may enhance the provision of learning materials, lessons, or toys. These learning opportunities could favorably influence children's intellectual development or achievement. Hence, what may appear to be differences in children's development due to maternal employment may be a result of greater learning opportunities afforded through increased family income. Effects on children's development must occur independently above and beyond these extraneous factors to be considered the result of maternal employment per se.

Employed vs. nonemployed categories are not homogeneous. Within these categories there may be vast differences between mothers, fathers, and families. For example, there is a broad range of occupations characteristic of employed mothers (A. E. Gottfried, A. W. Gottfried, & K. Bathurst, 1988). Further, within the employed and nonemployed categories, mothers do not all share the same attitudes towards employment and parenting (Galambos, Petersen, & Lenerz, 1988; A. E. Gottfried & A. W. Gottfried, 1988b; A. E. Gottfried, A. W. Gottfried, & Bathurst, 1988; Greenberger & Goldberg, 1989; Lerner & Galambos, 1988), the same work hours or schedules (A. E. Gottfried &   A. W. Gottfried, 1988a), or satisfactions and stresses with employment (A. E. Gottfried & A. W. Gottfried, 1988a; Hoffman, 1989)   Hence, comparisons between nonemployed and employed mothers without considering the specific variables of occupation, work hours, attitudes, and stress would mask the specific processes which may be accounting for child outcomes.

Directly comparing employed vs. nonemployed categories of mothers prevents looking at the family setting within which maternal employment occurs. Maternal employment is a family issue, and families respond to mothers' employment with a variety of strategies such as increased involvement of the father with the child (A. E. Gottfried, A. W. Gottfried, & Bathurst, 1988; Hoffman, 1989). The simple categorization of mothers as employed or nonemployed describes the mothers but imparts no information about the specific nature of family environment which may be related to the employment status of the mother.

Research indicates that it is the proximal home environment, that is, the array of specific cognitive, social-emotional, and physical stimulation available to children as well as family interpersonal relationships that impacts children's development (A. W. Gottfried & A. E. Gottfried, 1984, 1986). In general, cognitive stimulation consists of the materials and activities in the home aimed at promoting the child's intellectual and language development. Specific experiences may include provision of toys, learning materials, books, language, reading to the child, or working with the child on academic skills. Higher levels of cognitive stimulation have been favorably related to children's early intellectual development (A. W. Gottfried, 1984) and to school achievement in upper elementary and secondary students (Marjoribanks, 1979).

Social-emotional environment consists of affection, warmth, and responsiveness between family members. Mothers' pride, affection, and warmth toward the child have been favorably related to young children's intellectual and language development (A. W. Gottfried & A. E. Gottfried, 1984); maternal rejection has been related to having young children with more difficult temperaments (Lerner & Galambos, 1988); and, as reviewed by Belsky and Isabella (1988), there is evidence that children tend to have more secure attachments when their mothers are more sensitive to them.

Physical stimulation typically refers to the nature of children's surroundings, which may include the inanimate environment as well as nonresponsive social stimuli (such as a person who is in the child's presence but is currently not attending to the child) (Wachs, 1989). Examples of the physical environment include number of noise sources (e.g., TV, radio) simultaneously available in the home; number and variety of toys; restriction of exploration of the home; access to books and newspapers; number of siblings; and number of persons in the home (Wachs, 1989). Early access to floor freedom and a greater degree of space in the home were favorably related to infant development and preschool intellectual development but having a greater degree of interfering noise sources and a larger number of siblings in the home was related to lower levels of early infant development and preschoolers' language and intellectual development (A. W. Gottfried & A. E. Gottfried, 1984).

Finally, family interpersonal relationships would appear to cut across both cognitive and social-emotional environment. The provision of cognitively stimulating experiences and the responsivity and warmth of environment would need to be mediated through the interactions of family members. There have been conceptualizations of interpersonal relationships that include family climate (Bathurst, 1988; Moos & Moos, 1981). For example, family cohesiveness and intellectual-cultural orientation correlated positively with young children's intellectual development (A. W. Gottfried & A. E. Gottfried, 1984). Positive family functioning (e.g., cohesiveness, cooperation) was favorably related to social maturity at age eight (Bathurst, 1988).

The extent to which maternal employment status relates to the proximal home environment may impact children's development. The role of maternal employment on children's development can only be understood within the context of the family environment. Hence, one of the major goals of this research program is to examine how maternal employment is related to the family setting and how this family setting, in turn, may be related to children's development.

Another issue related to the role of maternal employment in the family context concerns child care. Child care may be considered an extension of the home. It is the number one need of families in which the mother is employed. The child care arrangements are part of the balance between maternal employment and family responsibilities. Types of child care that families arrange are examined in this chapter to ascertain how they fit into the family context.

Described below is a longitudinal study that addresses the issues presented above. A longitudinal perspective studying the effects of maternal employment on children's development over time, provides a significant contribution because maternal employment may have both immediate and/or long-term impact on the child and the family (A. E. Gottfried & A. W. Gottfried, 1988b). A longitudinal perspective allows for determining whether a child's age at the time of employment and stability of employment over time make a difference with regard to children's development (Bronfenbrenner, 1986; Heyns, 1982; Hoffman, 1984).

This longitudinal study examines maternal employment status in the context of the proximal family environment and examines the short- and long-term impact of maternal employment status on the cognitive, social-emotional, and physical home environment and children's development. The position taken in this research is that if maternal employment has any impact on children at all, it is through the proximal home environment that such influence occurs. The present study examines the period from infancy through the early school years. Implications for social policy will be addressed as well.

Method

Subjects

This longitudinal study began in the fall of 1979 when 130 one-year-olds and their families were selected from birth notifications of hospitals surrounding a university in Southern California. All infants were full-term and of normal birthweight with no visual or neurological abnormalities (A. W. Gottfried & Gilman, 1983). Of the 130 infants, 68 were male, 62 were female, 117 were white, and 13 were from other racial groups. The sample represented a broad middle-class range. This chapter will focus upon maternal employment and children's development through the early childhood years, through age seven, and will also include specific analyses of data available at age eight.

Evaluations took place in a university laboratory where the children were administered a battery of standardized psychological tests. Throughout the investigation the participation rate was substantial, ranging from 99 percent (128) at one-and-one-half years, to 82 percent (107) at eight years. Families discontinued in the study primarily because of relocation. Evaluations consisted of a complete set of psychological assessments that lasted 1.5 to 2 hours. While the children were being assessed, the parent filled out a variety of inventories assessing family demographics and surveys of parenting and work attitudes, activities and stimulation provided in the home, and family functioning. Direct home observations were conducted at 15 and 39 months, and eight years.

Developmental Domains

Throughout the study children have been evaluated on infant developmental status, cognition, intelligence, academic achievement, temperament, social competence, and behavioral adjustment. Where available, major standardized measures were used. Information was also gathered from teachers and parents regarding children's behavioral adjustment and academic achievement. (See A. E. Gottfried, A. W. Gottfried, & Bathurst, 1988 for a complete description.)

Home and Family Environment

An extensive array of home environment measures have been collected throughout the course of this longitudinal study (A. E. Gottfried, A. W. Gottfried, & Bathurst, 1988; A. W. Gottfried & A. E. Gottfried, 1984). This chapter concentrates on home environmental measures tapping cognitive, social-emotional, and physical stimulation including, for example, responsivity of the parent, variety of stimulation, educational orientation, availability of play and learning materials, and fathers' involvement in the home. With regard to these variables, analyses are discussed for the following: direct home observations conducted at ages 15 months, 39 months, and eight years using the Home Observation for Measurement of the Environment (HOME) (Bradley, Caldwell, Rock, Hamrick, & Harris, 1988; Caldwell & Bradley, 1984); the Home Environment Survey (HES) (A. E. Gottfried, A. W. Gottfried, & Bathurst, 1988) administered to mothers at the 5- and 7-year assessments; and the Father Involvement Checklist (Bathurst, 1988; A. E. Gottfried, A. W. Gottfried, & Bathurst, 1988) administered to mothers at the 6- and 7-year assessments.

Child Care

When children were ages five and seven years, mothers were surveyed regarding the types of child care they used. Arrangements surveyed included family and center day care, babysitters, spouses and other relatives, school and after school programs, and use of more than one type of care.

Maternal Employment and Demographic Data

At each laboratory assessment, a survey was completed by mothers regarding employment status (full-time, part-time, or not employed)[2]. Family social history also provided information about marital status, number of children in the home, and socioeconomic status (SES) (Hollingshead, 1975). These latter variables were used as controls to determine that any effect of maternal employment would occur above and beyond these extraneous factors (marital status, number of children, SES). When children were age one, 36.2 percent of the mothers were employed. The rate of employment increased through age eight at which time 71 percent of mothers were employed. Virtually all parents were high school graduates with most having attended college or beyond. Parents' age averaged in the late twenties when the children were born. Fifty-five percent of children were first-borns at age one, and the average number of children in the family increased from 1.5 (one year) to 2.3 (age eight). Additional demographic data can be found in A. E. Gottfried, A. W. Gottfried, and Bathurst (1988) and A. W. Gottfried and A. E. Gottfried (1984).

Maternal Occupation, Hours of Employment, and Attitudes

Maternal occupation data were analyzed from infancy through age seven assessments and coded using the Hollingshead scale. Hours of weekly employment were collected from age five and analyzed through age seven. Work hours averaged 31-32 hours at ages five through seven. Maternal attitudes towards employment and

---

[2]There were no consistent differences in results between full- and part-time employment status, and throughout the study these two categories were combined.

parenting were surveyed during the laboratory assessments at ages five and seven, and included satisfaction with work and parenting, stress and spillover from work to family, personal satisfaction, and perceptions of dual responsibilities of work and parenting (A. E. Gottfried, A. W. Gottfried, & Bathurst, 1988). Higher scores indicated more favorable attitudes and perceptions and less stress.

Findings

Is maternal employment related to children's development?

This key question concerns whether maternal employment relates to children's development independently, that is, above and beyond SES, sex of child, marital status, number of children in the home, and home environment. It is essential to determine whether maternal employment has any immediate (contemporaneous) effects on children's development or whether it has a long-term (prospective) impact on later development. For example, the relationship of 12-month maternal employment status to 12-month child development was assessed (contemporaneous analyses) and was also examined as to its relationship to subsequent development at later ages. Contemporanous analyses were conducted through age eight and prospective analyses were conducted through age seven.

Results showed that maternal employment status was not consistently, significantly related to children's development either contemporaneously or prospectively. Children of working and nonworking mothers developed comparably from infancy through early childhood on measures of infant developmental status, cognition, intelligence, achievement, temperament, social competence, and behavioral adjustment. Developmental timing of employment (i.e., when the mother was employed) was not a significant factor in any of these developmental outcomes (A. E. Gottfried, A. W. Gottfried, & Bathurst, 1988).

Among the significant predictors of children's development were environmental measures, SES, and to a much lesser extent sex of child, and number of children in the home. Only the first will be discussed here as the latter three were primarily included as controls.

A higher degree of cognitive and social-emotional stimulation was favorably related to a variety of intellectual, language, and achievement outcomes both contemporaneously and across time from the preschool years onward. Educational stimulation (e.g., reading to the child and taking child to the library) and higher educational aspirations for the child were also related to intellectual development and school achievement both contemporaneously and over time from age five onward.

Is maternal employment related to home environment and fathers' involvement?

The degree to which home environment is related to maternal employment was a major interest of this research, since it is the view of the investigator that any effects of maternal employment on children's development occur through the home environment. Hence, in order to pursue this question, analyses were conducted to determine if maternal employment bore a relationship to home environment above and beyond SES, sex of child, number of children in the home, and marital status. Regarding father involvement, the question is significant as it deals with the balance of roles between mothers and fathers in homes where the mother is employed vs. not employed. It was expected that fathers would be more involved with their children when the mother was employed as time constraints and energy may make it necessary to share these functions.

Results showed that there were no significant differences in the home environments of employed and nonemployed mothers regarding the amount of cognitive, social, or physical stimulation (availability of play or learning materials), or in parent-child interactions, all of which had been observed using the HOME inventories at 15 months, 39 months, and eight years.

However, there were several aspects of the home environment that were related significantly to maternal employment. One concerned an environmental variable measured on the parent-completed Home Environment Survey. At ages five and seven years, maternal employment status significantly predicted the Educational

Attitudes factor of this survey. Analyses showed that mothers' Educational Attitudes were higher when they were employed. At age five, Educational Attitudes consisted of mothers' educational aspirations for the child (high school through professional), amount of TV viewing by child and mother, and child's possession of a real musical instrument. Higher scores on this factor indicated higher aspirations, less TV viewing by mother and child, and possession of a musical instrument. At age seven, Educational Attitudes consisted of the same items except that child receiving private lessons replaced possession of a musical instrument.

This relationship was observed not only in contemporaneous analyses, but it was also obtained in the prospective analyses. Earlier maternal employment status predicted subsequent educational attitudes beginning when the child was three-and-one-half years. Mothers who were employed when the children were ages three-and-one-half, five, and six were significantly more likely to score higher on the Educational Attitudes factor when children were age seven. These results occurred above and beyond SES, marital status, number of children, and sex of child.

Father involvement with the child showed a significant relationship with maternal employment. Father involvement was measured using a checklist, completed by mothers in the laboratory, at the 6- and 7-year assessments. It consisted of items pertaining to caretaking, doing chores and errands, provision of intellectually stimulating activities, and sharing of other activities with the child. The final measure at each age consisted of the total number of items checked as having been engaged in by the father.

At age six, fathers of children with employed mothers were significantly more involved than fathers of children with nonemployed mothers. Moreover, father involvement at age six was significantly predicted by maternal employment status at age five beyond the influence of SES, sex of child, marital status, and number of children in the home.

The Network of Relationships between Maternal Employment, Home Environment, and Children's Development

Although the children of employed vs. nonemployed mothers developed comparably and the home environments were also generally equivalent, there were some differences in their home environments, particularly with regard to mothers' educational attitudes and fathers' involvement. In order to understand the intricate network of relationships between maternal employment status on the one hand and children's development on the other, analyses relating educational attitudes, fathers' involvement, and children's development were conducted.

At age five, higher educational attitudes were related to higher intellectual functioning. Mothers' educational attitudes when the child was five also positively predicted reading and math achievement, and social adjustment in subsequent years. (Higher educational attitudes were related to more favorable child outcomes.) Results occurred above and beyond the influence of SES (A. E. Gottfried, A. W. Gottfried, & Bathurst, 1988).

Greater father involvement was related to more mature social adjustment at age six, higher IQ (ages six and seven), and higher achievement (ages six and seven) (A. E. Gottfried, A. W. Gottfried, & Bathurst, 1987, 1988). Thus, mother's educational attitudes and father involvement, both associated with the mother's employment were, in turn, predictive of more favorable aspects of children's development.

Child Care

Results of survey data on child care used by families are presented. There were no sex differences in any of the results to be reported, and hence, this issue will not be considered further.

Overall, results of the survey data indicated that child care choices were diverse. Data concern the child care choices of employed mothers when children were school age, that is, age five and age seven. At age five, the child care choices included school (nursery or kindergarten); day care in a home; day care in a center; babysitter in mother's home; babysitter in another's home; husband or other immediate family member; or live-in help. Mothers ($\underline{N}$ = 59) predominantly reported using two or more arrangements (67.8 percent). Of those reporting using one arrangement, school was the most frequent type (22 percent), with day care (5.1 percent) and family member (5.1 percent) being the least used.

At age seven, child care was surveyed for after school, evening, and weekend work hours. Of those reporting using child care ($\underline{N}$ = 57), 26 percent used babysitters at another home, 17.5 percent used husband or other family member; 13.5 percent used an after-school program; 3 percent used babysitters in the home; 2 percent used live-in help; 7 percent reported using "other" types of care; and 30 percent used a combination of 2 or more types of care.

Summary of Other Findings

Sex Differences. Analyses showed that there were no consistent gender differences in the effect of maternal employment on children's development nor in the role of maternal employment in home environment. Hence, the hypothesis that middle-class boys are disadvantaged by maternal employment (Bronfenbrenner, 1986; Hoffman, 1984) was not supported.

Consistency of Employment. In addition, the data through age seven were analyzed to determine if mothers' consistency of employment status (that is, consistently employed, consistently nonemployed, or change in employment status either into or out of the work force) had any relationship to children's development or home environment. Consistency or inconsistency of employment status bore little relationship to development or environment from infancy on.

Mothers' Occupation. Maternal occupational status was positively related to some developmental and environmental outcomes, however, these were not pervasive. Higher occupational levels were associated with higher levels of cognitive development (ages two, three-and-one-half, six and seven), achievement (ages six and seven), and more mature social adaptiveness (age six). Mothers with higher occupational statuses also had higher educational attitudes and aspirations (ages five and seven).

Hours of Employment. The hours a mother worked were related to developmental and environmental measures at ages five, six, and seven. While most relationships were nonsignificant, those that were significant showed that a greater number of hours was associated with higher educational attitudes (age five), but lower achievement (ages five and seven), and less educational stimulation in the home (age seven).

Mothers' Attitudes. At age five, more positive attitudes towards employment and dual roles of career and family were related to children's higher interest and participation in school and higher educational stimulation in the home. At age seven, when mothers were more available to children, had more job flexibility, and worried less about their children, mothers provided more educational stimulation. When mothers had more confidence and less stress with regard to their dual roles, children had higher achievement (age seven). More positive attitudes were also related to fewer child behavior problems (ages five and seven). In addition, mothers were more involved with their children if they had more favorable employment-related attitudes.

Satisfaction with parenting was positively related to higher achievement in children and more educational stimulation and maternal involvement at age seven but only for employed mothers. Parenting satisfaction was not related to children's development or home environment among nonemployed mothers.

Overall, although results for mothers' occupation, hours of employment, and attitudes were not entirely pervasive across all variables, there was enough consistency to indicate that mothers with higher occupational status, more favorable attitudes towards parenting and employment, and less stress tend to have children with higher cognitive development and/or achievement and homes that are higher in educational stimulation. On the other hand, as work hours increased there were some instances of lower achievement and educational stimulation. Even so, mothers who worked longer hours had higher educational attitudes and also tended to have higher occupational status, and both of these latter variables are positively related to developmental outcomes. All results were above and beyond family SES.

Conclusions and Issues

It is clear from the results of this extensive longitudinal study that children develop similarly well whether or not their mothers are employed. This is true from infancy through childhood and across varied developmental domains. Consistency and inconsistency of employment also bore no relationship to development. These findings are supported by other longitudinal studies (A. E. Gottfried & A. W. Gottfried, 1988b). Children of employed mothers are simply *not harmed* by their mothers' employment status. Rather, it is the proximal environment that is critical to children's development (A. E. Gottfried & A. W. Gottfried, 1988a; A. E. Gottfried, A. W. Gottfried, & Bathurst, 1988; A. W. Gottfried & A. E. Gottfried, 1984; 1986). For example, current and previous research (A. E. Gottfried, A. W. Gottfried, & Bathurst, 1988; A. W. Gottfried & A. E. Gottfried, 1984) indicates that provision of appropriately stimulating and responsive toys, reading to the child, taking the child to the library, allowing exploration of the home surroundings, encouraging a variety of experiences, having high aspirations for the child, spending time with the child encouraging academic activities, developing a warm, expressive, and cohesive family interaction style, and having the father involved with the child's activities are important for optimizing children's development. It is essential that parents be attuned to the needs and developmental progress of their children and move them to a level beyond their current one.

Analyses also showed that employed mothers are capable of providing a quality environment that is supportive of children's development. The provision of cognitive, social, and physical stimulation was equivalent in the homes of employed and nonemployed mothers. The variables that were significantly different between employed and nonemployed mothers seem particularly pertinent to employment itself. These were educational attitudes and fathers' participation with the child. Hoffman (1989) has recently reviewed literature indicating increased personal satisfaction for employed relative to nonemployed mothers. It seems logical that if employed mothers derive personal satisfaction from their careers, they would hold higher aspirations for their children. Additionally, their TV viewing is less frequent, as is their children's, which may reflect less time for such activities. They also provide more out of school lessons, and children are more likely to have musical instruments, again reflective of educational emphasis. The greater participation of fathers in employed-mother families is consistent with other maternal employment literature (Crouter, Perry-Jenkins, Huston, & McHale, 1987; Radin & Harold-Goldsmith, 1989). Interestingly, both of these factors--educational attitudes and fathers' participation--are positively related to children's development. Hence, although there is no direct relationship between maternal employment status and children's development, there is a network of factors that relate to development. Maternal employment is positively related to educational attitudes and father involvement, and these factors are positively related to children's development.

The network applies to other areas as well. For example, A. E. and A. W. Gottfried (1988a) suggested that maternal work hours may be associated with phenomena which provide both positive and negative effects on development. Higher work hours tend to be associated with higher occupational status and higher educational attitudes, both of which are positively related to children's development. However, longer work hours are also associated with lower educational stimulation (A. E. Gottfried, A. W. Gottfried, & Bathurst, 1988) and higher maternal anxiety (Owen & Cox, 1988). Together, these two trends may operate within a single home so that longer work hours can have both positive and negative relationships to a child's development. Overall, the two trends may result in no net influence on children's development. To the extent that one trend is predominant in any home, then longer work hours may be either more positive or negative. The family must be sensitive to stress or lowered stimulation that could result from undue work hours. Increased father involvement with children when mother is employed may also offset the role of maternal work hours since greater father participation is associated with more favorable development.

Hence, there may be no net difference between the children of employed and nonemployed mothers because there are networks of positive and negative factors operating in both types of homes. There may only be a visible impact where the home is noticeably imbalanced toward one kind of environmental factor.

It is suggested that maternal employment status will only have an impact on children's development to the extent that it influences the child's environment (A. E. Gottfried, A. W. Gottfried, & Bathurst, 1988). Where research reports either positive or negative effects of maternal employment status, one must look beyond these broad categories into the specific environment to determine what factors are related to this trend.

The data on child care were presented in this paper to indicate that balances made by families are varied. A. E. Gottfried and A. W. Gottfried (1988a) suggested that the manner in which families balance the demands of employment is the relevant next step in research on maternal employment. Although our present data on this issue pertain only to school-age children, several conclusions can be reached. Disentangling the impact of different child care arrangements on children's development involves the same issues that pertain to maternal employment. Specific proximal environmental variables within the child care setting are likely to impinge on children's development. For example, recent evidence indicates that the quality and stability of child care are related to children's development (Andersson, 1989; Howes, 1988; Goldberg & Easterbrooks, 1988). Research must examine proximal environmental variables in child care settings as they relate to children's development. When there are different types of child care across families or when a single family is using more than one type of care, it is essential to distinguish the child care type from the nature of environment (e.g., the social and emotional environment and the degree of stimulation and stability in the environment) with regard to its impact on development.

Second, child care can be considered to be an extension of the family. It has already been shown that mothers' attitudes towards separation from their children are related to child care use during the infancy and preschool period (Hock, DeMeis, & McBride, 1988). Child care choices may also be related to parental screening of the environment. Hence, child care may not randomly operate but may augment the parents' own attitudes and types of home environment provided.

On the other hand, the lack of availability of child care, particularly for infants (McMillan, 1989), may hamper parents' efforts to find the kind of child care consistent with their own proclivities, and the use of multiple forms of child care may represent this lack of availability.

Two caveats must be noted. First, while the data suggest that maternal employment affects home environment and home environment affects children's development, causality between these variables must be verified by statistical analyses. Second, the impact of maternal employment on children's development and home environment needs to be studied in families differing with regard to SES, ethnicity, and parenting status (e.g., in single parents).

Implications and Social Policy

Maternal employment is a social issue. We now have available a body of scientific evidence indicating that maternal employment per se is not detrimental to children's development. Relevant social policies can be based upon such knowledge (A. E. Gottfried & A. W. Gottfried, 1988).

A major social policy is to make the public aware of these findings. Not only can this occur through the media, but professionals who work with families (e.g., educators, mental health professionals, pediatricians, nurses) must be aware of the current findings and be able to work objectively with their clients' needs. Moreover, decisions about mothers' employment should be based on scientific knowledge rather than myth. Guilt about mothers' employment harming their children's development is not warranted in light of a body of evidence about the role of maternal employment in children's development.

Increased knowledge by professionals and lawmakers can help to promote programs aimed at helping families. The need for family responsiveness on the part of work supervisors is essential (Hughes & Galinsky, 1988), and research results can help to promote such attitudes.

In the field of law, this research has already made an impact. In a California Supreme Court ruling (Burchard v. Garay, 1986), it was decided that a mother's employment status could not be used to discriminate against her in deciding a child's custody arrangement. Our results (A. E. Gottfried, A. W. Gottfried, & Bathurst, 1985) regarding the absence of differences in the development of children with employed and nonemployed mothers provided a basis for this decision.

The results for father involvement indicate that increased father-child interaction is desirable. Hence, parental leave policies that include fathers would be beneficial. Further, sensitive supervisors in the workplace should allow fathers to be available for school events or child care responsibilities. Hughes and Galinsky (1988) found that fathers' work-family interference was greater when they worked more hours, when supervisors were insensitive to family issues, and when job demands and challenges were higher.

The most profound and immediate need for families is the availability of stable, quality child care from infancy through childhood. Increasing the availability of after school care is also in order judging from the multiple child care arrangements found in the present study. The number of child care arrangments must be reduced. If families use several arrangements, it is likely that there will be an increased incidence of child care breakdown, a phenomenon that affects women more than men (Galinsky, 1986; Hughes & Galinsky, 1988). Alternative types of child care are also needed to accommodate nontraditional schedules or parental preferences. The quality of the proximal environment needs to be developed to support the cognitive and social-emotional needs of children.

Finally, now that there is a body of evidence indicating that maternal employment is not detrimental to children, we need to support social policies and programs that will maximize the opportunities for all families to provide quality environments for their children.

Annotated Bibliography

Gottfried, A. E., & Gottfried, A. W. (Eds.). (1988b). *Maternal employment and children's development: Longitudinal research.* New York, NY: Plenum.

This is a compendium of longitudinal studies dealing with the role of maternal employment in children's development from infancy through adolescence and early adulthood. The focus of the research is on the family processes that mediate the impact of maternal employment. Each author provides an extensive review of the literature as well as original data from their own studies. There are six longitudinal studies as well as a chapter on corporate policies. In the final chapter, conclusions are drawn based upon the studies presented, and implications for public policy are advanced. Citations to specific chapters appear in the reference list.

Gottfried, A. W., & Gottfried, A. E. (1984). Home environment and cognitive development in young children of middle-socioeconomic-status families. In A. W. Gottfried (Ed.), *Home environment and early cognitive development: Longitudinal research* (pp. 57-115). New York: Academic Press.

This chapter focuses upon early home environment and its relationship to cognitive development from infancy through the preschool years. It provides the reader with additional information on the specific nature of home environment and types of factors consistently related to development. Other chapters in the book deal with the same issues in different populations. The final chapter integrates findings across studies and provides conclusions.

Hoffman, L. W. (1989). Effects of maternal employment in the two-parent family. *American Psychologist, 44,* 283-292. In this article the author reviews research dealing with family processes that modify the impact of maternal employment on children's development. Factors considered include parental attitudes, mothers' and fathers' roles, and parent-child interactions.

Howes, C. (1988). Relations between early child care and schooling. *Developmental Psychology, 24,* 53-57. Results of a longitudinal study are presented in which early day care, maternal employment, and quality and stability of day care are examined with regard to their impact on children's subsequent elementary school achievement.

Bibliography

Andersson, B. (1989). Effects of public day care: A longitudinal study. *Child Development, 60,* 857-866.

Bathurst, K. (1988). The inventories of family functioning: A psychometric analysis. *Dissertation Abstracts International, 49* (7), 2918B (University Microfilms No. DA88-22158).

Belsky, J., & Isabella, R. (1988). Maternal, infant, and social-contextual determinants of attachment security. In J. Belsky & T. Nezworski (Eds.), *Clinical implications of attachment* (pp. 41-94). Hillsdale, NJ: Lawrence Erlbaum.

Bradley, R. H., Caldwell, B. M., Rock, S. L., Hamrick, H. M., & Harris, P. (1988). Home observation for measurement of the environment: Development of a home inventory for use with families having children 6 to 10 years old. *Contemporary Educational Psychology, 13,* 58-71.

Bronfenbrenner, U. (1986). Ecology of the family as a context for human development: Research perspectives. *Developmental Psychology, 22,* 723-742.

Burchard v. Garay, 42 Cal.3d 531; *Cal.Rptr.,* P.2d (Sept. 1986).

Caldwell, B. M., & Bradley, R. H. (1984). *HOME observation for measurement of the environment.* Little Rock, AR: University of Arkansas at Little Rock.

Crouter, A. C., Perry-Jenkins, M., Huston, T. L., & McHale, S. M. (1987). Processes underlying father involvement in dual-earner and single-earner families. *Developmental Psychology, 23,* 431-440.

Galambos, N. L., Petersen, A. C., & Lenerz, K. (1988). Maternal employment and sex typing in early adolescence: Contemporaneous and longitudinal relations. In A. E. Gottfried & A. W. Gottfried (Eds.), *Maternal employment and children's development: Longitudinal research* (pp. 155-189). New York, Plenum.

Galinsky, E. (1986). Contemporary patterns of child care. In N. Gunzenhauser & B. M. Caldwell (Eds.), *Group care for young children* (pp. 13-24). Johnson & Johnson Baby Products Company Pediatric Round Table Series, 12. Skillman, NJ: Johnson & Johnson.

Goldberg, W. A., & Easterbrooks, M. A. (1988). Maternal employment when children are toddlers and kindergartners. In A. E. Gottfried & A. W. Gottfried (Eds.), *Maternal employment and children's development: Longitudinal research* (pp. 121-154). New York: Plenum.

Gottfried, A. E. (1988). Maternal employment and children's development: An introduction to the issues. In A. E. Gottfried & A. W. Gottfried (Eds.), *Maternal employment and children's development: Longitudinal research* (pp. 3-8). New York: Plenum.

Gottfried, A. E., & Gottfried, A. W. (1988a). Maternal employment and children's development: An integration of longitudinal findings with implications for social policy. In A. E. Gottfried & A. W. Gottfried (Eds.), *Maternal employment and children's development: Longitudinal research* (pp. 269-287). New York: Plenum.

Gottfried, A. E., & Gottfried, A. W. (Eds.). (1988b). *Maternal employment and children's development: Longitudinal research.* New York, NY: Plenum.

Gottfried, A. E., Gottfried, A. W., & Bathurst, K. (1985, August). *Maternal employment and children's development: A longitudinal study.* Paper presented at the annual convention of the American Psychological Association, Los Angeles.

Gottfried, A. E., Gottfried, A. W., & Bathurst, K. (1987, August). *Fathers' involvement, maternal employment, and young children's cognitive, academic, and social development.* Paper presented at the annual convention of the American Educational Research Association, Washington, DC.

Gottfried, A. E., Gottfried, A. W., & Bathurst, K. (1988). Maternal employment, family environment, and children's development: Infancy through the school years. In A. E. Gottfried & A. W. Gottfried (Eds.), *Maternal employment and children's development: Longitudinal research* (pp. 11-58). New York: Plenum.

Gottfried, A. W. (1984). Home environment and early cognitive development: Integration, meta-analyses, and conclusions. In A. W. Gottfried (Ed.), *Home environment and early cognitive development: Longitudinal research* (pp. 329-342). New York: Academic Press.

Gottfried, A. W., & Gilman, G. (1983). Development of visual skills in infants and young children. *Journal of the American Optometric Association, 54,* 541-544.

Gottfried, A. W., & Gottfried, A. E. (1984). Home environment and cognitive development in young children of middle-socioeconomic-status families. In A. W. Gottfried (Ed.), *Home environment and early cognitive development: Longitudinal research* (pp. 57-115). New York: Academic Press.

Gottfried, A. W., & Gottfried, A. E. (1986). Home environment and children's development from infancy through the school entry years: Results of contemporary longitudinal investigations in North America. *Children's Environments Quarterly, 3,* 3-9.

Greenberger, E., & Goldberg, W. A. (1989). Work, parenting, and the socialization of children. *Developmental Psychology, 25,* 22-35.

Hayghe, H. (1982). Dual-earner families: Their economic and demographic characteristics. In J. Aldous (Ed.), *Two paychecks: Life in dual-earner families* (pp. 27-40). Beverly Hills, CA: Sage.

Heyns, B. (1982). The influence of parents' work on children's school achievement. In S. Kamerman & C. D. Hayes (Eds.), *Families that work: Children in a changing world* (pp. 229-267). Washington, DC: National Academy Press.

Hock, E., De Meis, D., & McBride, S. (1988). Maternal separation anxiety: Its role in the balance of employment and motherhood in mothers of infants. In A. E. Gottfried & A. W. Gottfried (Eds.), *Maternal employment and children's development: Longitudinal research* (pp. 191-229). New York: Plenum.

Hoffman, L. W. (1984). Maternal employment and the young child. In M. Perlmutter (Ed.), *Parent-child interaction and parent-child relations in child development: The Minnesota Symposia on Child Psychology,* (Vol. 17, pp. 101-127). Hillsdale, NJ: Lawrence Erlbaum.

Hoffman, L. W. (1989). Effects of maternal employment in the two-parent family. *American Psychologist, 44,* 283-292.

Hollingshead, A. B. (1975). *Four factor index of social status.* Unpublished manuscript, Yale University (avaliable from Department of Sociology).

Howes, C. (1988). Relations between early child care and schooling. *Developmental Psychology, 24,* 53-57.

Hughes, D., & Galinsky, E. (1988). Balancing work and family lives: Research and corporate applications. In A. E. Gottfried & A. W. Gottfried (Eds.), *Maternal employment and children's development: Longitudinal research* (pp. 233-268). New York: Plenum.

Lerner, J. V., & Galambos, N. L. (1988). The influences of maternal employment across life: The New York Longitudinal Study. In A. E. Gottfried & A. W. Gottfried (Eds.), *Maternal employment and children's development: Longitudinal research* (pp. 59-83). New York: Plenum.

Marjoribanks, K. (1979). Family environments. In H. J. Walberg (Ed.), *Educational environments and effects* (pp. 15-37). Berkeley, CA: McCutchan Publishing Corp.

McMillan, P. (1989, July 24). Child care comes of age as issue, yet need grows. *Los Angeles Times,* pp. 1, 22.

Moos, R. H., & Moos, B. S. (1981). *Family Environment Scale manual.* Palo Alto, CA: Consulting Psychologists Press.

Owen, M. T., & Cox, M. J. (1988). Maternal employment and the transition to parenthood. In A. E. Gottfried & A. W. Gottfried (Eds.), *Maternal employment and children's development: Longitudinal research* (pp. 85-119). New York: Plenum.

Radin, N., & Harold-Goldsmith, R. (1989). The involvement of selected unemployed and employed men with their children. *Child Development, 60,* 454-459.

Wachs, T. D. (1989). The nature of the physical microenvironment: An expanded classification system. *Merrill-Palmer Quarterly, 35,* 399-419.

Maternal Employment and Adolescents[1]

Maryse H. Richards and Elena Duckett

I think I use my family as a crutch. They really help me out a lot,
but sometimes I just feel like breaking away from the crutch. I just
want to be on my own. But when I think about that, it scares me.
I think how lonely I'll feel. I worry that I won't be able to make
it. I don't even know where to begin. (*Changing Bodies, Changing
Lives,* p. 138)

The adolescent experience of family is paradoxical in nature,
marked by changes in needs for dependence and independence.
These changing needs have to be understood within the current
context of most families where both parents work outside the home
(Hayghe, 1986; Matthews & Rodin, 1989). Although research has
demonstrated no consistent effects of maternal employment on young
children, less is known about its effects during the critical biological,
social, and cognitive changes of early and mid-adolescence. The little
attention paid to the adolescent age groups (Hoffman, 1979) may be
the result of a belief that younger children need more constant
contact with their mothers than do older children (Montemayor &
Clayton, 1983).

In this chapter, we will discuss the effects of maternal
employment within the developmental periods of adolescence: early
adolescence (ages eleven to thirteen), and mid-adolescence (ages
fourteen to seventeen). We begin by addressing the developmental
needs of adolescents and the experience of their mothers. The
"larger picture" is considered next--in other words, the overall effects
of maternal employment on adolescent boys and girls. We then turn
to the family environment as a mediator of these effects. For
example, maternal employment may affect the amount and quality of

[1]This work was supported by NIMH grant number MH42618, "Effects of Maternal
Employment on Young Adolescents," awarded to Maryse H. Richards. We gratefully
acknowledge Christine Wittstock's assistance with this chapter.

interaction that adolescents have with parents, and this difference may, in turn, affect adolescent well-being. Research will be used to illuminate the impact of maternal employment on the following mediators: mother's role, parental availability, familial relations, and single-mother families. In conclusion, we discuss the after-school environment of the adolescent, with a focus on types of supervision and the necessity of community support for after-school activities.

The Adolescent

Adolescence, particularly early adolescence, is an age of transition during which children do not require baby sitters when parents are away from home but still need some measure of adult supervision and guidance. It is a time when children optimally receive a balance between autonomy and support from family. Regarding maternal employment and the developmental needs of the adolescent, Hoffman (1979) wrote, "The adolescent child needs guidance, love, and understanding, but he or she also needs autonomy, parental confidence and trust."

Because of the numerous changes occurring during this stage of life, adolescence forms a particularly important period in the life span to study the effects of parents' emotional and physical availability on the child. First, within the early adolescent years, the child's body becomes transformed into an adult one as a consequence of pubertal development (Richards, Abell, & Petersen, 1991). This major transformation will inevitably influence the perceptions a child has about him or herself, the ways of relating within and without the family, and the sense of a role within this world (Simmons & Blyth, 1987; Tobin-Richards, Boxer, & Petersen, 1983). Second, numerous social disruptions may take place at this time. Included in these are the transition from primary school to a relatively larger and more anonymous junior high or middle school, the initiation of heterosocial and heterosexual activities, changes in friendships and friendship groups, and changes in the family (Hill & Holmbeck, 1987; Simmons & Blyth, 1987; Steinberg, 1988). Third, cognitive change during early adolescence is associated with the emergence of qualitatively different reasoning abilities (Neimark, 1975). Fourth, gender intensification during adolescence means more time and energy is paid to gender-typed behaviors and experiences (Bush & Simmons, 1988; Richards & Larson, 1989). The physical appearance of sexual characteristics at puberty is believed to increase pressures to conform to traditional masculine and feminine gender roles (Hill & Lynch, 1983). The adolescent organizes and interprets daily occurrences in new ways and hence, people, events, and experiences are assigned new meanings. These developmentally related changes are then overlaid with the larger historical shifts of changing gender roles (Scanzoni & Fox, 1980).

The changes that describe adolescence mean gradually less time is spent with family and more time is spent with friends and alone (Larson & Richards, 1991). The gradual shift away from family appears to result in a different experience of maternal employment for adolescents relative to children, still requiring parents to be available but not omnipresent. This chapter will consider what this experience is.

The Adolescent's Mother

In addition to the developmental differences in the experience of maternal employment for the adolescent, the *mother* of an adolescent may experience employment differently than the mother of a younger child. As her child needs less day-to-day care, the adolescent's mother may have more time available for a paid job. Thus, employment is expected to be a more positive experience for the mother of a teenager than the mother of a much younger child. Hoffman (1979) suggests that the mother of an adolescent experiences a diminution of function when her child spends more time away from home and has less need for her companionship or daily guidance. This may be especially acute for the homemaker mother and in particular, the middle-class mother, who tends to have a smaller family and fewer demands on her time. With employment, Hoffman observes, "The mother is psychologically freer to encourage the child's independence and to communicate confidence in the child and the child's independence is more compatible with the needs of the [family] system" (p. 864).

Mothers of adolescents appear to detach to some extent from their children; mothers of eighth through twelfth graders reported more satisfaction when they participated in activities that did not include their adolescent children. In contrast, mothers of sixth and seventh graders reported more satisfaction when with their children (Montemayor & Brownlee, 1982). Finding no connection between maternal role satisfaction and the nature of the mother-adolescent relationship, Galambos, Petersen, and Lenerz (1988) suggest the impact of maternal role satisfaction is stronger when the child is younger, more dependent, and spends more time with the mother.

Beyond the family, the effects of maternal employment on adolescents need to be placed in the larger picture of society. There is often a tendency in the maternal employment literature to discuss the family in isolation of the community or larger context. As Bronfenbrenner, Garbarino, and Moen (1984) have noted, "In spite of the recent resurgence of interest in the ecological embeddedness of families in a wider network of social systems, the amount of empirical work in the [child development] area is still meager" (p. 283). What are the needs of the employed-mother family with regard to adolescents? What is society doing to meet such needs?

Effects of Maternal Employment: The Larger Picture

The effects of maternal employment on adolescents are not always consistent across studies (Table 1). This has led to the conclusion that maternal employment itself does not consistently or directly contribute to adolescent adjustment but is instead mediated by other characteristics (Bronfenbrenner & Crouter, 1982; Montemayor & Clayton, 1983). One of the more salient of these characteristics is the gender of the child. Maternal employment affects male and female adjustment differently (Montemayor & Clayton, 1983). For girls, maternal work appears to either enhance or not affect adjustment. Adolescent daughters of employed mothers have demonstrated greater independence, a more positive concept of the female role (Hoffman, 1979), less "fear of success" (Gilroy, Talierco, & Steinbacher, 1981), better personality and social adjustment (Gold & Andres, 1978a), and a tendency for higher academic achievement than daughters of nonemployed mothers (Query & Kuruvilla, 1975; Rees & Palmer, 1970). When maternal employment is not related to positive adjustment in girls, it tends to be associated with no effects (D'Amico, Haurin, & Mott, 1982; Dellas, Gaier, & Emihovich, 1979; Lerner & Galambos, 1988; Nelson 1971; Trimberger & MacLean, 1982). For boys, the pattern is less clear, with some suggestion of better adjustment with employed mothers (Gold & Andres, 1978a; Nelson, 1971; Trimberger & MacLean, 1982), counteracted by findings that maternal employment is associated with poorer adjustment (McCord, McCord, & Thurber, 1963), a strained father-son relationship in working-class families (Douvan & Adelson, 1966; Gold & Andres, 1978b; Propper, 1972), and lower academic achievement for sons in middle-class families (Banducci, 1967; Gold & Andres, 1978b). Other research indicates no relationship at all between adolescent boys' adjustment and maternal employment (Burchinal, 1963; D'Amico, Haurin, & Mott, 1982; Dellas et al., 1979; Lerner & Galambos, 1988).

The majority of these studies have focused on how maternal work might affect adolescent adjustment. We have little information, however, on what adolescents do from day to day under conditions of maternal employment and nonemployment. An on-going concern of society is whether children with employed mothers are properly supervised. It has been assumed that when activities are not supervised, adolescents will engage in less constructive, if not destructive, pursuits. The data on adolescents' activities reveal few differences between children of employed and nonemployed mothers in leisure pursuits (Medrich, Roizen, Rubin, & Buckley, 1982), though children of employed mothers, especially girls, have been found to do more household chores (Douvan & Adelson, 1966; Propper, 1972; White & Brinkerhoff, 1981). (See Bartko and McHale, this volume, for a discussion of this issue).

The impact of social change on attitudes toward maternal employment may also influence outcomes for children. In particular, research conducted prior to 1960 demonstrated more negative associations for male than female children (Bronfenbrenner & Crouter, 1982). Negative effects on boys found in the past were often based on lower-class samples with a focus on delinquency (Glueck &

Table 1
Summary of Studies

Adjustment and Emotional Well-Being

Studies	Number of Boys	Number of Girls	Age or Grade	Family Structure	Socio-Economic Status	Results
Gold & Andres, 1978b	114	109	10 years old	Two-parent	Working & middle class	Working class boys with employed mothers were described more negatively by their fathers and were more shy and nervous. Girls did not differ by maternal employment status.
Woods, 1972	61	47	5th graders	————	Lower class	Children of full-time employed mothers had better social adjustment scores[a]. The quality of the mother-child relationship and attitudes toward employment were also associated with better adjustment.
Dellas, Gaier, & Emihovich, 1979	54	55	9 - 12 years old	Two-parent	————	Maternal employment was unrelated to children's perceptions of their personal problems.

Adjustment and Emotional Well-Being (Continued)

Studies	Number of Boys	Number of Girls	Age or Grade	Family Structure	Socio-Economic Status	Results
Richards & Duckett, under review	165	169	5th - 8th graders	Two-parent	Working & middle class	Children of part-time employed mothers reported higher self-esteem and higher daily affect and arousal. No differences emerged between children of non-employed and full-time employed mothers.
Duckett & Richards, 1989	218	222	5th - 9th graders	Two-parent & single parent	Working & middle class	Children of full-time employed single mothers had higher daily emotional well-being[a].
Rosenthal & Hansen, 1981	274	281	7th - 9th graders	Two-parent & single parent	————	No differences were found between children of employed and nonemployed mothers in self-concept or vocational maturity.

Adjustment and Emotional Well-Being (Continued)

Studies	Number of Boys	Number of Girls	Age or Grade	Family Structure	Socio-Economic Status	Results
Nelson, 1971	156	156	9th graders	Two-parent	Working class	Boys had better personality adjustment when mothers worked full-time[a]. Girls with nonemployed mothers had better adjustment scores than girls with mothers who worked part time or full time.
Gold & Andres, 1978a	98	155	14 - 16 years old	Two-parent	Working & middle class	Children of employed mothers had better personality adjustment and total adjustment. They reported a greater sense of personal worth, personal freedom, a greater sense of belonging, and better family relations. Girls of employed mothers also had better overall social adjustment.
Propper, 1972	92	137	9th - 12th graders	Two-parent	Working class	Children's degree of participation in social activities did not differ consistently by maternal employment.

Adjustment and Emotional Well-Being (Continued)

Studies	Number of Boys	Girls	Age or Grade	Family Structure	Socio-Economic Status	Results
Whitmarsh, 1965	0	72	16 - 18 years old	Two-parent	Lower & middle class	Daughters of employed mothers reported fewer problems than daughters of full-time homemakers. Middle-class daughters of full-time employed mothers made the best adjustment in home and family life.
Lerner & Galambos, 1988	66	67	16 - 22 years old	Two-parent & single parent	Middle & upper-middle class	Maternal employment did not have an effect on adjustment or temperament.

Academic Achievement

Studies	Number of Boys	Girls	Age or Grade	Family Structure	Socio-Economic Status	Results
Gold & Andres, 1978b	114	109	10 years old	Two-parent	Working & middle class	Middle-class boys of employed mothers had lower scores on language and mathematics achievement tests. Working-class boys of employed mothers reported greater dislike of school and lower grades. Girls did not differ by maternal employment status.
Woods, 1972	61	47	5th graders	———	U p p e r - lower class	Children of full-time employed mothers had better intelligence scores[a]. The quality of the mother-child relationship and attitudes toward employment were also associated with high achievement.
Rosenthal & Hansen, 1981	274	281	7th - 9th graders	Two-parent & single parent	———	No differences were found between children of employed and nonemployed mothers in school achievement.

Academic Achievement (Continued)

Studies	Number of Boys	Girls	Age or Grade	Family Structure	Socio-Economic Status	Results
Query & Kuruvilla, 1975		225[b]	9th graders	Two-parent	————	Children of employed mothers, especially girls, tended to perform better on achievement tests. Daughters of mothers with higher levels of occupation and education performed significantly better on achievement tests.
Nelson, 1969	156	156	9th graders	Two-parent	Working class	There was no difference in school achievement among children with nonemployed, part-time, or full-time employed mothers.
Gold & Andres, 1978a	114	109	14 - 16 years old	Two-parent	Working & middle class	No differences were found between children of employed and nonemployed mothers in achievement scores.
Banducci, 1967	1520	1494	High school seniors	Two-parent	Working & middle class	There was a trend for all children of employed mothers to have higher educational aspirations except for middle-class boys of employed mothers who had lower grade point averages and lower educational aspirations. Working class boys of employed mothers had higher grade point averages.

Academic Achievement (Continued)

Studies	Number of Boys	Girls	Age or Grade	Family Structure	Socio-Economic Status	Results
D'amico, Haurin & Mott, 1983	143	174	Longitudinal study; 14-17 years old when study began; 24-27 years old at time of results	Two-parent	————	Maternal employment had no pervasive effect on the educational or career paths of children.

Sex-Role Concepts

Studies	Number of Boys	Girls	Age or Grade	Family Structure	Socio-Economic Status	Results
Marantz & Mansfield, 1977	0	98	5-11 years old	————	Middle class	Overall, daughters of employed mothers showed fewer sex-role stereotypes. However, 9-11-year-olds showed little stereotyping regardless of maternal employment status.
Bacon & Lerner, 1975	0	126	2nd, 4th, and 6th	————	Working class	Although girls in all grades expected that they themselves would engage in traditional female vocations, daughters of employed mothers were more likely to see male-dominated occupations as open to both sexes.

Sex-Role Concepts (Continued)

Studies	Number of Boys	Number of Girls	Age or Grade	Family Structure	Socio-Economic Status	Results
Gold & Andres, 1978b	114	109	10 years old	Two-parent	Working & middle class	Children of employed mothers had the most egalitarian sex-role concepts.
Dellas, Gaier, & Emihovich, 1979	54	55	9 - 12 years old	Two-parent	————	Only the pre-adolescent children showed more liberal sex-role concepts. Older children did not differ by maternal employment.
Galambos, Peterson, & Lenerz, 1988	153	182	6th - 8th graders	Two-parent & single parent	Middle & upper middle class	Maternal employment was associated with more egalitarian sex-role attitudes only in sixth grade.
Rosenthal & Hansen, 1981	274	281	7th - 9th graders	Two-parent & single parent	————	No differences were found between children of employed and nonemployed mothers in occupational aspirations.
Chandler, Sawicki, & Stryffeler, 1981	225	213	8th graders	————	————	Children of employed mothers expressed more liberal attitudes toward women's role, but maternal employment was not associated with more liberal attitudes toward women workers.

Sex-Role Concepts (Continued)

Studies	Number of Boys	Number of Girls	Age or Grade	Family Structure	Socio-Economic Status	Results
Stephan & Corder, 1985	171	156	8th - 12th graders	Two-parent	Middle class	Children from dual-career families had more liberal sex-role attitudes and greater preferences for dual-career families. However, peers and same-sex parents had the greatest influence on children's sex-role models.
Gold & Andres, 1978a	98	155	14 - 16 years old	Two-parent	Working & middle class	Children with employed mothers had the most egalitarian sex role concepts; however, this was primarily related to their mothers' greater satisfaction with their roles.
Gilroy, Talierco, & Steinbacher, 1981	0	90	13 - 17 years old	Two-parent	Middle class	Daughters of employed mothers were more androgynous and demonstrated less fear of success than daughters of nonemployed mothers.

Sex-Role Concepts (Continued)

Studies	Number of Boys	Number of Girls	Age or Grade	Family Structure	Socio-Economic Status	Results
Gardener & LaBrecque, 1986	~	~ 172	High school seniors	Two-parent & single parent	Middle class	Children of employed mothers had a more liberal sex-role orientation and attitude toward division of household tasks.
Almquist & Angrist, 1971	0	110	College students	-------	-------	College women with employed mothers were more likely to be career-oriented.
Altman & Grossman, 1977	0	51	College seniors	-------	-------	Daughters of employed mothers were more career-oriented. Daughters of nonemployed mothers who perceived their mothers as dissatisfied were also more career-oriented than those who perceived mothers as satisfied.

Family Relations

Studies	Number of Boys	Girls	Age or Grade	Family Structure	Socio-Economic Status	Results
Richards & Duckett, under review	226	225	5th - 8th graders	Two-parent	Working & middle class	Maternal employment was not associated with amount of time children spent with family. Fifth and sixth graders spent less time with employed mothers. Fathers compensated for decreased time with mother so that there was no difference in overall time with parents.
Rosenthal & Hansen, 1981	274	281	7th - 9th graders	Two-parent & single parent	————	Maternal employment was not associated with children's perceptions of their parents.
Propper, 1972	92	137	9th - 12th graders	Two-parent	Working class	Children of employed mothers had slightly more household responsibility. Parent-child disagreement was more common when mother was employed, but perceptions of parental interest and closeness were similar to children with nonemployed mothers.

Family Relations (Continued)

Studies	Number of Boys	Girls	Age or Grade	Family Structure	Socio-Economic Status	Results
Montemayor, 1984	30	34	10th graders	Two-parent	Middle class	Boys of employed mothers had more arguments with their mothers and siblings than those with nonemployed mothers. Both boys and girls spent less time with their parents and more time with their peers when mothers were employed. Boys who spent the most time alone had mothers who worked full-time.
Douvan & Adelson, 1966	700	1162	Boys: 14 - 16 years old. Girls: 11 - 18 years old	Two-parent	Working & middle class	Daughters of part-time employed mothers were closest to their parents and most often chose their mothers as their adult ideal relative to girls with nonemployed or full-time employed mothers. Daughters of employed mothers did more household chores. Maternal employment was related to few differences among boys except in the working class. Working class boys with employed mothers were less likely to choose their fathers as their adult ideal.

Family Relations (Continued)

Studies	Number of Boys	Number of Girls	Age or Grade	Family Structure	Socio-Economic Status	Results
Jenson & Borges, 1986	0	53	18 - 26 years old	Two-parent	Middle & upper-middle class	Daughters of employed mothers recalled a less close relationship with their fathers, perceived them as less happy and friendly, and recalled more anger and tension in the home during their adolescence.

Self-Care

Studies	Number of Boys	Number of Girls	Age or Grade	Family Structure	Socio-Economic Status	Results
Rodman, Protto, & Nelson, 1985	54	42	4th - 7th graders	Two-parent & single parent	Working & middle class	No differences were found between children in self care and children in adult care on measures of social and psychological functioning.
Woods, 1972	61	47	5th graders	-------	Lower class	More girls than boys were unsupervised, and the unsupervised girls had deficits in cognitive functioning.

Self-Care (Continued)

Studies	Number of Boys	Number of Girls	Age or Grade	Family Structure	Socio-Economic Status	Results
Trimberger & MacLean, 1982	22	29	5th - 7th graders	Two-parent	Middle class	Older children, girls, and children who stayed alone after school felt more negatively affected by their mothers' employment than younger children, boys, and children who were supervised after school.
Steinberg, 1986	394	468	5th - 9th graders	Two-parent & single parent	Working & middle class	Adolescents who went home after school were not different from those who were supervised by their parents after school. However, the more removed from supervision that children were, the more susceptible they were to peer pressure. Adolescents who were at home alone were less susceptible to peer pressure than those who were at a friend's house, who were, in turn, less susceptible than those who "hung out" after school.

[a]Mothers' full-time employment was contrasted with part-time and nonemployment.
[b]Number of boys and girls was not provided.

Glueck, 1957; Gold, 1961). In these studies, mothers may have been forced to seek employment out of economic necessity and not out of choice. In addition, their employment status placed them in the minority. In a review of more recent literature (1960 to 1980), Bronfenbrenner and Crouter (1982) came to the conclusion that maternal employment does not produce predictable effects. With large numbers of mothers currently working outside the home, maternal employment has become the norm. Historical time appears to constitute an important moderating variable; the more recent years may reflect a greater acceptance of maternal employment by society.

The mixed picture suggests that it is not maternal employment status alone that affects adolescent development. As Maccoby (1958) pointed out over 30 years ago and as others have re-emphasized (Bronfenbrenner & Crouter, 1982; Montemayor & Clayton, 1983), the inconsistent results in the literature suggest the existence of mediating factors. The underlying processes that might be affected by maternal employment must be addressed. As Galambos et al. (1988) observe "... studies that compare groups of adolescents according to maternal work status provide only a limited understanding of relationships .... The state of contemporary research ... requires a more fine-grained analysis of family processes" (p. 183). We turn now to those processes which mediate the effects of maternal employment with a discussion of the adolescent's experience of family.

The Adolescent's Family

Perhaps the most critical variable mediating the impact of maternal employment on adolescent development is the family environment. As Bronfenbrenner (1986) observes, the family is a principal context in which young people develop, but it is not secluded from the influences of other domains. Parental work outside the home shapes a host of factors in the familial climate, the most salient of which is parents' ability to create a nurturing environment for their children. In their recent study of the effects of maternal employment on children's development, Gottfried, Gottfried, and Bathurst (1988) emphasized the importance of family environmental processes over the single fact of employment status:

Maternal employment itself is a distal variable. It categorizes
mothers on the basis of employment or nonemployment. Such
categorization gives no information regarding the quality of home
environment provided to children. Additionally, maternal
occupation, attitudes, and number of hours may vary within the
proximal home environment. Hence, to understand the effects of
maternal employment on children, one must examine the proximal
home environment and its relationship to both maternal
employment and children's development. (p.13)

In response to the physical, cognitive, and social changes that occur
during early adolescence, patterns of familial interaction may also
change. As youths move toward greater autonomy in their
relationships with parents, many families experience increased parent-
child conflict and emotional distance (Hill & Holmbeck, 1987; Papini,
Datan, & McCluskey-Fawcett, 1988; Steinberg, 1988). This tension
appears to be most pronounced between adolescents and their
mothers (Hill & Holmbeck, 1987). But the issue of maternal
availability ought not to be overlooked during the child's adolescence.
Although teenagers' growing sense of autonomy may lead to greater
discord with family, there is evidence to suggest that the parent-
adolescent relationship does not appear to dissolve but instead
changes (Richardson, Galambos, Schulenberg, & Peterson, 1984).
Young adolescents' total amount of time with family members has
been found to gradually decrease, but quantity of time with *parents*
remains unchanged (Larson & Richards, 1991). Parents continue to
function as a basis of supervision, guidance, and support even as the
parent-child relationship is altered.

The Availability of Mother

One of the persistent underlying assumptions about the
effects of maternal employment on children is that mothers' paid
employment will mean less availability of mothers to their children,
and that this lessened availability is detrimental to children's welfare.
The vast majority of the research on maternal employment and
quantity of time with mother has focused on young children with the
assumption that because adolescents spend most of their waking
hours in school, they do not suffer any decrement in time with an
employed mother. Potential negative effects of less time with
mother, however, include lack of supervision, "latchkey" status, and

heightened negative peer influence (see Galambos & Maggs, this volume). And yet, lessened maternal availability may have positive consequences; for example, greater father involvement, less restrictive childrearing attitudes and practices, and greater adolescent independence.

The first question that must be addressed is whether mothers employed outside the home actually spend *less time* with their adolescent children than full-time homemakers. Montemayor (1984) examined maternal employment and the amount of time that adolescents spend with parents. Teenagers were found to spend less time with both parents when mothers were employed, particularly when mothers worked full time (Montemayor, 1984). In our recent study of early adolescence, developmental differences were revealed in the effects of maternal employment on time spent with parents, with fifth and sixth graders spending less time with employed mothers while seventh and eighth graders of employed mothers did not experience diminished maternal contact (Richards & Duckett, 1990). Although time with mother was diminished, time with parents did not differ by mothers' employment status.

The little research that has directly studied time spent with parents seems to point to some diminution of time with employed mothers for some children but not others and some compensatory increase in father time. Our findings lead us to speculate that the pre-adolescent may need the parent to establish contact while young and middle adolescents are more capable of seeking parental contact themselves. Because the studies on adolescents are scarce, more research is needed before we can confidently say that maternal employment definitely diminishes the time these youths spend with their parents.

Maternal Availability: Boys versus Girls

When adolescents are negatively affected by lessened maternal availability, boys appear most vulnerable. The negative effects of maternal employment on boys may be explained by a relative lack of parental structure. In particular, the lower academic achievement found more often among boys than girls when mothers work outside the home (Gold & Andres 1978a; Nelson, 1969; Query & Kurvilla, 1975; Rosenthal & Hansen, 1981) may be attributed to less parental supervision. Boys may experience greater difficulty making parental contact when mother is less available. We have found that boys are generally less involved with family life than girls are (Richards & Larson, 1989), a tendency that mothers' employment may enhance. Additionally, parents may seek boys out less often than girls, perhaps on the assumption that boys do not need as much parental contact and supervision as girls. Yet in fact, boys may actually need more structure (Bronfenbrenner & Crouter, 1982) in the form of monitoring homework, peer contact, sports participation, and television viewing. As discussed above, maternal employment is not always associated with negative effects for boys, but those that do emerge may reflect the adolescent male's lack of developmental readiness for the relative freedom that an employed mother may, at times, allow.

Maternal employment does *not* appear to increase family conflict or peer contact among girls as it does among boys (Montemayor, 1984). These findings are consistent with the generally positive effects of maternal employment on adolescent girls' psychological adjustment (Bronfenbrenner & Crouter, 1982; Hoffman, 1979) and the lack of detrimental effects on academic performance (Gold & Andres, 1978a, 1978b; Nelson, 1969; Rosenthal & Hansen, 1981).

Mother as Role Model

Maternal employment affects children, especially daughters, in ways other than availability. Researchers have suggested that the employed mother may be a positive role model, particularly for her daughter. Girls with employed mothers have been found to express greater admiration for their mothers, report a more positive concept of the female role, and display greater independence (Baruch, 1972; Douvan & Adelson, 1966). Boys and girls report more liberal sex-role concepts[2] when their mothers are employed (Gold & Andres, 1978a, 1978b; Stephen & Corder, 1985). Not only do adolescents from dual-worker families tend to have less traditional sex-role attitudes, but relative to adolescents from traditional single-earner families, they expect to have a dual-career family themselves (Banducci, 1967; Stephan & Corder, 1985) and they report more liberal attitudes toward the division of household tasks (Gardner & LaBrecque, 1986).

Accompanying more liberal sex-role concepts, high school senior girls and college females with employed mothers tended to have higher educational aspirations and expectations (Banducci, 1967; Stein, 1973), demonstrated less fear of success (Gilroy, Talierco, & Steinbacher, 1981), believed most occupations should be open to both sexes (Bacon & Lerner, 1975; Chandler, Sawicki, & Struffeler, 1981; Gold & Andres, 1978a), and were more career-oriented than the daughters of nonemployed mothers (Almquist & Angrist, 1971; Altman & Grossman, 1977). Maternal employment has been said to be the most consistent correlate of a female's departure from the traditional feminine role as evidenced by her desire to pursue a career (Huston-Stein & Higgins-Trenk, 1978). An employed mother may model an entire range of behaviors that affect her children's attitudes, especially those of her daughter. For example, the employed mother may display characteristics of independence and competence in areas beyond the domestic environment as well as the nurturant and care-giving behaviors that are traditionally associated with the female role.

Not surprisingly, the sex-role concepts of boys are not as strongly affected as girls. While there is some evidence that boys with employed mothers have more liberal sex-role perceptions than those with homemaker-mothers (Chandler et al., 1981; Gold & Andres, 1978a; 1978b), other studies have found no difference (Dellas et al., 1979; Gold & Andres, 1980). The role model theory offers one

---

[2]Sex role concepts, attitudes, perceptions and ideology will be used interchangeably here to represent the expectations that certain behaviors, thoughts, and emotions are appropriate to one gender or the other.

explanation for the greater frequency of positive effects found for girls with employed mothers and not for boys.

In contrast to these findings are the lack of differences found with samples of older adolescents. Sex-role ideology was found to differ by maternal employment status only for preadolescents and not adolescents (Dellas et al., 1979). In one of the few longitudinal studies of maternal employment and adolescents, Galambos et al. (1988) found a slight effect of maternal employment status on the sex-role attitudes of sixth graders but no effects on eighth graders. Similar differences were reported by Gold & Andres (1978a) when comparing fifteen-year-olds with younger children. Maternal employment was related to nontraditional sex-role concepts in middle-childhood, but the strength of this relationship was diminished in early adolescence (Chandler et al., 1981; Marantz & Mansfield, 1977). In adolescence, peer pressure may become a more salient influence on sex-role concepts than mothers' employment (Montemayor & Clayton, 1983). These findings may reflect developmental differences; in contrast to younger children, the sex-role identity of an adolescent may not be influenced by maternal work status.

Maternal Role Satisfaction

Mother's satisfaction with her role and her psychological health may contribute more to a child's adjustment than employment per se. Lerner and Galambos (1985) describe a "process of influence" model in which maternal role satisfaction affects mother-child interaction and this affects child adjustment. They found that mothers who are more satisfied with their roles, employed or not, have more positive interactions with their children and these children were better adjusted than those of dissatisfied mothers (Lerner & Galambos, 1985). Other studies confirm that when the mother's attitude about working outside the home matches her employment status, positive outcomes for the child are the result (Gold & Andres, 1978b; Woods, 1972). In addition, a match of education and employment (high education and full-time employment; low education and non- or part-time employment) contributes to enhanced self-esteem and diminished depression in mothers, and their young adolescent children report more positive daily affect when mothers also report high affect (Joebgen & Richards, 1990). Inversely related to role satisfaction, mother's role difficulty appears to predict lessened male athletic competence (Lerner, Hess, & Banerjee, 1986).

But the relationship between mother's role satisfaction and child adjustment seems to diminish in later adolescence. Again, developmental differences may explain why maternal role satisfaction affects adolescents less than younger children. In explaining the lack of a relationship between role satisfaction and adolescent well-being, Galambos and colleagues (1988) wrote that this "may reflect the greater amount of time spent with peers (during later adolescence) relative to time spent with family in early adolescence. That is, the mother's role satisfaction might influence the nature of the mother-child relationship when the child is young and there is extensive contact between them, but the nature and quantity of time spent with the mother in early adolescence may decrease the likelihood of such a relationship" (Galambos et al., 1988, p. 183).

Contact and Interaction with Father

Relationships with mothers are not singularly affected by maternal employment; fathers also may relate to their adolescent children differently when their wives work outside the home. In our study, the fifth and sixth graders with employed mothers experienced less maternal contact than those with homemaker mothers, but the total quantity of time that these children spent with at least one parent was not reduced by maternal employment. We found that fathers compensated for less time with mother so that there was no decrement in the amount of overall parental contact (Richards & Duckett, 1990). Older adolescents, however, were found to spend less time with both mother and father when mother was employed (Montemayor, 1984).

Mothers have been called the "gatekeepers" of children's time with fathers. Turning to animal studies, when circumstances ensure that a male rat has sufficient exposure to his young, he will demonstrate care giving behavior (Rosenblatt, Siegel, & Meyer, 1979). Human fathers may be more likely to supervise their children as well as interact with them when mothers are less available to engage in these activities. Because mother's work outside the home may decrease her availability to her children, maternal employment may influence, in part, the extent of a father's involvement with his children.

In a comprehensive review of the research on fathers' involvement with their children, Pleck (1983) suggested that the data reveal very few differences between husbands of employed and nonemployed wives in amount of participation in child rearing. Instead, the *proportion* of family work in which husbands engaged was higher for those with employed wives simply because employed women spent less time on these tasks (Pleck, 1983). Most of this research has focused on time spent in care or play with young children. Consequently, there is a considerable gap in the data on older children and adolescents. If we are to fully understand paternal participation in child rearing, further research is needed on fathers' interaction with older children.

Adolescents' Experience of Family Interaction

The quantity of time that adolescents spend with parents is perhaps less important than what occurs during that time. An area in need of study is how maternal work status influences the kinds of activities in which parents and children engage (Bronfenbrenner & Crouter, 1982). Adolescents with employed mothers were found to spend less "free time" with their parents than those with homemaker mothers, but the quantity of chores done with parents was not associated with mother's work status (Montemayor, 1984). In our sample of younger adolescents, boys and seventh and eighth grade girls with employed mothers experienced less leisure with family. In contrast, daughters of employed mothers spent more time doing homework with parents (Richards & Duckett, 1990).

We know very little about how maternal employment might affect the way that children *feel*. In our study, maternal work status had few effects on the moods of children from two-parent families when they were with family or with parents (Richards & Duckett, 1990). These findings are consistent with more recent research that shows no difference by mothers' employment status in children's perceptions of their parents (Rosenthal & Hansen, 1981) or family relationships and interactions (Dellas et al., 1979).

In considering the effects of mothers' work status on their relationships with adolescent children, two views have dominated the literature. On the one hand, maternal employment is thought to lead to better mother-child relations, particularly for girls, by fostering adolescents' autonomy and contributing to their sense of family (Hoffman, 1979). Evidence for this view is garnered from several studies. Daughters of employed mothers reported fewer home-related problems than daughters of homemakers (Whitmarsh, 1965) and also tended to express more admiration for their mothers (Baruch, 1972; Douvan & Adelson, 1966). Hoffman (1979) points out that girls and boys alike gain a better sense of belonging with family from the household responsibilities they take on while their mothers work outside the home.

On the other hand, maternal employment has been associated with increased familial conflict. The most frequent explanation for these tensions is that home chores lead to more strained mother-adolescent relations if the child resents the additional household responsibility. Older children, who tend to have greater responsibility for household tasks and caretaking of siblings, feel more negatively affected by their mother's employment than younger children (Trimberger & MacLean, 1982). Women whose mothers worked full-time recalled more anger and tension during their adolescence than women whose mothers were not employed (Jenson & Borges, 1986). Adolescent sons reported more arguments with their mothers and siblings when their mothers were employed (Montemayor, 1984). Other studies have also found more disagreements between parents and children in employed-mother households, but the disagreements are attributed to the adolescent's greater autonomy--these children are more likely to question parental restriction than those with nonemployed mothers (Douvan & Adelson, 1966; Propper, 1972).

Less restrictive childrearing attitudes may also facilitate greater maturity and independence in adolescents. Gold and Andres

(1978a) felt that less restrictive childrearing contributed to the better adjustment they found in adolescents with employed mothers. The greater opportunity for independence in the employed-mother family may be particularly beneficial to girls. Chodorow (1978) suggests that mothers and daughters can become enmeshed in their relationships, making it difficult for girls to develop a distinct sense of separate self. Employment compels the mother to expand her role psychologically as well as physically beyond the home, consequently lessening the intensity of the mother-daughter relationship.

The number of hours that mothers work have been found to moderate these effects. In a major study of maternal employment and adolescents, Douvan and Adelson (1966) found that daughters of part-time employed mothers experienced the closest relations with their parents and reported the strongest emotional bond with their parents in comparison to mothers who worked full time or not at all. In contrast, daughters of nonemployed and full-time employed mothers experienced less mature relationships with their parents. Douvan and Adelson suggest that full-time and part-time employment each render a qualitatively different experience for the child, with part-time employment appearing to offer maternal availability as well as a model of competence for adolescent daughters. Part-time employment may enhance general well-being; the seventh and eighth graders in our sample with part-time employed mothers reported higher self-esteem and higher daily affect and arousal than those with non employed or full-time employed mothers. There were no significant differences between the non employed and full-time employed groups (Richards & Duckett, 1990). Part-time maternal employment may achieve the appropriate balance of parental availability for meeting the adolescent's simultaneous needs for dependence and independence (Douvan & Adelson, 1966; Nye, 1963). It may foster an atmosphere of parental protection that also allows the child to begin the necessary tasks of individuating and separating.

Single-Mother Families

It is important to note that family structure may influence the effects of maternal employment on adolescents. In our study, the experience of maternal work differed dramatically for young adolescents of single mothers. While mothers' work status did not directly affect the emotional well-being of children living in two-parent families, *full-time* maternal employment was linked to enhanced daily affect and arousal as well as self-esteem for adolescents of *single mothers* (Duckett & Richards, 1989). The consistent pattern of these findings despite the removal of socioeconomic and community effects suggests that there is something beyond income that is influencing well-being in these youths.

We also found that the quality of parent-child interaction was linked to maternal employment solely for children of single mothers. They reported higher affect while with mother, perceived their fathers as friendlier, and felt closer to their fathers than those children with part-time employed or nonemployed single mothers (Duckett & Richards, 1989). With the absence of longitudinal data, however, we cannot assume maternal employment is causing positive experience. The lower well-being observed among youths in the nonemployed and part-time groups might be related to the distress of mothers or children that prevented mothers from taking a full-time job. But rather than familial well-being affecting a mother's decision to work, we speculate that it is the employment situation which fosters her psychological health and, in turn, affects her child. For single women, psychological well-being is strongly associated with paid employment (Warr & Parry, 1982). The higher well-being of employed single mothers may positively affect mother-child interaction as manifested in adolescents' daily moods and self-esteem during this time.

The enhanced moods that these youths also experienced with their fathers are possibly related to the mother's desire and ability to maintain cordial relations with the non-custodial parent. The full-time employed mother may experience time constraints that necessitate reliance on the father as a resource of supervision and care for children. Consequently, the children of these mothers experience more frequent contact with their fathers, a situation which seems to foster a better relationship. Furthermore, employment compels the mother to expand her role beyond the home, thus lessening the intensity of the mother-child relationship. Full-time employed single mothers may possess a greater capacity to permit a close relationship between children and their fathers.

The After-School Environment

A concern that both single parents and two-parent families share is what happens to their children after school. This can be particularly troubling for adolescents who are too old for certain types of supervision but too young to be left completely on their own.

Self-care

A more recent focus of research in this area concerns the supervision of children and adolescents (see Galambos & Maggs, this volume). Once again the research is spotty with adolescents; because adolescents are often believed to be mature enough to care for younger children they are not expected to need supervision themselves (Long & Long, 1983). Although self-care, also known as "latchkey" or "unsupervised," arrangements are believed to have detrimental consequences for children, the little research evidence that exists is equivocal. Certain studies demonstrate negative effects (Long & Long, 1983; Woods, 1972), while others find no significant differences in social and psychological functioning between older children and adolescents in self-care and adult care arrangements (Galambos & Garbarino, 1983; Rodman, Pratto, & Nelson, 1985).

Variations in these studies are illuminating. Studying fifth to seventh graders, Galambos and Garbarino (1983) found no differences between self-care, adult-care, and mother-care children on measures of academic achievement, fear of going outdoors alone, classroom orientation, and teacher-rated adjustment. Similarly, Rodman, Pratto, and Nelson (1985) found no differences in self-esteem, locus of control, or teachers' ratings of social adjustment and interpersonal relations between fourth and seventh graders in self-care and adult care. In a Canadian study of fourteen- to sixteen-year-olds, Gold and Andres (1978b) found no differences between supervised and unsupervised adolescents on measures of sex-role concept, adjustment, academic achievement and intelligence.

In contrast, fifth through seventh graders who stayed alone after school felt more negatively affected by their mothers' employment than children who were supervised after school (Trimberger & MacLean, 1982). In a lower class sample, Woods (1972) found impoverished cognitive development in fifth graders in self-care relative to those who were supervised by adults. Although Long and Long (1983) found higher levels of fear among first through sixth graders in self-care, their findings are based on individual case histories. In examining the variations in self-care experiences, Steinberg (1986) found no differences in "latchkey" adolescents who are at home alone after school versus those who are at home under adult care, but greater susceptibility to peer pressure was found among fifth, sixth, eighth and ninth graders who spend time at a friend's house without adult supervision or who "hang-out" after school. The further adolescents were removed from adult supervision, the more susceptible they were to peer pressure.

These studies converge in suggesting that self-care by itself is not critical to adolescent well-being. Instead, the larger community "safety net" (Galambos & Garbarino, 1983) and the type of self-care arrangements (Steinberg, 1986) available to adolescents emerge as important to their psychological welfare. As Steinberg (1986) observed, "... variations in the setting in which self-care takes place, variations in the extent to which absent parents maintain distal supervision of their children, and variations in patterns of child rearing--are more important than variations between adult care and self-care, broadly defined" (p. 438).

The need for more research on the nature of self-care arrangements is very apparent. What does a child actually do and feel under self-care? Are children lonely, scared, or bored, or are they able to structure their time in a satisfying manner? Furthermore, researchers have not begun to explore times other than the after-school hours when children's parents are not at home. Many employed mothers have schedules that require their absence from home during mornings, evenings, or nights. What happens to children then? How do their experiences differ from children who are without adult supervision only after school?

Adolescents and After-School Activities

With increasing numbers of children in self-care, there is a need for extracurricular and community-sponsored activities to help structure their time. The importance of out-of-school services is emphasized in a study of children's time use headed by Medrich (1982):

> A surprisingly large proportion of children are "heavy users" of four facilities commonly located in neighborhoods -- school yards, parks, recreation centers, and libraries.... But few can be happy with the situation that is unfolding, for young adolescents' needs are coming into focus just as many communities are withdrawing fiscal support for these out-of-school activities. (p. 2)

As Medrich points out, community services and government policies often overlook the needs of young people. The data have shown that maternal employment status does not directly affect adolescents' well-being but has different outcomes under different circumstances. Rather than debating whether mothers should or should not work, parents and the elected officials who represent them need to ensure that children have choices in how to spend their leisure time. The opportunity for supervised activities enhances the conditions of maternal employment for adolescents and also reduces the strain on parents. Since employed mothers are not always available to chauffeur their children to various events, after-school programs must be located in the neighborhood.

But it is not only employed-mother families that would benefit from these programs. The lack of after-school offerings is a concern among all parents (Medrich et al., 1982). The programs that do exist tend to be offered to children between the ages of six and thirteen; there are few programs available for children past the age of thirteen who may not be ready for self-supervision (Galambos & Dixon, 1984). Healthy development requires systems other than family, such as peers, teachers, and others in the community (Bronfenbrenner, 1986). Quality after-school services and resources are likely to foster contact with peers and adults in a safe and structured setting.

Conclusions

The current information on maternal employment generates new questions. Further research is needed to examine maternal employment in relation to the *entire* family, not simply mother and child. For example, how do fathers and siblings mediate the effects of maternal employment on adolescents? Most of these studies have focused on white working and middle-class populations. More attention should be given to families of varied contexts and cultures, such as single-parent families, those of lower socioeconomic status, Blacks, Hispanics, and other minorities.

Maternal employment by itself does not affect adolescent development. Instead, the quality of guidance, support, and after-school activities available to the adolescent by his or her family, school, and community appear to be salient to the adolescent's adjustment. The transitional nature of this age period renders the needs of a young adolescent different from those of an older adolescent. Programs and supervision must reflect these varying needs.

Annotated Bibliography

The following annotated bibliography for and about adolescents was selected from two reliable sources. Unfortunately, we were unable to review all of the listed materials ourselves. In addition, we annotate two other pieces that review self care literature and programs. The first list of sources was selected from the appendix of B. E. Robinson, B. H. Rowland and M. Coleman's book, *Latchkey Kids: Unlocking Doors for Children and their Families,* Lexington Books, Lexington, Massachusetts, 1986. We included those sources which mentioned adolescents in the title or description.

Books for Adults

Child Care Programs

Dorman, Gayle, (1985). *3:00 to 6:00 P.M.: Planning programs for young adolescents.* Chapel Hill.: Center for Early Adolescence. A comprehensive curriculum designed to help youth-serving agencies improve services for 10 to 15 year olds, this book provides eight instructional modules to teach youth workers and administrators what young adolescents want and need in program development.

Lefstein, Leah, & Lipsitz, Joan. (1983). *3:00 to 6:00 P.M.: Programs for Young Adolescents.* For youth workers, directors of youth-serving organizations, and planners of community services for young people; describes twenty-four after-school programs around the United States that are especially effective in serving the needs of young adolescents.

Marzollo, Jean. (1986). *Superkids: Creative activities for Children 5-15.* St. Paul, MN: Toys N' Things. Activities especially for school-age kids include making movies, planning parties, baking bread, planting gardens, and building bird-houses. A good resource for school-age child care teachers.

Oregon, Boy. (1986). *The incredible indoor games book.* St. Paul, MN: Toys N' Things. An unlimited resource for games and activities that require little preparation and are designed for children between the ages of 6 and 16.

Rosenzweig, Susan. (1986). *Resources for youth workers and program planners.* Carroboro, NC: Center for Early Adolescence. Describes resources helpful to those who work with 10-15 year olds in out-of-school settings, such as churches, recreation departments, community education programs, youth organizations, libraries, museums, clubs, and volunteer programs. Topics covered include program development and implementation, model programs, funding, youth participation, community collaboration, social trends and public policy, racial, ethnic, and gender differences, and promoting physical and emotional health.

Latchkey Kids

Center for Early Adolescence. (1985). *Setting policy for young adolescents in the after-school hours.* Carroboro, NC: Center for Early Adolescence. Proceedings of national conference at the Wingspread Conference Center sponsored by the Center for Early Adolescence and the Johnson Foundation. Identifies program initiatives and policy barriers to increasing and improving opportunities for 10 to 15 years olds when school is out and recommends policies and strategies for reducing risks and increasing opportunities for young adolescents.

Lefstein, Leah; Kerewsky, Williams; Medrich, Elliot; & Frank, Carol. (1982). *Young adolescents at home and in the community.* Carroboro, NC: Center for Early Adolescence. Examines the developmental needs of young adolescents and how these needs can be best met in the out-of-school hours.

Lipsitz, Joan. (1986). *After-school: Young adolescents on their own.* Carroboro, NC: Center for Early Adolescence. A comprehensive report that discusses the effects of the so-called latchkey problem on the early adolescent age group, public policy initiatives that have addressed public responsibility for adolescent socialization, current municipal, state, and federal policies that either help or impede health growth of young adolescents, and possible options for the future.

Medrich, Elliott; Roizen, Judith; Rubin, Victor; & Buckley, Stuart. (1982). *The serious business of growing up: A study of children's lives outside of school.* Los Angeles: University of California Press. Looks at how 11- and 12- year-olds spend their time when not in school. Based on a five-year research project in Oakland, California.

Growth and Development of School-Age Children

Collins, W.A. (ed.). (1984). *Development during middle childhood: The years from six to twelve.* Washington, DC: National Academy Press. Assesses the status of knowledge on middle childhood within the framework of three areas: The distinctive developmental characteristics of school-age children, the influence of new settings and changing relationships during the elementary years, and the long-term implications of developmental difficulties experienced during middle childhood.

Farel, Anita. (1982). *Early adolescence: What parents need to know.* Carroboro, NC: Center for Early Adolescence. An easy-to-read handbook for parents seeking to understand the rapid physical, emotional, intellectual, and social changes their 10- to 15-year-old children are experiencing.

Hill, John. (1980). *Understanding early adolescence: A framework.* Carroboro, NC: Center for Early Adolescence. A comprehensive examination of early adolescent development for professionals, parents, volunteers, and policymakers.

Books for Children

Kyte, K.S. (1983). *In Charge, a Complete Handbook for Kids with Working Parents.* New York: Knopf, 115 pages. Addressed to the *young adolescent* in self care or to the babysitter, this book is written in a breezy style which emphasizes the normalcy of the self-care experience. The family conference is seen as the key to establishing agreement on roles, rules, and chores. The major sections of the book deal with the following topics: getting organized, coping with crises (minor and major), cooking, and clothing care. The book suggests approaches to thinking through difficult situations and encourages the young reader to assume responsibility for family maintenance. It is one of very few resources directed toward young adolescents.

Long, L. (1984). *On My Own: The Kids' Self Care Book.* Washington, DC: Acropolis Books, 176 pages. Directed toward children *8 to 12* years old, this paperback book of step-by-step exercises is attractive and provides specific guidance to children in self-care. Much of the emphasis is on the dangers inherent in the situation (for example, the young reader is informed that every year over 12,000 people in the U.S. die in fires). Some of the suggested rules (for example, absolutely no use of the stove) are quite strict. The tone of the material suggests the author believes children really should not be staying alone.

Swan, H. & Huston, V. (1985). *Alone at Home: Self-Care for Children of Working Parents.* Englewood Cliffs, NJ: Prentice Hall. This volume is perhaps the most balanced and comprehensive training manual for children in self-care to date. Focusing on children from 9 to 14, it includes separate sections for parents, school-age children, and early adolescents. For each of the major safety threats discussed, an actual situation is described. Included is a description of how the child followed the suggested approaches in the book to solve the problem and how the parent reacted to support the child's competence. The book doesn't pull any punches about potential dangers but gives useful guidance about how to meet and master them.

Additional books for children on self-care that include adolescents were annotated by Hyman Rodman and Cynthia Cole in "Latchkey Children: A Review of Policy and Resources", published in *Family Relations* 1987, *36,* pages 101-105. This article reviews the major policy issues and questions about self-care, with a focus on what self-care means, the consequences of self-care on children's development, policy implications and resources for family life educators.

Two additional pieces that review self-care literature and programs are the following:

Coolsen, P., Seligson, M., & Garbarino, J. (1985). *When school's out and nobody's home.* National Committee for Prevention of Child Abuse. 332 South Michigan Avenue, Suite 950, Chicago, Illinois 60604-4357. (312) 663-3520. This pamphlet describes programs local communities can develop to meet the needs of school age children when not in school. These alternatives include educational programs, community help lines, check-in and block parent programs, sick child programs, and employer-based initiatives.

Robinson, B. E., Rowland, B. H., & Coleman, M. (1986). Taking action for latchkey children and their families. *Family Relations, 35,* 473-478. This article, by the authors of the book described above, summarizes research findings on children in self-care. In addition, activities and programs for teachers, parents and communities are suggested. Last, resources for parents are noted.

Sources of Help

Organizations

This section, describing the major organizations concerned with adolescents and latchkey adolescents, is divided into two types of organizations: assistance and professional. Assistance organizations provide such services as dissemination of resources on latchkey and other adolescent children, materials for replicating model care programs, and other types of technical assistance in the area of latchkey situations. Professional organizations are national associations of professionals dedicated to the improvement of those who work with adolescents. These organizations generally charge membership dues, publish journals and sponsor an annual meeting where members gather for seminars, speeches, and workshops.

Assistance Organizations

Center for Early Adolescence, Suite 221, Carr Mill Mall, Carroboro, North Carolina 27510. As part of the Department of Maternal and Child Health at the University of North Carolina at Chapel Hill, the center disseminates information such as resource lists and bibliographies that deal with school-age and early adolescent children. The center's quarterly newsletter is filled with valuable resources such as programs, research, books, films, and conferences for professional who work with 10-15 year olds.

Family Day Care Check-in Project. Fairfax Country office for Children, 10396 Democracy Lane, Fairfax, Virginia 22030. Provides a comprehensive package of materials for agencies and organizations interested in adapting the Family Day Care Check-in Project in their communities. The package contains step-by-step procedures for starting up, administering, supervising, and evaluating a program. In addition to addressing such issues as licensing, zoning, and liability, the materials include a section on community outreach, describing methods of educating the community about the needs and problems of unsupervised young adolescents and procedures for recruiting day care providers and families.

School-Age Child Care Project. Center for Research on Women, Wellesley College, 828 Washington Street, Wellesley, Massachusetts 02181. A national information and technical assistance resource started in 1979 and committed to promoting the development of programs and services for children between the ages of 5 and 12, before and after school at such times when there is a need for care and supervision. Offers technical assistance throughout the country regarding the design and implementation of school-age child care programs, publishes a newsletter, and acts as a clearinghouse for national programs and publications on latchkey children and school-age child care.

Professional Organizations

Association for Childhood Education International. 11141 Georgia Avenue, Suite 200, Wheaton, Maryland 20902. A professional medium for those concerned with the education and well-being of children from infancy through early adolescence: classroom teachers, teachers in training, teacher educators, parents, day care workers librarians, supervisor, administrators, and other practitioners.

National Center for Youth Law (NCYL). 1663 Mission Street, San Francisco, California 94103. Devoted to improving the lives of poor children in the United States by providing advice and technical assistance to legal services attorneys regarding the law affecting poor children and adolescents.

Society for Research in Child Development. 5801 Ellis Avenue, Chicago, Illinois 60637. A professional platform for researchers and theoreticians interested in the study and development of children from infancy to adolescence.

Audiovisuals

The audiovisual section includes a number of good resources organized by type of audiovisual.

16 MM Films

Better Safe Than Sorry. Film Fair Communications, 10900 Ventura Boulevard, Studio City, California, 91604. Presents a series of vignettes on children encountering strangers under potentially dangerous circumstances-for example, when children walk home alone from school or a stranger comes to their door. The film has three versions, each for a different age level: (I) For primary and elementary children; (II) For kindergarten and primary children; (III) for adolescents. Dramatized examples are followed by commonsense rules for personal safety and avoidance to match age levels.

Videotapes

Friends: How   They   Help...How   They   Hurt.   Sunburst
Communications,   Room   A   7575,   39   Washington   Avenue,
Pleasantville, New York 10570.   Examines for fifth through ninth
graders the meaning of friendship during the difficult transition from
childhood to adolescence.   Open-ended dramatizations encourage
discussion and provide a nonthreatening forum in which children can
gain practice in solving their own problem with friendships.

Nutrition   on   the   Run: Snacks   and   Fast   Foods.   Sunburst
Communication, Room Q 7575, 39 Washington Avenue, Pleasantville,
New York 10570.   Especially helpful for latchkey kids who prepare
their own snacks when in self-care.   Encourages teens to question the
nutritional quality of the food they buy and consume by examining
their own eating habits.

Filmstrips/Cassettes

*Planning After-School Programs for Young Adolescents: What Works
and Why.*   Center for Early Adolescence, University of North
Carolina at Chapel Hill, Suite 223, Carr Mill Mall, Carroboro, North
Carolina 27510.   Explains the characteristics of effective programs,
shows several examples of popular activities, and offers a model for
successful planning.   Filmstrip.

*You and Your Parents: Making it Through the Tough Years. Parts I
and II.*   Sunburst Communications, Room H6262, 39 Washington
Avenue, Pleasantville, New York 10570-9971. Designed for children
between fifth and ninth grades to help them understand and cope
with the tensions in parent-child relationships that often accompany
the developmental years between 10 and 14.   Part I shows the years
between 10 and 14 and times of physical and emotional change that
can trouble parents and children.   Notes that conflict is normal and
that there are techniques for handling it.   Part II outlines a simple
version for better communication and includes an introduction to
skills of negotiation as a method for resolving conflict.   Two filmstrips
and two cassettes with teacher guide.

Bibliography

Almquist, E. M., & Angrist, S. S. (1971). Role model influences on college women's career aspirations. *Merrill-Palmer Quarterly, 17,* 263-279.

Altman, S. L., & Grossman, F. K. (1977). Women's career plans and maternal employment. *Psychology of Women Quarterly, 1,* 365-376.

Bacon, C., & Lerner, R. M. (1975). Effects of maternal employment status on the development vocational-role perception in females. *The Journal of Genetic Psychology, 126,* 187-193.

Banducci, R. (1967). The effect of mother's employment on the achievement, aspirations, and expectations of the child. *Personnel and Guidance Journal, 46,* 263-267.

Baruch, G. K. (1972). Maternal influences upon college women's attitudes toward women and work. *Developmental Psychology, 6,* 32-37.

Bell, R. (1980). *Changing bodies, changing lives.* New York: Random House.

Bronfenbrenner, V. (1986). Ecology of the family as a context for human development: Research perspectives. *Developmental Psychology, 22,* 723-742.

Bronfenbrenner, V., & Crouter, A. C. (1982). Work and family through time and space. In S. B. Kamerman, & C. D. Hayes (Eds.), *Families that work: Children in a changing world* (pp. 39-83). Washington, DC: National Academy Press.

Bronfenbrenner, U., Garbarino, J., & Moen, P. (1984). Child, family, and community. In R. D. Parke (Ed.), *Reviewing child development research: The family.* (Vol. 7, pp. 283-328). Chicago: University of Chicago Press.

Burchinal, L. B. (1963). Personality characteristics of children. In F. I. Nye, & L. W. Hoffman (Eds.), *The employed mother in America.* Chicago: Rand McNally.

Bush, D. M., & Simmons, R. (1988). Gender and coping with the entry into early adolescence. In R. C. Barnett, L. Biener, & G. K. Baruch (Eds.), *Gender and Stress.* New York: The Free Press.

Chandler, T. A., Sawicki, R. F., & Struffeler, J. M. (1981). The relationship between adolescent sexual stereotypes and working mothers. *Journal of Early Adolescence, 1,* 72-83.

Chodorow, N. (1978). *The reproduction of mothering and the sociology of gender.* Berkeley: University of California Press.

D'Amico, R. J., Haurin, R. J., & Mott, F. L. (1983). The effects of mothers' employment on adolescent and early adult outcomes of young men and women. In C. D. Hayes & S. B. Kamerman (Eds.), *Children of working parents: Experiences and outcomes* (pp. 130-219). Washington, DC. National Academy Press.

Dellas, M., Gaier, E. L., & Emihovich, C. A. (1979). Maternal employment and selected behaviors and attitudes of preadolescents and adolescents. *Adolescence, 14,* 579-589.

Douvan, E., & Adelson, J. (1966). *The adolescent experience.* New York: Wiley.

Duckett, E., & Richards, M. H. (1989, April). *Maternal employment and young adolescents' daily experience in single-mother families.* Paper presented at the Biennial Meeting of the Society for Research on Child Development, Kansas City, Missouri.

Galambos, N. L., & Garbarino, J. (1983, July-August). Identifying the missing links in the study of latchkey children. *Children Today,* pp. 2-4, 40-41.

Galambos, N. L., & Dixon, R. A. (1984). Toward understanding and caring for latchkey children. *Child Care Quarterly, 13,* 116-125.

Galambos, N. L., Petersen, A. C., & Lenerz, K. (1988). Maternal employment and sex typing in early adolescence: contemporaneous and longitudinal relations. In A. E. Gottfried, & A. W. Gottfried (Eds.), *Maternal employment and children's development.* New York: Plenum.

Gardner, K. E., & LaBrecque, S. V. (1986). The effects of maternal employment on sex role orientation of adolescents. *Adolescence, 21,* 875-885.

Gilroy, F. D., Talierco, T. M., & Steinbacher, R. (1981). Impact of maternal employment on daughters' sex-role orientation and fear of success. *Psychological Reports, 49,* 963-968.

Glueck, S., & Glueck, E. (1957). Working mothers and delinquency. *Mental Hygiene, 41,* 327-352.

Gold, M. (1961). *A social-psychology of delinquent boys.* Ann Arbor, MI: Institute for Social Research.

Gold, D., & Andres, D. (1978a). Comparisons of adolescent children with employed and nonemployed mothers. *Merrill-Palmer Quarterly, 24,* 75-84.

Gold, D., & Andres, D. (1978b). Developmental comparisons between ten-year-old children with employed and non-employed mothers. *Child Development, 49,* 75-84.

Gold, D., & Andres, D. (1980). Maternal employment and development of 10-yr-old Canadian francophone children. *Canadian Journal of Behavioral Science, 12,* 233-240.

Gottfried, A. E., Gottfried, A. W., & Bathurst, I. C. (1988). Maternal employment, family environment, and children's development: Infancy through the school years. In A. E. Gottfried & A. W. Gottfried (Eds.), *Maternal employment and children's development* (pp. 11-58). New York: Plenum.

Grossman, A. S. (1982). More than half of all children have working mothers. *Monthly Labor Review, 105,* 41-43.

Hayghe, H. (1986). Rise in mothers' labor force activity includes those with infants. *Monthly Labor Review, 109,* 43-45.

Hill, J. P., & Holmbeck, G. (1987). Families adaptation to biological change during adolescence. In R. M. Lerner and T. T. Foch (Eds.), *Biological-psychosocial interactions in early adolescence* (pp. 207-224). Hillsdale, NJ: Erlbaum.

Hoffman, L. W. (1979). Maternal employment. *American Psychologist, 34,* 859-865.

Hoffman, L. W. (1983). Work, family, and the socialization of the child. In R. D. Parke (Eds.), *Review of child development research, Vol. 7: The family.* Chicago: University of Chicago Press.

Huston-Stein, A., & Higgens-Trenk, A. (1978). Development of females from childhood through adulthood: Career and feminine role orientations. In P. B. Baltes (Ed.), *Life-span development and behavior* (Vol. 1, pp. 257-296). New York: Academic Press.

Jensen, L., & Borges, M. (1986). The effects of maternal employment on adolescent daughters. *Adolescence, 11,* 659-666.

Joebgen, A., & Richards, M. H. (1990). Maternal employment and education, maternal emotional adjustment, and adolescent emotional adjustment. *Journal of Early Adolescence, 10,* 329-343.

Larson, R. W., & Richards, M. H. (in press). Daily companionship in childhood and adolescence: changing developmental contexts. *Child Development.*

Lerner, J. V. & Galambos, N. L. (1985). Maternal role satisfaction, mother-child interaction, and child temperament: A process model. *Developmental Psychology, 21,* 1157-1164.

Lerner, J. V., & Galambos, N. L. (1988). The influences of maternal employment across life: The New York longitudinal study. In A. E. Gottfried, & A. W. Gottfried (Eds.), *Maternal employment and children's development.* New York: Plenum.

Lerner, J. V., Hess, L. E., & Banarjee, P. (1986, March). *Maternal employment, maternal role satisfaction and early adolescent outcomes.* Paper presented at the first Meeting of the Society for Research in Adolescence, Madison, Wisconsin.

Long, T. J., & Long, L. (1983). *The handbook for latchkey children and their parents.* New York: Arbor House.

Maccoby, E. (1958). Effects upon children of their mothers' outside employment. In *Work in the lives of married women.* Proceedings of a conference sponsored by the National Manpower Council. New York: Columbia University Press.

McCord, J., McCord, W., & Thurber, E. (1963). Effects of maternal employment on lower-class boys. *Journal of Abnormal and Social Psychology, 47,* 177-182.

Marantz, S. A., & Mansfield, A. F. (1977). Maternal employment and the development of sex-role stereotyping in five-to eleven-year-old girls. *Child Development, 48,* 668-673.

Matthews, K. A., & Rodin, J. (1989). Women's changing work roles: Impact on health, family, and public policy. *American Psychologist, 44,* 1389-1393.

Medrich, E. A. (1982). Adolescents need community-sponsored after-school programs. *Common Focus, 4,* 2.

Medrich, E. A., Roizen, J., Rubin, V. & Buckley, S. (1982). *The serious business of growing up: A study of children's lives outside school.* Berkeley: University of California Press.

Montemayor, R., & Clayton, M. D. (1983). Maternal employment and adolescent development. *Theory into Practice, 22,* 112-118.

Montemayor, R. (1984). Maternal employment and adolescents' relations with parents, siblings and peers. *Journal of Youth and Adolescence, 13,* 543-557.

Montemayor, R. & Brownlee, J. R. (1982). *The mother-adolescent relationship in early and middle adolescence: Differences in maternal satisfaction.* Unpublished Manuscript.Department of Family and Consumer Studies. University of Utah.

Neimark, E. (1975). Intellectual development during adolescence. In F. Horowitz (Ed.), *Review of child development research: Vol. 4,* Chicago: University of Chicago Press.

Nelson, D. D. (1969). A study of school achievement among adolescent children with working and nonworking mothers. *Journal of Educational Research, 62,* 456-457.

Nelson, D. D. (1971). A study of personality adjustment among adolescent children with working and nonworking mothers. *Journal of Educational Research, 64,* 328-330.

Nye, F. I. (1963). The adjustment of adolescent children. In F. I. Nye, & L. W. Hoffman (Eds.), *The employed mother in America.* Chicago: Rand McNally.

Papini, D. R., Datan, N., & McCluskey-Fawcett, K. A. (1988). An observational study of affective and assertive family interactions during adolescence. *Journal of Youth and Adolescence, 17,* 477-486.

Pleck, J. H. (1983). Husbands' paid work and family roles: Current research issues. In H. Lopata, & J. Pleck (Eds.). *Research in the interweave of social roles: Vol. 3, Families and job* (pp. 233-251). Greenwich, CT: JA1.

Propper, A. (1972). The relationship of maternal employment to adolescent roles, activities, and parental relationships. *Journal of Marriage and the Family, 34,* 417-421.

Query, J. M., & Kuruvilla, T. C. (1975). Male and female adolescent achievement and maternal employment. *Adolescence, 10,* 353-356.

Rees, A. N., & Palmer, G. H. (1970). Factors related to change in mental test performance. *Developmental Psychology Monograph, 3,* (2, Pt. 2).

Richards, M. H., & Larson, R. W. (1989). The life space and socialization of the self: Sex differences in the young adolescent. *Journal of Youth and Adolescence, 18,* 617-626.

Richards, M. H., & Duckett, E. (1990). *Maternal employment and young adolescents' daily experience.* Manuscript submitted for publication.

Richards, M. H., Abell, S., & Petersen, A. C. (in press). Pubertal development and the psychological well-being of adolescents. In P. Tolan, & B. Cohler (Eds.), *Handbook of Clinical Research and Practice with Adolescents.* New York: Wiley.

Richardson, R. A., Galambos, N. L., Schulenberg, J. E., & Petersen, A. C. (1984). Young adolescents' perceptions of the family environment. *Journal of Early Adolescence, 4,* 131-153.

Rodman, H., Pratto, D. J., & Nelson, R. S. (1985). Childcare arrangements and children's functioning: A comparison of self-care and adult care children. *Developmental Psychology, 21,* 413-418.

Rosenblatt, J. S., Siegel, H. I., & Meyer, A. D. (1979). Progress in the study of maternal behavior in the rat: Hormonal, non-hormonal, sensory, and developmental aspects. In J. S. Rosenblatt, R. A. Hinde, C. Beer, & M. C. Bushnel (Eds.), *Advances in the study of behavior.* (Vol. 10, pp. 225-311). New York: Academic Press.

Rosenthal, D., & Hansen, J. (1981). The impact of maternal employment on children's perceptions of parents and personal development. *Sex Roles, 1,* 593-598.

Scanzoni, J. & Fox, G. L. (1980). Sex roles, family & society: The seventies and beyond. *Journal of Marriage and the Family, 11,* 743-756.

Simmons, R. G., & Blyth, D. A. (1987). *Moving into adolescence.* New York: Aldine DeGruyter.

Stein, A. H. (1973). The effects of maternal employment and educational attainment on the sex-typed attributes of college females. *Social Behavior and Personality, 1,* 111-114.

Steinberg, L. (1986). Latchkey children and susceptability to peer pressure: An ecological analysis. *Developmental Psychology, 22,* 433-439.

Steinberg, L. (1988). Reciprocal relation between parent-child distance and pubertal maturation. *Developmental Psychology, 24* (1), 122-128.

Stephan, C. W., & Corder, J. (1985). The effects of dual-career families on adolescents' sex-role attitudes, work and family plans, and choices of important others. *Journal of Marriage and the Family, 11,* 921-929.

Tobin-Richards, M., Boxer, A., & Petersen, A. C. (1983). The psychological significance of pubertal change: Sex differences in perceptions of self during adolescence. In J. Brooks-Gunn & A. C. Petersen (Eds.), *Girls at puberty: Biological and psychosocial perspectives.* New York: Plenum.

Trimberger, R., & MacLean, M. J. (1982). Maternal employment: The child's perspective. *Journal of Marriage and the Family, 44,* 469-475.

Warr, P., & Parry, G. (1982). Paid employment and women's psychological well-being. *Psychological Bulletin, 91,* 498-516.

White, L. K., & Brinkerhoff, D. B. (1981). The sexual division of labor: Evidence from childhood. *Social Forces, 60,* 170-181.

Whitmarsh, R. E. (1965). Adjustment problems of adolescent daughters of employed mothers. *Journal of Home Economics, 52,* 201-204.

Woods, M. B. (1972). The unsupervised child of the working mother. *Developmental Psychology, 6,* 14-25.

Children in Self-Care:
Figures, Facts, and Fiction[1]

Nancy L. Galambos and Jennifer L. Maggs

During the past decade, members of the media, the child care and educational professions, and the child development fields have paid increasing attention to children who care for themselves after school or who are not supervised by an adult when school is out for the day. Mention of this unsupervised situation brings to mind the picture of a lonely child sitting on the doorstep and waiting for a parent to return home. Indeed, one company that markets computer equipment designed to prevent the loss of data advertises its products by playing on this image. The magazine advertisement presents a poignant photo of a sad child alone on the doorstep, complete in costume, waiting for mother's arrival late on Halloween night. Accompanying the picture is the caption, "lost data means lost opportunities."

The above picture captures the notion of what is popularly known as the "latchkey child," so named because the child carries a key, opens the door, and remains in an empty house for some amount of time after school. Although the term latchkey child implies that the child stays home, many unsupervised children spend their time in places other than home (Rodman, Pratto, & Nelson, 1988; Steinberg, 1988). The term latchkey child also evokes the image of a lonely and neglected child, when in fact, many children who care for themselves for some time after school live in happy, loving, and caring homes. Therefore, in the present chapter we use the broader term "self-care children" to refer to children who are not supervised by an adult when school is out, regardless of where they spend their time.

---

[1]Preparation of this manuscript was supported by Social Sciences and Humanities Research Council of Canada and University of Victoria Faculty Research Grants to N. Galambos.

The purpose of this chapter is to discuss what is currently known about self-care children. To this end, we present information on the scope of the self-care phenomenon--how widespread this after-school arrangement is and what families are likely to be involved. Because it is the consequences of self-care versus adult-care that are of most concern to parents and others interested in child welfare, we examine next the research that has addressed the implications of self-care for a child's development, including results from our study of children in dual-earner families. Finally, we discuss some examples of innovative programs that are designed to provide alternatives to or meet the needs of children in self-care, and we present an annotated bibliography that should be useful for parents, children, and professionals interested in knowing more about how to deal with the self-care situation.

The Scope of the Self-Care Phenomenon

Although the issue of children in self-care is not a new one (Herzog, 1960), concerns for the welfare of these children grew in the late 1970s and 1980s in response to the increasing numbers of mothers joining the labor force. It was assumed that as the proportion of employed mothers and single-parent families increased, the numbers of children in self-care would rise dramatically. Hence, a host of popular press articles examining the perceived negative and positive implications of self-care appeared in the 1980s (see Galambos & Dixon, 1984) as did research on the consequences of self-care for children (e.g., Galambos & Garbarino, 1985; Rodman, Pratto, & Nelson, 1985; Steinberg, 1986).

With estimates reaching as high as 10 or 15 million children in the United States in self-care (about half of all school-age children), some writers became alarmed about the prevalence of self-care arrangements and its implications for the health and welfare of American children (see Long & Long, 1983 for a discussion of various estimates). As argued by Cain and Hofferth (1989), however, most estimates of the number of children in regular self-care have been based on *inferences* made from the labor force participation rates of mothers. Without direct assessment of the alternative after-school arrangements that mothers may make for their school-age children, including care by the spouse, the estimates are inflated.

The most recent nationally representative survey was conducted by the U.S. Bureau of the Census (1987); parents were interviewed specifically about child care arrangements for their school-age children. This report found that about 2.1 million children between the ages of five and thirteen (about 7 percent of all such children in the United States) were regularly unsupervised by an adult after school in 1984. This figure a decade earlier was 1.8 million (U.S. Bureau of the Census, 1976). Thus, the actual increase was small relative to what might be expected based on increasing female labor force participation and divorce rates.

How can the relatively low estimate of the U.S. Bureau of the Census be reconciled with higher estimates based on the labor force patterns of mothers? If one is to dismiss the Census figure as an invalid or unreliable estimate, and accept higher estimates as more accurate, then one would also have to assume that *most* parents whose children are in self-care make false reports. Although there may be some underreporting by parents, it is not clear that this would amount to the tune of many millions of self-care children going unreported. Indeed, Richardson et al. (1989) found that when parents and their adolescents were asked independently about the number of *days* the adolescent spent in self-care, 55-65% of the parent-adolescent pairs reported the same number. Where there was discordance, parents did not systematically underreport; many reported that their adolescents spent more days in self-care, relative to what the adolescents reported. However, parents were more likely to underreport the number of *hours* per day spent in self-care, as compared to the adolescents' reports. If parents do in general provide valid reports of whether their children are in self-care, then the high non-Census-based estimates of the number of U.S. children in self-care are overestimates. Most likely, what the higher estimates fail to take into account is that parents can and do make a variety of after-school care arrangements for their children, including sitters, going to a neighbor's or relative's house, and care by an older sibling. Furthermore, given that one-third of dual-earner couples with children are involved in some form of shiftwork, it is common for parents to arrange child care by working different shifts (Presser, 1986). Morgan (1981) found that over 25 percent of working parents with children under twelve years used split shifts as their form of child care. Taking all possible care arrangements such as split shifts into consideration, we believe that the Census figures give the most accurate representation of the scope of the self-care phenomenon.

Results from the U.S. Bureau of the Census show that the percentage of children in self-care differs by mother's employment status, age of the child, income, and race. The child in self-care is likely to have an employed mother, is more often older than younger (e.g., 1 percent of five-year-olds are in self-care and 14 percent of thirteen-year-olds care for themselves), is more likely to be white than black (the percentages of children in self-care are twice as high for whites), and is more likely to come from a higher- rather than lower-income household. The notion that self-care is prevalent among single-parent households seems to be a misconception, as 6.8 percent of two-parent households had children in self-care, relative to 8.1 percent of households headed by a woman, a difference that is unremarkable (U.S. Bureau of the Census, 1987). Rodman and Pratto (1987) also found that in a sample of over 1,100 mothers across the United States, marital status was unrelated to the use of self-care arrangements. In Cain and Hofferth's (1989) analyses of the Census data, self-care was found to be more common in rural or suburban areas and less common in central cities. Self-care, then, is not seen disproportionately in poor, single-parent families in urban centers, as implied by some authors (Long & Long, 1983), but is an arrangement more likely to be made for early adolescent children with middle-class backgrounds living in relatively safe neighborhoods.

The U.S. Bureau of the Census (1987) showed that 88 percent of children in self-care after school are without adult supervision for two hours or less per day. Parents in general do not leave their children alone for long periods of time. Moreover, the number of children who are left without supervision before school is relatively small (1.9 percent) and those left unsupervised at night is even smaller (.9 percent). All of these figures suggest that the case for alarm over the numbers of children in self-care has been overstated. This is not to suggest that attention should not be paid to this issue, or that it is appropriate for children to be in self-care, or that self-care may not have negative consequences. The point is that the Census estimates do not support dire predictions of a nation of children going largely unsupervised after school because their mothers are in the labor force or are single parents.

Although the majority of school-age children are, in fact, under some form of adult supervision after school, it is relevant to consider how the 7 percent of children in self-care are affected by their after-school situations. The following section reviews the research that has examined the consequences of self-care for the behavior and development of children.

The Consequences of Self-Care

Images from the Media

It is probably the media that is primarily responsible for bringing the issue of self-care children to the attention of the general public as well as child development researchers. Quite frequently this issue is discussed in magazines and newspapers and is sometimes the topic for talk shows and television reports. An article in *Newsweek* recently proclaimed that "Divorce and working parents strain the family's ability to cope. Latchkey kids are the rule more than the exception" (Baker & Gore, 1989, p. 7). Teenage suicide, drug use, pregnancy, and violence were attributed in part to self-care.

Galambos and Dixon (1984) discussed the contrasting images of children in self-care presented in the popular press. On the one hand, some articles emphasize the supposed benefits of being a self-care child, drawing attention to the independence and responsibility that might accompany caring for oneself. On the other hand, some articles captivate the audience by concentrating on the dangers of the self-care situation, the fears purportedly experienced by self-care children, and the guilt felt by mothers who are away from home. It is the rare article that actually presents a fair picture of potential negative and positive consequences and an even rarer one that admits to the general lack of knowledge about these children. For, despite the attention by the media, what we know about self-care children is really very little.

Investigations of Self-Care Children

The earliest investigations touching on the issue of self-care were not explicitly designed to address the self-care issue but were primarily focused on determinants of delinquent behavior. In the course of these investigations an absence of adult supervision was implicated as a potentially important variable.

Thus, in a study of juvenile delinquency and mothers' employment (Glueck & Glueck, 1957) boys who were delinquent were more likely to be left at home alone or with an irresponsible person than were nondelinquent boys. Devereaux (1970) reported that sixth-grade boys and girls with preferences for frequent association with a large group of friends experienced lower adult supervision and engaged in more misconduct than did children who preferred being with parents or just a few friends. Nye (1958) found that both high and low levels of supervision in the evening were related to higher delinquency in adolescent girls, compared with girls experiencing moderate levels of supervision. These studies point to a possible link between the peer activities and delinquent behaviors of children and a lack of adequate adult supervision.

Woods (1972) conducted the first study specifically designed to examine the effects of self-care on children, interestingly before self-care became a topic of widespread concern. Woods administered a battery of intelligence, personality, and social adjustment measures to a sample of black ghetto children in the fifth grade, all of whom had employed mothers. Hospital (illness and accident) and police records were also obtained. Children were divided into two groups (supervised and unsupervised) according to whether they were regularly cared for by an adult. A comparison of the supervised and unsupervised boys revealed no pattern of association between supervision status and personality, intelligence, or social adjustment. Unsupervised girls, on the other hand, showed poorer cognitive, personality, and social adjustment than did supervised girls. They were no more likely than supervised girls to have police records or to have experienced accidents or illness. Although the Woods (1972) study is a key investigation into self-care, the results may not be generalizable to children living in other than urban environments.

Indeed, the physical context of self-care or the type of area in which the self-care child lives is important to consider. In studies of supervised and unsupervised children and adolescents living in suburban Montreal, there were no significant differences in performance on achievement, personality, and social adjustment measures (Gold & Andres, 1978a; 1978b). Vandell and Corasaniti (1988) reported that among middle-class third graders in a suburban school system, self-care children performed similarly to mother-care children with respect to grades, standardized achievement test scores, interpersonal relations, and perceptions of self-competence. Galambos and Garbarino (1985) found that in a rural setting, there were no differences between supervised and unsupervised subjects (fifth- and seventh-grade boys and girls) on academic achievement and orientation or behavioral adjustment in school. Galambos and Garbarino (1985) emphasized the importance of the community setting in which self-care takes place. Self-care might be more likely to have some negative consequences in an environment that is dangerous or unsafe, for example, an urban ghetto where crime rates are high.

In fact, Long and Long (1982; 1983) reported that self-care children in an inner city were beset with fears, nightmares, and other behaviors indicative of some psychological disturbance. This study was based on semistructured interviews with 53 unsupervised and 32 supervised black children living in Washington, DC. Long and Long (1983) present vivid and frightening examples of the fears and dangers faced by the children in their sample. Their research, however, is marked with methodological flaws, including interviewer bias, the use of unstandardized measures, and unsophisticated analyses with no controls for socioeconomic status or other demographic variables. Although it could be the case that self-care children in an inner city experience a higher incidence of psychological disturbances than adult-care children, it is impossible to draw this conclusion on the basis of the Long and Long research. Moreover, even if there were convincing data showing that self-care children in an urban center were functioning poorly relative to adult-care children (as found in the Woods, 1972, research), the applicability of the findings to children in suburban or rural neighborhoods would be questionable.

The most recent published study on self-care children examined substance use in a sample of nearly 5,000 eighth-grade adolescents living in the Los Angeles and San Diego metropolitan areas (Richardson et al., 1989). This study explored the relations between the adolescent's report of time spent in self-care, ranging from 0 to 11 hours or more per week, and lifetime use of alcohol, cigarettes, and marijuana. High use was defined as having ever had 11 or more alcoholic drinks, smoked one or more packs of cigarettes, or tried marijuana at least once. The results showed that among eighth-grade girls and boys, those in self-care for 11 or more hours per week were about twice as likely to be high users of alcohol, cigarettes, and marijuana as those who never cared for themselves. This relationship was seen even when controlling for a host of variables such as income, parental marital status, grades in school, and parents' substance use. Although the majority of the adolescents in the sample were not high users (e.g., less than 25 percent of the subjects who were in self-care for more than 11 hours had drunk a total of 11 or more alcoholic drinks over the course of their lives), this study provides convincing evidence that a higher amount of time in self-care is associated with an increased risk of substance use, at least in the setting studied.

Other recent investigations of children in self-care were conducted by Rodman et al. (1985) and Steinberg (1986). Rodman et al. (1985) investigated whether 48 fourth and seventh graders in self-care after school (those who stayed home without adult supervision) differed from 48 children in adult-care on measures of self-esteem, locus of control, and social adjustment. The children in this study were from varied family backgrounds and neighborhoods. The research found that the self-care children did not differ from the adult-care children, and Rodman et al. (1985) concluded that "the growing public and professional concern about the negative effects of self-care arrangements...is premature and may not be warranted" (p. 417).

Steinberg (1986) took issue with this claim and argued, on the basis of two points, that the Rodman et al. study provided insufficient evidence for calling into question the presumed negative effects of self-care. First, Rodman et al. selected only those subjects who stayed home after school, thereby omitting children who go elsewhere, still without supervision. As argued by Steinberg, the self-care children who do not stay home in the afternoons may engage in different, perhaps undesirable, activities than self-care children who stay home. Second, Steinberg argued that the measures selected by Rodman et al. (1985)--locus of control, self-esteem, and social adjustment--are less likely to be directly affected by the self-care situation than are other variables. For example, because many children in self-care spend time with their friends it is relevant to look at peer activities, involvement with friends, and participation in minor delinquent acts.

To overcome the purported deficiencies of past research, Steinberg (1986) examined suburban children (in grades 5, 6, 8, and 9) in adult-care and several types of self-care, including self-care children who stay home after school, those who go to a friend's home (where no adult is present), and those who merely "hang out" (e.g., at shopping malls). Additionally, Steinberg (1986) selected a dependent variable that might be expected to be sensitive to the effects of self-care--susceptibility to antisocial peer pressure, or the likelihood of engaging in antisocial acts if pressured by peers. Although this variable was measured by the child's responses to hypothetical situations, it was assumed that the responses would be indicative of real-life behaviors.

Steinberg (1986) made comparisons between the adult-care and self-care children and also compared children in the different self-care situations to each other on susceptibility to antisocial peer pressure. It was found that the children who were home unsupervised after school did not differ from those who were supervised by an adult after school. However, the children who were unsupervised at a friend's home were more susceptible to antisocial peer pressure than the self-care children at home, and the unsupervised children who were hanging out were most susceptible. Thus, susceptibility to antisocial peer pressure was shown to be a function, not of self-care per se, but of where the child spent time unsupervised after school, with distance from home a crucial feature of the self-care arrangement. The conclusion to be drawn from this research is that self-care children living in a suburban setting may be more likely to get into trouble if they are not at home in the afternoon.

Steinberg (1986) also found that more self-care children at home reported that their parents knew their whereabouts after school, relative to self-care children who were at a friend's or hanging out. Moreover, the more that parents knew about the child's whereabouts (according to the child), the less susceptible was the child. Self-care children who were reared more authoritatively (i.e., parents maintain control but consider the child's opinion) were also less susceptible to antisocial peer pressure than other self-care children. This set of results suggests that parenting patterns, then, may operate to reduce the risk of greater susceptibility to peer pressure among self-care children who spend time away from home.

Steinberg (1986) advanced the study of self-care children by showing that we should consider where the child spends the afternoon when not supervised by an adult. Variation in self-care experience is more important for predicting behavior than simply knowing that the child is in self-care. Nevertheless, there are some limitations to Steinberg's study. First, the dependent measure-- susceptibility to antisocial peer pressure--was based on responses to hypothetical situations. Although susceptibility to peer pressure in hypothetical situations might have some relationship to behavior in real situations, it may be more fruitful to determine whether children in self-care away from home actually commit more antisocial acts (cf. Richardson et al., 1989) and whether they are more likely to associate with friends who get into trouble.

Second, although Steinberg criticized Rodman et al.'s choice of measures, it is too soon to close the chapter on measures of self-esteem, locus of control, and other global indicators of well-being and adjustment. These indicators might be less likely to be directly influenced by self-care in the short term, but over time, it is possible that the cumulation of experiences in self-care might result in changes on these variables. Moreover, the study by Woods (1972) refutes the notion that it is futile to examine global indicators. After all, there were consistent differences between self- and adult-care girls on cognitive, personality, and social adjustment measures. Even if future research finds that self-care influences peer experiences and behavior more than it influences more stable personality attributes, then it is important to be certain that this is the case. It is suggested here that future research consider global indices of adjustment as well as more directly relevant behaviors, for example, activities with peers.

There are some limitations that apply to all of the above studies. One is that the studies have asked only whether there is a relationship between self-care and child behavior on a given occasion and have not looked into long-term consequences of self-care. Another limitation is that, with the exception of the Richardson et al. (1989) study, research has not attempted to assess the amount of time spent in self-care. The child who is unsupervised away from home once a week for an hour is probably less likely to get into trouble with peers than is the child who is away from home for three hours a day, five days a week. In fact, Richardson et al. showed that successively higher levels of self-care were accompanied by an increased risk of substance use. A third limitation of available studies is that self-care is usually considered in the context of after-school time. What happens to children who care for themselves during the summertime, with the potentially larger number of hours that parents are away?

The following section describes a study that attempted to overcome some of the limitations of earlier research. First, it examined the consequences of self-care for peer activities *and* global indices of self-image. Second, it examined the effect of self-care at one point in time on behavior six months later. Third, it assessed the self-care experience of children in the summertime. And fourth, it took into account an indication of the amount of time that parents are not at home when school is not in session.

The Two-Earner Family Study

Sample. Using data from a study of two-earner families with sixth-grade children, Galambos and Maggs (1989) contrasted adult-care children with children in three self-care situations (unsupervised at home, unsupervised at a friend's home, and unsupervised "hanging out"). The subjects in the study were 112 sixth graders from two-parent families in which both parents were employed on a part- or full-time basis. The families cut across the working- and middle-classes in a largely suburban setting. The parents and children completed questionnaires at two points in time (six months apart), once in the winter of 1988 and once in the summer of 1988.

This study examined three research questions: (a) Do children in adult- and self-care situations differ with respect to peer experience (peer involvement, association with deviant peers, and problem behavior or minor delinquency) and self-image (impulse control, mastery, and emotional tone)? (b) Does the number of hours that both parents are at work influence peer experience and self-image? and (c) Does the season during which self-care takes place (winter afternoons vs. summer days) have any effect on the relationship between self-care, peer experience, and self-image?

Measures. Sixth graders were categorized into one of four supervision categories based on their responses to a series of questions designed by Steinberg (1986) to assess the after-school care situation. The four categories were: supervised by an adult (e.g., at home by a parent or other adult, in an after-school program), unsupervised at home, unsupervised at a friend's home, and unsupervised, "hanging out." Although Steinberg examined more categories than those used here, his results indicated that it was these categories that discriminated most among children with respect to susceptibility to antisocial peer pressure. In the summertime questionnaire, the questions were revised to reflect supervision status during the day, and to reduce the number of items necessary to determine supervision status.

The work schedules of both parents were used to compute the number of hours they are at work simultaneously. For the winter measurement we obtained the number of hours per week *both* parents were at work between 3:00 and 6:00 P.M. For the summer measurement we assessed the number of hours per week *both* parents were at work between 8:00 A.M. and 6:00 P.M. These variables were important for determining the amount of time neither parent was at home after school and in the summertime.

There were six measures on which the adult- and self-care children were compared. Three assessed the nature of peer experience: (a) peer involvement, or the frequency of activities with friends in the past month, for example, going out to a movie or out to eat (Brown, Clasen, & Eicher, 1986), (b) deviant peers, or the extent to which the sixth grader associates with peers who engage in misconduct or problem behavior, for example, shoplifting or damaging property, and (c) problem behavior, or the frequency of misconduct by the sixth grader in the previous month, for example, shoplifting, drinking, or failing an exam (Brown et al., 1986; Kaplan, 1978).

Three additional measures (Petersen, Schulenberg, Abramowitz, Offer, & Jarcho, 1984) examined the sixth grader's self-image: (a) impulse control, or the sixth grader's calmness under pressure, (b) mastery, or the sixth grader's confidence in coping, and (c) emotional tone, or the degree of positive affect in the sixth grader.

Results: Winter, 1988. A series of analyses was conducted in order to examine how self-care and parental work hours were associated with peer experience and self-image in the wintertime. The results were that self-care was important for predicting peer experience but not self-image. Peer involvement was higher among sixth-grade girls and boys who were unsupervised and further away from home. Also, self-care girls who were at a friend's house or hanging out were more likely to have contact with friends who got into trouble than were self-care girls at home or adult-care girls. There was no such effect of self-care on boys. Similarly, the results indicated that unsupervised girls away from home reported a higher number of problem behaviors than did unsupervised girls at home or the adult-supervised girls. There was no relationship between self-care and problem behavior among boys. The number of hours both parents were away from home made no difference with respect to the child's peer involvement, association with deviant peers, or problem behavior.

Results: Summertime. The second set of analyses was identical to the first but pertained to self-care during the summer days. The results were that unsupervised girls who were further away from home associated more with deviant peers and reported a higher number of problem behaviors relative to unsupervised girls at home and supervised girls. There was no relationship between self-care and peer experiences in boys. Self-image was not related to self-care for boys or girls, and the number of hours both parents were away had no bearing on the peer experiences or self-image of the subjects.

Long-term consequences. The third set of analyses was designed to determine whether self-care in the winter predicted peer experiences and self-image six months later (in the summer). Indeed, self-care in the winter was associated with increased problem behavior in girls the following summer but only among those who spent their winter afternoons away from home. There was also some indication that self-care girls who were away from home in the winter had lower impulse control the following summer and also felt less able to cope. There were no such consequences for boys.

From the above pattern of results, Galambos and Maggs (1989) concluded that sixth-grade girls in self-care *away from home* may be at risk for problem behavior and contact with friends who get into trouble. It might be that unsupervised girls who are not at home are perhaps hanging out with older boys and girls. Perhaps the unsupervised girls are early maturing girls whose parents believe they can handle more responsibility and autonomy. Magnusson, Stattin, and Allen (1986) showed that early maturing girls are more apt to associate with an older crowd and, therefore, to engage in the kinds of activities (e.g., drinking) in which older adolescents more frequently participate. Some girls, then, may reach their peak in problem behavior earlier than do other girls and boys, and self-care could potentially play a role in this process. Essentially, these results support the conclusion of Steinberg (1986) that *where* the child spends unsupervised time is very important. Further, this study suggests that it may be fruitful to consider how self-care is related to aspects of self-image such as impulse control and feelings of mastery.

Parental Monitoring

No discussion of children in self-care is complete without considering the notion of parental monitoring. Parental monitoring, or the extent to which the parent knows the child's whereabouts, has been identified as an important predictor of antisocial behavior. Patterson (1986; Patterson & Stouthamer-Loeber, 1984; Snyder, Dishion, & Patterson, 1986) has shown that inept monitoring by parents is linked to delinquent behavior in boys. Crouter, MacDermid, McHale, and Perry-Jenkins (1990) reported that less well-monitored boys from single- and dual-earner families had lower school achievement than their well-monitored counterparts. In addition, this research found that less well-monitored boys from dual-earner families had more unfavorable self- and parent-ratings of their behavior, relative to single-earner boys and to well-monitored boys from dual-earner families.

One reason that children who are unsupervised away from home may be more likely to get into trouble is that their working parents are less likely to be able to monitor the child's whereabouts, although it is not impossible for a parent to stay informed. In fact, Steinberg (1986) found that self-care children whose parents knew their whereabouts were no more susceptible to antisocial peer pressure than adult-care children. Whether the child is unsupervised at home or away from home after school, parents should make an effort to be aware of where the child is and what the child is doing. Steinberg (1987) suggested that employed parents should maintain some control over their children's activities by setting up after-school routines and/or requiring contact by telephone. Of course, parents must be careful not to overcontrol their children, especially in the early adolescent years when increasing autonomy is a delicate issue.

Conclusions about Implications of Self-Care

With respect to the consequences of self-care for the behavior and development of children, it is clear that there are far more questions to ask than those that have been answered. A summary of findings from research on self-care is as follows.

1. Although the popular press has discussed potentially positive effects of self-care (e.g., learning responsibility), not one study has found that as a group children in self-care show more advanced personal, social, or cognitive skills than children in adult-care.

2. Some forms of self-care may set up conditions in which children are more likely to engage in peer activities conducive to problem behavior. Specifically, self-care children away from home may associate with peers who get into trouble and may engage in more misconduct. Self-care children in the home appear to be no different from adult-care children.

3. Whether self-care influences more stable personality attributes is open to question. The results of Woods (1972) and Galambos and Maggs (1989) suggest that self-care can be associated with global aspects of personality and self-image.

4. Whether self-care influences boys or girls differently is also open to question. In two studies where differences between self-care and adult-care children have been found, girls seemed to be at a disadvantage (Galambos & Maggs, 1989; Woods, 1972). However, Steinberg (1986) found that boys and girls unsupervised away from home were equally susceptible to antisocial peer pressure, and Richardson et al. (1989) found no sex difference in the positive relationship between self-care and substance use.

5. It is important to consider the context of self-care. Parents in suburban and rural areas make greater use of self-care arrangements, but even children in these settings may be susceptible to peer pressure if they spend time away from the home. A priority

for future research is to consider self-care children in many different settings within one study.

6. As previously discussed by Galambos and Dixon (1984), the age of the child may make a difference with respect to responses to the self-care situation. It is doubtful that children under the ages of eight or nine should be left unsupervised, because it is unlikely that they have the cognitive and social skills necessary to deal with an emergency. As for older children, only the parent can assess whether that child is able to handle self-care, and the decision has to be based on a thorough understanding of the child's cognitive, social, and behavioral skills. Some thirteen-year-olds may not have the judgment to care for themselves, whereas some other precocious ten-year-olds may be able to do so quite adequately.

Sources of Help

Families' decisions regarding children's after-school care arrangements depend on many factors. Parents must consider, for example, the options that are available in their community, financial costs, transportation, and the age, number, personal characteristics, and preferences of the children themselves. What after-school care options are available to parents of school-age children? In this section we examine a variety of existing formal and informal after-school programs and arrangements, followed by an annotated list of resources that may help parents to make informed decisions and help children to adapt positively to after-school care situations (see also Richards & Duckett, this volume, for additional related materials).

Structured After-School Programs

For many reasons, *schools* seem to be the logical location for after-school programs. Classrooms, gyms, equipment, and playing fields are already set up for and familiar to children, school facilities are empty at the end of the day, and transportation to an after-school care setting is unnecessary. Indeed, many extended-day programs in the United States already take advantage of otherwise unused school facilities, most often initiated and administered by parents or community groups, in cooperation with the schools. However, caregivers in school-based programs must make extra efforts to create an environment that is fun, relaxing, and that provides as much of a change from school as possible, so that children do not feel that the school day has simply been extended to eight, nine, or ten hours (see Robinson, Rowland, & Coleman, 1986, for a discussion of how after-school care can best meet the needs of school-age children).

In the rural mountains of North Carolina, a flexible, community-operated after-school program, *Agelink,* has been developed by the Center for Improving Mountain Living at Western Carolina University. This unique approach aims to bring together children who are alone after school with older volunteers who enjoy them. The seniors spend time with children alone and in small groups, often teaching traditional skills that are no longer being passed on from generation to generation. This approach to after-school care typically occurs in a group setting (e.g., in a school or community center), but Agelink has also developed three other models: older volunteers may (a) care for up to five children in licensed private homes; (2) provide transportation to sports or scouts programs; or (3) staff telephone call-in services. The program is now being expanded with different activities and emphases to include adolescents up to age fifteen.

Another approach to intergenerational after-school care is operated in nursing homes in Massachusetts by Genesis Health Ventures. The *Intergenerational Latchkey Program* operates in cooperation with local schools to provide quality after-school care while fostering mutual respect and understanding in a creative, enriching environment (Ziemba, Roop, & Wittenberg, 1988).

Community Centers and organizations such as the YM/YWCA also provide supervised after-school care and recreational opportunities for children, often with a fun, club-like atmosphere. These centers may offer daily after-school programs as well as informal swimming and other sports programs, courses (e.g., first-aid, computers), and drop-in games rooms. The flexibility offered by such recreational centers allows families with children who are old enough for a limited amount of self-care to tailor-design their own after-school care schedule. For example, a child could attend planned activities on Tuesday and Thursday afternoons, thereby never having to spend more than a day in a row in self-care and without relinquishing valued unorganized free time or incurring the greater costs of daily care. Some of these programs overcome the problem of transportation by having buses pick children up from school.

The *School-Age Child Care Project* (SACC) at Wellesley College, Massachusetts, plays a prominent role in promoting the establishment of high-quality after-school care programs. SACC maintains a clearinghouse for research and information on supervised care programs, undertakes rigorous program demonstration and evaluation, and also provides consultation for professionals who wish to implement after-school care programs. SACC has numerous publications (see annotated bibliography), including the new *Action Research Papers from the School-Age Child Care Project*, a series of in-depth reports on such issues as the changing role played by libraries in the out-of-school lives of children.

Schools and community centers may be the most familiar locations for after-school programs, but day care centers, libraries, churches, and parental workplaces are other possible candidates for providing school-age child care programs (see Dowd, 1988; Long & Long, 1983; Robinson et al., 1986; Ziemba et al., 1988 for a more complete discussion of these options). Of course, the context and needs of individual communities and the relative merits and disadvantages of all possible options must be carefully evaluated by parents and local child care professionals in order to arrive at optimal decisions about the establishment of after-school child care programs.

Family Day-Care (before- or after-school care in a neighbor's house) can offer families more flexible, child-appropriate supervision than formal programs. For example, the *Family Day-Care Check-In Program* developed by the Fairfax County Office for Children in Virginia recognizes that preadolescents may be unhappy in traditional child care programs yet may not be ready for the responsibility of full self-care. In this Check-In Program, after school the child checks in with the family day-care provider for a snack and a chance to talk about the day. The child may then spend the afternoon wherever and in whatever activities the parents and child have agreed upon: activities with the provider, playing outside in the yard or elsewhere in the neighborhood, or even at the child's home. Check-in programs are an affordable care option that give older children more independence and freedom than formal programs, but provide the loving supervision and companionship that may be difficult to maintain with self-care. This type of family day-care can be arranged informally between neighbors or friends or, as in Fairfax County, can be sponsored and coordinated by a community agency that matches providers with interested families.

Support for Self-Care Children

Many families live in areas where ideal, high quality after-school care is unavailable or is too costly. In addition, many families decide that children are mature enough to look after themselves after school and indeed would be happier doing so than attending an organized program. As a result, 2.1 million children in the United States are in self-care for some period of time every week. What resources can families turn to as they consider and adapt to self-care? What help is available for self-care children and their parents?

Project Home Safe is a national demonstration and advocacy program for self-care children and their families. Project Home Safe maintains an extensive resource center and a toll-free information line, sponsors research related to children in self-care, trains professionals in the development of community resources for self-care children, and advocates the establishment and implementation of standards for school-age child care. Remarkably comprehensive bibliographies of self-care guides for children and adults, activity and hobby ideas, books on self-care safety, fiction about kids in self-care, and audio-visual resources are available from the Project Home Safe address listed in the annotated bibliography.

A growing number of helpful books are available for both self-care children and their parents. These publications generally combine a positive attitude about self-care with practical suggestions for making the self-care experience fun, safe, and productive. These guides vary in the topics covered, target ages, and reading levels. A selection of these books is reviewed in the annotated references. Swan and Houston's (1986) book, *Alone After School: A self-care guide for latchkey children*, deserves a special recommendation for parents considering and preparing their children for self-care. This book presents one of the most comprehensive and thought-provoking discussions of all aspects of the self-care situation. The authors emphasize the active role played by parents and children in carefully designing a tailor-made "self-care plan" that best serves the family's particular needs.

A practical source of support for self-care children is a phone line that children at home alone can call for advice, help, or companionship. In 1982 a pioneer of these innovative call-in "hotlines" or "warmlines," *PhoneFriend*, was established in State College, PA (Guerney & Moore, 1983); today more than 250 such phone lines have been established in the United States. Staffed by volunteers trained in empathic listening, these centers aim to enhance children's coping abilities and to provide reassurance and support to self-care children. PhoneFriend has now started a networking project to aid other communities in establishing call-in phone services (see annotated bibliography). Other networks of phone lines for children at home alone in the United States are operated by Kidsline and Contact Teleministries. In Canada, a national, 24-hour toll-free Kids Help Phone for children has recently been established (see annotated bibliography).

In the many areas where formal programs or call-in lines are not available, some families have been able to form links with individuals in the community (e.g., grandparents, adults who are housebound) who are willing to be available to children by phone when they arrive home from school. Such a relationship may be very meaningful both to the child and to the supporting adult.

Organizations

Agelink
Center for Improving Mountain Living
Western Carolina University
Cullowhee, NC 28723
(704) 227-7492

Center for Early Adolescence
University of North Carolina
Suite 223, Carr Mill Mall
Carrboro, NC 27510

Fairfax County Office for Children
11212 Waples Mill Road
Fairfax, VA 22030

National Committee for the Prevention of Child Abuse
332 South Michigan Ave., Suite 950
Chicago, IL 60604-4357

Project Home Safe
American Home Economics Association
2010 Massachusetts Ave., N.W.
Washington, DC 20036
Hotline: (800) 252-SAFE

School-Age Child Care Project
Center for Research on Women
Wellesley College
Wellesley, MA 02181
(617) 431-1453 extension 2546

Phone Lines

PhoneFriend Central
State College, PA
(814) 466-7524

Kids Help Phone
P.O. Box 513
Toronto, ON M4W 3E2
Canada
(800) 668-6868

Annotated Bibliography

Books for Self-Care Kids and Parents

Chaback, E., & Fortunato, P. (1981). *The official kids' survival kit: How to do things on your own.* Boston: Little, Brown, & Co., pp. 223.
    A practical guide that assumes that kids do many things on their own and therefore includes advice on many topics other than self-care situations. Information on handling emergencies may be difficult to find quickly, however, as it is not listed in a single section. This book is attractively designed and illustrated, but its length will make it most appropriate for children who enjoy reading.

Kleeburg, I.C. (1985). *Latchkey kid.* New York: Franklin Watts, pp. 102.
    This fun and easy-to-read book is written from a child's point of view and includes useful advice on such topics as how to make the house look tidy fast and what to do when bored. The section on emergencies emphasizes weather-related dangers rather than crime prevention, which may make it more applicable to rural-rather than urban-dwelling families. Although it is not a comprehensive reference guide, this is a funny, upbeat book which may promote positive feelings about the self-care experience.

Kyte, K.S. (1983). *In charge: A complete handbook for kids with working parents.* New York: Knopf, pp. 115.
    This book, which is written for the independent and self-directed pre- or early adolescent, emphasizes the active role taken by the self-care individual. The strong emphasis on chores may make this less fun reading, but the simple recipes, laundry tips, and suggestions for dividing chores equitably between family members will

be of interest to children and parents alike. Much more information about what to do in emergencies is provided than in the first two volumes reviewed.

Long, L., & Long, T. (1983). *The handbook for latchkey children and their parents.* New York: Berkley Books, pp. 305.

Although this book would appear to be a guide for self-care children and their parents, very few suggestions are made for improving the self-care experience. Instead, the authors use disturbing anecdotes to emphasize the manifold dangers and negative consequences of the latchkey "problem." A more positive aspect of the book is its discussion of innovative employer-based child care programs.

Swan, H.L., & Houston, V. (1985). *Alone after school: A self-care guide for latchkey children and their parents.* Englewood Cliffs, NJ: Prentice-Hall, pp. 200.

This comprehensive guide offers thoughtful suggestions to help determine whether self-care is appropriate for children and to prepare them practically and emotionally for the experience. Included in the complete section on emergencies are descriptions of actual situations and how a self-care child might respond; this section may facilitate parent-child discussion and preparation for handling emergencies effectively. Other chapters cover sibling relations, summer vacation, and special needs of self-care adolescents, making this one of the best books available for parents of self-care children.

Resources for Professionals

Chawla, L. (Ed.). (1986). Latchkey children in their communities (Special issue). *Children's Environments Quarterly, 3,* (2).

Articles by expert child-care professionals and researchers cover a wide range of after-school options and ideas, including self-care, block parent and after-school check-in programs, Agelink, and principles of neighborhood design. Book reviews and a list of school-age child care resources are also included.

Cole, C., & Rodman, H. (1987). When school-age children care for themselves: Issues for family life educators and parents. *Family Relations, 36,* 92-96.

Rodman, H., & Cole, C. (1987). Latchkey children: A review of policy and resources. *Family Relations, 36,* 101-105.

Two articles about self-care children and an excellent annotated bibliography of books, organizations, and audio-visual materials within this issue of *Family Relations* are a particularly valuable source of additional information.

Bibliography

Brown, B. B., Clasen, D. R., & Eicher, S. A. (1986). Perceptions of peer pressure, peer conformity dispositions, and self-reported behavior among adolescents. *Developmental Psychology, 22,* 521-530.

Cain, V. S., & Hofferth, S. L. (1989). Parental choice of self-care for school-age children. *Journal of Marriage and the Family, 51,* 65-77.

Crouter, A. C., MacDermid, S. M., McHale, S. M., & Perry-Jenkins, M. (1990). Parental monitoring and perceptions of children's school performance and conduct in dual- and single-earner families. *Developmental Psychology, 26,* 649-657.

Devereaux, E. C. (1970). The role of peer-group experience in moral development. In J. P. Hill (Ed.), *Minnesota Symposia on Child Psychology,* (Vol. 4, pp. 94-140). Minneapolis: University of Minnesota Press.

Dowd, F. A. (1988). Latchkey children in the library. *Children Today, 17,* 5-8.

Galambos, N. L., & Dixon, R. A. (1984). Toward understanding and caring for latchkey children. *Child Care Quarterly, 13,* 116-125.

Galambos, N. L., & Garbarino, J. (1985). Adjustment of unsupervised children in a rural setting. *Journal of Genetic Psychology, 146,* 227-231.

Galambos, N. L., & Maggs, J. L. (1989, April). The after-school ecology of young adolescents and self-reported behavior. In C. J. Carpenter (Chair), *Effects of maternal employment on the social ecology of pre-adolescents.* Symposium conducted at the Biennial Meeting of the Society for Research in Child Development, Kansas City, MO.

Glueck, S., & Glueck, E. (1957). Working mothers and delinquency. *Mental Hygiene, 41,* 327-352.

Gold, D., & Andres, D. (1978a). Comparisons of adolescent children with employed and nonemployed mothers. *Merrill-Palmer Quarterly, 24,* 243-253.

Gold, D., & Andres, D. (1978b). Developmental comparisons between ten-year-old children with employed and nonemployed mothers. *Child Development, 49,* 75-84.

Guerney, L., & Moore, L. (1983). PhoneFriend: A prevention-oriented service for latchkey children. *Children Today, 12,* 5-10.

156   Nancy L. Galambos and Jennifer L. Maggs

Herzog, E. (1960). *Children of working mothers* (Children's Bureau Publication 382). Washington, DC: U.S. Government Printing Office.

Kaplan, H. B. (1978). Deviant behavior and self-enhancement in adolescence. *Journal of Youth and Adolescence, 7,* 253-277.

Long, L., & Long, T. (1983). *The handbook for latchkey children and their parents.* New York: Berkley Books.

Long, T. J., & Long, L. (1982). *Latchkey children: The child's view of self care.* Washington, DC: Catholic University of America. (ERIC Document Reproduction Service No. ED 211 229).

Magnusson, D., Stattin, H., & Allen, V. L. (1986). Differential maturation among girls and its relation to social adjustment: A longitudinal perspective. In P. B. Baltes, D. L. Featherman, & R. M. Lerner (Eds.), *Life-span development and behavior* (Vol. 7, pp. 135-172). Hillsdale, NJ: Erlbaum.

Morgan, J. N. (1981). Child care when parents are employed. In S. Hill, D. H. Hill, & J. N. Morgan (Eds.), *Five thousand American families: Patterns of economic progress* (Vol. 9, pp. 441-456). Ann Arbor: University of Michigan, Institute for Social Research.

Nye, F. I. (1958). *Family relationships and delinquent behavior.* New York: Wiley.

Patterson, G. R. (1986). Performance models for antisocial boys. *American Psychologist, 41,* 432-444.

Patterson, G. R., & Stouthamer-Loeber, M. (1984). The correlation of family management practices and delinquency. *Child Development, 55,* 1299-1307.

Petersen, A. C., Schulenberg, J. E., Abramowitz, R. H., Offer, D. D., & Jarcho, H. D. (1984). A self-image questionnaire for young adolescents (SIQYA): Reliability and validity studies. *Journal of Youth and Adolescence, 13,* 93-111.

Presser, H. B. (1986). Shift work among American women and child care. *Journal of Marriage and the Family, 48,* 551-563.

Richardson, J. L., Dwyer, K., McGuigan, K., Hansen, W. B., Dent, C., Johnson, C. A., Sussman, S. Y., Brannon, B., & Flay, B. (1989). Substance use among eighth-grade students who take care of themselves after school. *Pediatrics, 84,* 556-566.

Robinson, B. E., Rowland, B. H. & Coleman, M. (1986). *Latchkey kids: Unlocking doors for children and their families.* Lexington, MA: D. C. Heath & Co.

Rodman, H., & Pratto, D. J. (1987). Child's age and mother's employment in relation to greater use of self-care arrangements for children. *Journal of Marriage and the Family, 49,* 573-578.

Rodman, H., Pratto, D. J., & Nelson, R. S. (1985). Child care arrangements and children's functioning: A comparison of self-care and adult-care children. *Developmental Psychology, 21,* 413-418.

Rodman, H., Pratto, D. J., & Nelson, R. S. (1988). Toward a definition of self-care children: A commentary on Steinberg (1986). *Developmental Psychology, 24,* 292-294.

Snyder, J., Dishion, T. J., & Patterson, G. R. (1986). Determinants and consequences of associating with deviant peers during preadolescence and adolescence. *Journal of Early Adolescence, 6,* 29-43.

Steinberg, L. (1986). Latchkey children and susceptibility to peer pressure: An ecological analysis. *Developmental Psychology, 22,* 433-439.

Steinberg, L. (1987). Familial factors in delinquency: A developmental perspective. *Journal of Adolescent Research, 2,* 255-268.

Steinberg, L. (1988). Simple solutions to a complex problem: A response to Rodman, Pratto, and Nelson (1988). *Developmental Psychology, 24,* 295-296.

Swan, H. L., & Houston, V. (1985). *Alone after school: A self-care guide for latchkey children and their parents.* Englewood Cliffs, NJ: Prentice-Hall.

U.S. Bureau of the Census. (1976). *Daytime care of children* (Current Population Reports, Series P-20, No. 298). Washington, DC: U.S. Government Printing Office.

U.S. Bureau of the Census (1987). *After-school care of school-age children; December 1984* (Current Population Reports, Series P-23, No. 149). Washington, DC: U.S. Government Printing Office.

Vandell, D. L., & Corasaniti, M. A. (1988). The relation between third graders' after-school care and social, academic, and emotional functioning. *Child Development, 59,* 868-875.

Woods, M. B. (1972). The unsupervised child of the working mother. *Developmental Psychology, 6,* 14-25.

Ziemba, J., Roop, K., & Wittenberg, S. (1988). A magic mix: After-school programs in a nursing home. *Children Today, 17,* 9-13.

The Household Labor of Children from Dual- Versus Single-Earner Families

W. Todd Bartko and Susan M. McHale

Parents differ in the extent to which they make maturity demands on their children, and these differences are thought to have important developmental consequences (e.g., Baumrind, 1971). Studies that have examined parenting styles as a function of husbands' and wives' work involvement suggest that, as a group, dual-earner parents tend to expect more mature behavior from their children than do single-earner parents (Hoffman, 1979; 1989). Presumably because of drains on their time and energy, parents who juggle work and family responsibilities tend to make greater demands for independent and autonomous behavior in their children, and they may expect their children to assume more adult-like roles in the family. Although such maturity demands are generally viewed in a positive light, there are few hard facts about the nature of parents' expectations for their children or about how specific kinds of maturity demands might affect children's psychosocial functioning.

In this chapter we consider one dimension of parents' expectations for mature and responsible behavior, namely, *children's involvement in household labor.* Although the nature and extent of children's tasks may vary, performing chores around the house seems to be a part of most children's daily lives (Goodnow, 1988). As such, household task performance is a good candidate for research that examines *differences in families* in the extent to which maturity demands are placed on children and explores the potential *consequences* of children's different experiences. In this chapter we discuss research related to each of these concerns. We begin by describing the extent to which boys and girls, particularly those from dual- versus single-earner families, are involved in housework. We then consider the household labor of mothers and fathers from these two family contexts in an effort to determine whether children's patterns of work involvement mirror those of their parents. Finally, we review evidence from our own and others' research pertaining to the potential implications of children's household labor, specifically in the area of children's psychosocial functioning.

Children's Involvement in Household Labor

Most children are regularly involved in household chores. One survey of nearly seven hundred United States children aged two to seventeen found that ninety percent of children were regularly required to perform chores by age nine or ten, and that children averaged about four hours per week of involvement (White & Brinkerhoff, 1981a). A British study revealed that fifty-five percent of seven year olds were expected to regularly perform chores, and eighty-two percent were expected to take care of their own toys, clothes, etc. (Newson & Newson, 1976).

Not surprisingly, parents' expectations for help around the house seem to vary depending on how old their children are and on whether they have sons versus daughters. Age differences in children's chores mean that young children may simply be asked to pick up after themselves, whereas older children and adolescents may be expected to take care of their own possessions as well as to engage in tasks (such as cooking, laundry, or yard work) that benefit the family as a whole . White and Brinkerhoff (1981b) note that:

> Children begin their involvement in household chores by assuming responsibility for themselves: picking up their own toys, making their own beds, and cleaning up their own rooms. By the time they are 10 years old, however, most children have moved beyond purely self-centered chores and are doing work for their family. As children grow older they move from helping their parents, say by setting the table or folding the clothes, to replacing their parents by assuming full responsibility for some tasks. (p. 792)

As we have noted, task assignments also differ for boys versus girls. Specifically, children's tasks tend to parallel those of their same-sex parents. Like their fathers, boys spend most of their time mowing the lawn, shoveling snow, and taking out the garbage. Girls, on the other hand, are more involved in "women's work": cleaning the house, cooking, and doing the laundry (White & Brinkerhoff, 1981a; Zill & Petersen, 1982). Some research has shown that these gender differences are already apparent in children as young as two to five years of age, and that they become even more pronounced as children move through adolescence (White & Brinkerhoff, 1981b). Although there are some tasks that tend to be done equally by boys and girls such as cleaning one's own room, feeding pets, and taking care of one's own possessions (Newson & Newson, 1976; White & Brinkerhoff, 1981b), most surveys indicate that girls spend more time doing household chores than do boys. One survey revealed that girls between five and nine years of age spent an average of about four hours per week performing chores while boys in this age group spent just over two hours (White & Brinkerhoff, 1981b). When girls come from larger families, when they are the oldest child in the family, or when their mothers are employed outside the home, their work load tends to be even heavier (White & Brinkerhoff, 1981b).

In this chapter, a question of special importance is how children's involvement in household chores is affected by their mothers' involvement in the labor force. Not surprisingly, several studies have shown that children of employed mothers, and as we have noted, girls in particular, spend more time in household work (Bartko, 1989; Hedges & Barnett, 1972; Propper, 1972). One study found that teenagers whose mothers were employed fifteen hours per week or more performed thirty percent of the family housework compared to twenty percent for those whose mothers were not employed or those whose mothers were employed fewer than fifteen hours a week (Hedges & Barnett, 1972). As we and others (e.g., Hoffman, 1979, 1989) have argued, it may be that time and energy demands on dual-earner parents mean that children are called upon to assume additional, seemingly more adult-like, responsibilities.

Results from White and Brinkerhoff's (1981b) sample of children from Nebraska highlight the fact that the effects of living in a dual-earner family may differ for boys as compared to girls: when both parents were in the labor force, the boys in this study took on a wider *range* of tasks (specifically, more "women's work"); girls, in contrast, simply performed more of the chores that they are allotted traditionally. As such, women's involvement in the paid labor force may tend to "sink their daughters even deeper into the domestic role" (White & Brinkerhoff, 1981b, p. 177).

Children's experiences in household labor may differ in other ways than the amount or kinds of work they undertake. In our own longitudinal research on children's family relationships (Crouter & McHale, 1989), for example, we have collected detailed information on the *extent* and *nature* of children's task involvement, as well as the social contexts of these activities (that is, whether children do chores alone or with others such as their parents or siblings) and children's evaluations of how stressful and enjoyable they find their household tasks. We began our study in the spring of 1987, focusing on approximately one hundred and fifty families in which the oldest child was in the fourth or fifth grade. We were particularly interested in how the daily lives of children differed depending on their parents' work involvement. Consequently, in approximately half of the families in our sample both parents were employed outside the home (dual-earners) and in the remainder only the fathers were employed (single-earners). ·

We first interviewed mothers, fathers, firstborn (target) children, and their secondborn siblings in their homes in order to obtain their evaluations of their family relationships, personal well-being, and various areas of family members' daily lives (e.g., parents' attitudes toward their paid labor, children's feelings of stress regarding their chores). During the two to three week period subsequent to the home interviews, we also telephoned each family on seven evenings (five weekdays and two weekend days), shortly before the children's bedtimes. During these calls, children used a list of thirty activities to report on their experiences during the day of the call.[1] Activities on this list included twelve household tasks, seven leisure activities, eight personal development activities, and three activities related to meals and chauffeuring (see Table 1 for examples). For each activity children reported, they also were asked how long the activity lasted, who else participated in the activity, and "how much fun" the activity had been (ranging from "not fun at all" to "very fun"). Mothers and fathers also reported on their own household tasks and their activities with the target child using a similar procedure during four of the seven calls.

---

[1]We did not include any activities that children were involved in while in school.

Table 1

Examples of Activities Reported by Mothers, Fathers, and Children During Seven Telephone Interviews

Household Tasks	Personal Development Activities	Leisure Activities
Making/changing bed[a]	Sports practice or performance	Watching TV
Cleaning[a]		Reading
Food Preparation[a]	Dance/music lesson or performance	Board games
Washing Dishes[a]	Religious activity	Listening to music
Laundry[a]	Paid job outside home	
Taking out garbage[b]	Homework	Working on a hobby/project
Outdoor work[b]	Visiting friends or relatives	Going to movie or concert
Washing/fixing car[b]	Outdoor recreation	Going to sports event
Household repairs[b]	Club activity	
Pet care		
Errands		
Caring for sibling(s)		

[a] Feminine Tasks
[b] Masculine Tasks

The information obtained from these phone calls has provided us with a detailed picture of how children spent their time over a week's period. Children spent more time watching television (an average of about one hour per day) than in any other kind of activity. In contrast, these children reported an average of about twenty minutes of homework, fifty minutes eating meals, and thirty-five minutes per day on household chores.

Tables 2 and 3 provide more detailed information on children's household tasks: boys' versus girls' and single-earner versus dual-earner children's involvement in different kinds of household chores. These data reveal that running errands is the most common task performed by all groups of children, followed by sibling caregiving. In contrast, activities such as doing laundry, washing the car, helping perform home repairs, and taking out the garbage consume a relatively small proportion of children's time.   These tables also indicate that, not surprisingly, children's rates of involvement in particular household task activities varied depending on their sex and on their parents' work status; these results are consistent with those of previous investigations. Our data replicate results showing that dual-earner children and girls spend a greater portion of their time involved in chores. We also found sex and earner status differences when we examined children's involvement in the specific household tasks shown in Tables 2 and 3.

The results of these analyses, in fact, have led us to qualify previous conclusions about the effects of mothers' work involvement on children's task participation. Specifically, the greater involvement of girls and dual-earner children seems to be limited to what we and others have described as "feminine" tasks; for example, laundry, house cleaning, and food preparation. These analyses also revealed that boys were more involved than girls in traditionally "masculine" activities: taking out the garbage, doing yardwork, or helping with home repairs.   In contrast, there were no differences between boys and girls or between dual- and single-earner children's involvement in "undifferentiated" chores such as sibling caregiving, running errands, or taking care of pets.

Table 2
Boys' and Girls' Rates of Involvement in
Household Tasks (minutes per week)

	Girls	Boys
Make bed	18.8	12.5
Cleaning	26.3	16.3
Food preparation	28.7	15.6
Wash dishes	22.1	15.6
Laundry	5.7	1.7
Take out garbage	1.5	5.4
Outdoor work	22.1	27.4
Wash/fix car	1.5	4.0
Household repairs	3.3	4.7
Pet care	34.4	28.1
Errands	81.3	55.2
Sibling care	52.6	52.9

Table 3
Dual and Single Earner Children's Rates of
Involvement in Household Tasks (minutes per week)

	Dual Earner	Single Earner
Make bed	17.2	15.8
Cleaning	16.4	26.8
Food preparation	20.5	25.4
Wash dishes	17.2	18.0
Laundry	3.4	4.8
Take out garbage	3.4	3.1
Outdoor work	28.6	19.7
Wash/fix car	4.2	1.7
Household repairs	5.7	2.3
Pet care	30.1	34.7
Errands	67.9	71.0
Sibling care	46.5	58.4

In addition to determining how much time children spent on their chores, we also were interested in how they evaluated their experiences. As mentioned earlier we asked children to rate "how much fun" each of the tasks they reported had been. Specifically, children used a three point scale (ranging from 0=not fun at all to 2=very fun), and we averaged their fun ratings across all the tasks they reported to create a rating for two categories of tasks: feminine and masculine chores. These data show, first, that masculine tasks tend to be rated as more fun than feminine tasks by most groups of children. As a group, boys and both single- and dual-earner children rate these tasks in the "sort of fun" to "very fun" range. In contrast, feminine tasks are rated by boys and by single-earner children less positively, in the "not fun at all" to "sort of fun" range. Group comparisons revealed that girls as well as dual-earner children rate feminine tasks as more "fun" whereas boys rate masculine tasks more positively.

Another issue of concern in our research was who was helping children with their chores. We thought that because of the time constraints on parents who were juggling work and family roles, children from dual-earner families might be asked to perform most chores on their own. We expected that in single-earner families, in contrast, children and parents might share their work more often. This hypothesis, however, was ony partly supported. The results of analyses examining the *social context* of children's household task activities revealed that children from single-earner families performed more *masculine tasks with their fathers* but did not differ from dual-earner children in the extent to which they performed chores in the company of their mothers. There were, however, sex differences in the social contexts of children's chores. Specifically, girls spent more time on feminine chores *with their mothers* and also spent more time on such chores undertaken *alone* than did boys. In contrast, boys performed more masculine tasks *with their fathers* than did girls.

These data on different dimensions of children's household tasks help us to paint a more detailed picture of how boys and girls from these two family contexts are spending their time. Findings across a number of studies suggest that, while children from dual-earner families are somewhat more involved in household tasks, the differences between boys' and girls' experiences may be more extensive than those between children from dual- versus single-earner families. Another important point to keep in mind is that while household chores do not appear to comprise an overwhelming proportion of most children's time, there is a great deal of variability in how much work children do around the house (variability that seems to be independent of parents' work situation). For example, the amount of time children reported spending in feminine tasks in our own research ranged from none at all by some children to *nine and one half hours per week* by others. Similarly, for masculine tasks, although a substantial number of children (almost forty percent of our sample) never reported performing tasks like taking out the garbage, raking leaves, or mowing the lawn, other children reported spending over *ten hours per week* on such chores. Given that such substantial differences exist between children, it would seem very important to address the question of what implications different amounts of household task participation have for children's well-being. This is the topic to which we now turn.

The Potential Consequences of Children's Household Task Involvement

> Janet is 10 years old but has many adult responsibilities. In addition to taking care of her clothes and room, she must prepare breakfast for herself and her younger sister and make sure that they get off to school on time. (Her mother leaves for work an hour before Janet needs to get to school.) When she gets home, she has to do some housecleaning, defrost some meat for dinner, and make sure her sister is all right....After Janet helps prepare dinner, her mother says, "Honey, will you do the dishes? I'm just too tired," and Janet barely has time to do some homework. (Elkind, 1981, p. 149)

As this scenario suggests, some parents make what seem to be excessive demands on their children for help with home and family responsibilities. A number of writers have argued that duties assigned to children by parents (who may be overburdened by their own responsibilities) may lead to heightened levels of stress and reduced feelings of competence and self-worth in children (Elkind, 1981; Postman, 1982; Winn, 1983). In addition, the extra time children spend carrying out family responsibilities may take away from time spent participating in activities outside the home, such as organized sports, clubs, or other peer-oriented involvement, which have important consequences for children's social adjustment (Propper, 1972). Finally, an indirect consequence of children's involvement in chores may be problems in the parent-child relationship. Specifically, parents' demands for children's help may give rise to increases in parent-child conflict. Some research suggests, in fact, that household responsibilities are one of the most common themes underlying arguments between parents and their children (Montemayor, 1983; Smetana, 1985). Because children from dual-earner families tend to be more involved in household chores, the likelihood of parent-child conflict may be increased in these families, though as yet, no research evidence relevant to this question is available.

Rather than focusing on these potential risks to children's development and adjustment, students of child development have argued that household task participation may benefit children by instilling in them "sound work habits, reliability, judgment, and in the case of household obligations, an awareness of the needs of others" (Elder, 1974, p. 71). In fact, both the U.S. and British surveys mentioned earlier showed that most parents require their children to perform household chores in an effort to help children develop a sense of responsibility as well as to learn the skills and values necessary for successful adaptation to adult life (Newson & Newson, 1976; White & Brinkerhoff, 1981a).

Unfortunately, there is little hard evidence to support either this view or the alternative conception that emphasizes the risks to adjustment of excessive demands on children. Available data provide an inconsistent account of the effects of household task participation. Early research on achievement motivation (McClelland, 1961) and moral development (Kohlberg, 1964), for example, suggested that high levels of task involvement may have a *negative* effect on children, possibly because of the pressures toward conformity inherent in demands for such activities. Another early investigation, however, found no connections between children's involvement in household tasks and either teachers' or parents' ratings of dependability or responsibility (Harris, Clark, Rose, & Valasek, 1963).

The Instrumental Value of Children's Household Tasks: Potential Implications

One line of evidence about children from different cultures suggests that the consequences of children's task involvement may vary depending on its instrumental value to the family. Some children have been shown to benefit from task involvement in terms of increases in prosocial and altruistic behavior; the consequences of task involvement appear to differ, however, depending upon whether children's work serves a meaningful role in their family and/or cultural context. Cross cultural studies have revealed that the least altruistic children are those who perform fewer household chores and whose involvement consists mainly of taking care of their own things. In contrast, the most altruistic or prosocial children are both more involved in work, in general, and their household responsibilities are clearly designed to benefit the family as a whole (Whiting & Whiting, 1975). Along these lines, Straus's (1962) study of children from farm families in the United States revealed that children who were highly involved in the family economy seemed to have a greater sense of responsibility and concern for others. Like Whiting and Whiting (1975), Straus argued that these consequences ensued *because* children's help was essential to the maintenance of the family as a whole. A third line of evidence for the proposition that children's task participation may have beneficial effects when it has instrumental value comes from an investigation of children in the Great Depression. Describing children's involvement in family work during this era, Elder (1974) noted that:

> Conditions in deprived families presented children with a moral challenge that called for their best effort...though most studies of children in affluent times have not found support for the developmental value of tasks in the home, economic and labor needs in deprived families created urgent, realistic, and meaningful demands which were not in any sense contrived. (p.71)

Taken together this group of studies suggests that an analysis of the possible effects of children's household task involvement must take into account not only the tasks children perform but the *meaning* of children's work in their family context. It appears from these data that the consequences of children's work experiences may differ across families, depending on the appreciation and support children receive for their endeavors. Dual-earner families may be one context, prevalent in contemporary western society, in which children's household work may serve an "urgent, realistic, and meaningful" function (Elder, 1974, p. 71). Indeed, a survey of parents' reasons for assigning household tasks to children revealed that parents from dual-earner families were twice as likely as those from single-earner families to report that they assigned chores because they *needed their children's help* (White & Brinkerhoff, 1981a). Although most parents said that they also assigned chores to children in an effort to instill a sense of responsibility, these data suggest that children's housework has a greater instrumental value in dual-earner families. Because the meaning or importance of children's work may differ in dual- and single-earner families, we might expect that the same level of participation will have different effects on these two groups of children.

Gender Roles in the Family

In addition to its instrumental value, the meaning of children's work may derive from other value or belief systems operating in the family (McHale, Bartko, Crouter, & Perry-Jenkins, in press). For example, besides altering the instrumental significance of the roles that parents and children play in the family economy, mothers' entry into the labor force also appears to affect family sex roles. For example, in terms of their family responsibilities, several studies have found that fathers in dual-earner families often become more involved in child care and, in addition, take on more of the household tasks traditionally performed by women (Atkinson & Huston , 1984; Robinson, 1977). Along with these alterations in their sex-role behaviors, dual-earner fathers may express less traditional sex role attitudes than do single-earner fathers (Atkinson & Huston, 1984). Some investigators, in fact, have argued that the ways in which mothers and fathers divide their family roles (i.e., as workers, homemakers, and child caregivers) may have an important influence on children's sex role socialization (Huston, 1983). As we have noted, data from our own and others' research suggest that the task performance of dual- and single-earner boys tends to mirror their fathers' patterns of involvement: like their fathers dual-earner boys tend to perform more traditionally feminine tasks. Because there has been little attempt to examine the tasks of parents and children in the same family, however, we do not yet know the extent to which sons and daughters actually model their fathers' and mothers' levels of task involvement. Such information may be important because the consequences of task involvement may depend on whether or not children's activities violate sex-role norms in the family, particularly the standards set by the same-sex parent. For example, a boy with a very traditional father who spends a good deal of time helping prepare dinner or cleaning the house may have a difficult time identifying with his father, with negative implications for his psychological well-being. Similarly, a girl with a nontraditional mother who herself embraces the domestic role, may experience less acceptance in her relationship with her mother and, consequently, lower self-esteem.

To explore these issues, we began by comparing the sex-typed household tasks as well as the sex-role attitudes of fathers and mothers from the dual- versus single-earner families in our sample. As we expected, these analyses revealed that the division of labor in single-earner families was more traditional when it came to feminine tasks: single-earner mothers performed *more* such tasks than did dual-earner mothers and single-earner fathers performed *fewer* feminine tasks than did dual-earner fathers (see McHale et al., in press). The results of the comparisons of parents' sex-role attitudes, likewise, revealed more traditional attitudes, specifically in fathers from single-earner families. As fathers generally have been shown to be more concerned about sex-role socialization than mothers, these attitudinal differences between dual- and single-earner fathers would seem to be particularly important.

We reasoned that the different sex role norms operating in these dual- and single-earner families might lead to different consequences for children's sex-typed task involvement. Because the single-earner families in our sample tended to be more traditional we expected that difficulties might arise for boys in single-earner families who performed *more feminine* tasks and girls who performed *more masculine* tasks; the family roles of both of these groups of children are likely to be incongruent with family sex-role norms including the division of household labor, fathers' sex-role attitudes, and the family structure itself (i.e., the fact that only the father was employed). In contrast, in the more nontraditional dual-earner families, more problems should arise in the case of boys who perform *fewer feminine* tasks and girls who perform *fewer masculine* tasks. In dual-earner families, children's help is sorely needed; thus, children who remain uninvolved in household labor, contrary to norms established by their parents, may be subject to more negativity from their parents, and in turn, feel more stressed about family responsibilities and less competent about their accomplishments. The results of our analyses were consistent with our prediction that the effects of household task performance would differ for children from dual-earner versus single-earner families but only in the case of boys (McHale, et al., in press). Specifically, there were two groups of boys who seemed better adjusted: dual-earner boys *high* in task involvement and single-earner boys *low* in involvement reported feeling more competent, less stressed by their chores, and also more positive about their relationships with both their mothers and fathers. In other words, high task involvement, specifically in traditionally feminine chores, seemed to be linked to positive functioning for dual-earner boys but to negative functioning for boys from single-earner families.

We followed up the findings on contextual differences for boys, focusing on the extent to which boys' feminine task involvement was congruent with their fathers' *sex-role behavior,* specifically their fathers' level of involvement in feminine tasks, and their fathers' *sex-role attitudes,* that is, ideas about how equal the roles of men and women ought to be. We anticipated that when sons modeled their fathers' level of task involvement or engaged in activities consistent with their fathers' sex role beliefs, these boys would likely exhibit more positive adjustment.

In our analyses we focused on two groups of boys whose task involvement was inconsistent with their fathers' behavior and attitudes and who therefore might be "at risk" for adjustment problems: (1) single-earner boys highly involved in feminine tasks whose fathers were more traditional in their sex-role attitudes or task involvement; and (2) dual-earner boys less involved in feminine tasks whose fathers were more liberal. As Table 4 suggests, our analyses revealed that these "at risk" boys scored more poorly on well-being measures than

Table 4
Boys' Reports of Stress,
Competence, and Father-Child Relationships

	Stress	Competence	Warm Father-Child Relationships
High-Risk Boys[1]	13.68	17.91	113.44
Low-Risk Boys	10.10	20.80	123.06

[1]The "High-Risk" group includes single-earner boys with *nontraditional* roles (more feminine tasks) whose fathers are more *traditional* in their sex-role attitudes and dual-earner boys with *traditional* roles (fewer feminine tasks) whose fathers are more *nontraditional* in their sex-role attitudes.

other boys. Specifically, they reported lower levels of perceived competence, greater feelings of stress regarding their family responsibilities, and less warmth and more rejection from their fathers (McHale, et al., in press). In brief, inconsistency between boys' involvement in feminine chores and their fathers' sex-role behavior and attitudes may be associated with boys exhibiting adjustment problems.

What we do not know from these findings, however, is whether these sex role incongruities *cause* boys' adjustment problems or, conversely, whether boys with personal and relationship problems are less likely to model their fathers' activities or behave in accordance with their fathers' sex-role attitudes. Only by examining family members' activities over time can we begin to draw firm conclusions about the causal processes linking children's household work with their well-being.

Turning to analyses of girls' task involvement our results revealed *no differences* across family contexts in girls' well-being as a function of their task involvement. Comparisons did indicate, however, that girls who performed more feminine tasks reported slightly higher levels of perceived competence, regardless of whether they came from dual- or single-earner families. We also found that girls from *both* dual- and single-earner families who performed *fewer* masculine tasks perceived more acceptance from their fathers than did girls who were highly involved in masculine tasks. Taken together, the findings for girls provide some evidence that sex-typed task involvement (high involvement in feminine tasks and low involvement in masculine tasks) may have the most positive implications for girls' adjustment and parent-child relationships, regardless of family context (McHale, et al., in press). The findings for girls, however, are much weaker than the findings for boys. Because involvement in feminine chores is so common for girls (all of the girls in this sample spent at least some time involved in tasks such as food preparation, washing dishes, or straightening up the house) such activities may not have a high level of emotion attached to them, and thus, have fewer implications for girls' well-being. On the other hand, because so few of the girls in this sample *ever* performed masculine tasks (only forty percent of girls spent more than five minutes a week on such chores), it is not surprising that links between such activities and measures of well-being were weak. Whereas girls' feminine task performance may be taken as a matter of course, the same activities may be highly salient when performed by boys, and subject to either elaborate praise or, in some cases, possibly teasing or ridicule.

Summary and Conclusions

We began this chapter by describing the household task activities of girls and boys from dual- versus single-earner families. A number of studies have shown that while most children are regularly involved in helping around the house, dual-earner children and girls tend to spend more time performing chores, particularly chores usually thought of as "women's work." Traditionally masculine tasks such as home repairs and yard work are performed less frequently but tend to be seen as more "fun" than feminine tasks. Group comparisons reveal, however, that dual-earner children and, again, girls, rate feminine tasks as more fun than do single-earner children and boys. That the same groups of children who are more involved in feminine tasks rate them as more fun may mean that greater exposure to certain tasks increases children's competence in those activities, resulting in more positive evaluations. Other factors, however, may also be responsible. This issue clearly deserves further exploration: parents who must beg or coerce their children into helping with chores would undoubtedly be grateful for information about how to help their children have more fun doing chores.

Analyses of the social contexts of children's housework, that is, who helps children with their chores, revealed few differences across single- versus dual-earner families, but not surprisingly, girls performed more tasks in the company of their mothers and boys performed more in the company of their fathers. Some writers have argued that children's experiences in performing household tasks may be an important mechanism of sex-role socialization (e.g., Huston, 1983). Both in terms of what kinds of tasks boys versus girls perform and in terms of opportunities to observe parental models, household task involvement may serve to prepare children for adult family roles.

Although most previous investigations of children's housework have focused on how much children are involved in chores and on what kinds of tasks they tend to perform, the research we have reported here suggests that children's work is multifaceted. Many dimensions of children's work remain unexplored, however, particularly those having to do with children's subjective evaluations of their work, such as whether *children* see their tasks as representing a significant and essential contribution to the maintenance of the family. Examining different dimensions of children's task performance may provide more clues about the connections between such experiences and children's development and well-being.

Although most parents assert that assigning chores to children will have the effect of fostering a sense of responsibility (White & Brinkerhoff, 1981a), as we have noted, the available evidence about the effects of children's task involvement is not so straightforward. Rather, the potential effects of children's task performance seem to vary depending on the *meaning* of children's work in their family context. The meaning of children's work has been examined in terms of its *instrumental value to the family* and in terms of the *congruence between children's sex-typed tasks and sex-role orientations* in the family. Because the meaning of children's work is likely to vary across dual-earner and single-earner family contexts, the same work experiences may have very different consequences in these two family contexts. As yet, however, there are few data available to substantiate this hypothesis, and more research is needed. At a more general level, the available data suggest that future studies of children growing up in dual- and single-earner families should focus on how the processes underlying children's development and well-being may differ across these two family contexts.

Annotated Bibliography

Elkind, D. (1981). *The hurried child.* Reading, PA: Addison-Wesley.
This widely-read book describes the unique pressures and burdens which today's children are experiencing and the emotional and behavioral consequences which may result. The author argues that children of the eighties often were forced to grow up too quickly;

to achieve more at an earlier age than children of previous eras. In turn, these "hurried children" may make up a large portion of those children who experience emotional problems, school failure, delinquency, and drug abuse. Strategies to help alleviate these stressors are discussed.

Medrich, E., Roizen, J., Rubin, V., & Buckley, S. (1982). *The serious business of growing up.* Berkeley: University of California Press.

This book describes a large-scale research project that examined the out-of-school lives of 764 sixth-grade students. The amount of time these boys and girls typically spent on activities such as chores, jobs, extracurricular activities, their time with family and their time with friends are all described in detail. Through these analyses we learn, among other things, that shared activities between parents and children are at a premium. The book concludes with a discussion of social policy issues relevant to children and families in contemporary American society.

Zelizer, V. (1985). *Pricing the priceless child.* New York: Basic.

This is a scholarly and immensely readable book about the changing role of children in American families and society. The author traces the development of our society's conceptualization of children and childhood from the mid-1800's when children's "economic" role in the family was fundamental, to the mid-1900's, as children came to be viewed as "sacred". The interplay among economic, moral, and social forces that underlie this change are vividly described. Zelizer concludes with the speculation that we may be witnessing a reversal of earlier trends: changes in the structure of the contemporary American family, including the increasing number of single-parent families and the unsurpassed entry of mothers into the labor force may mean that the "economically useless but emotionally sacred" child may be put back to work and, once again, assigned a significant role in the maintenance of family life.

Bibliography

Atkinson, J., & Huston, T. (1984). Sex role orientation and division of labor in early marriage. *Journal of Personality and Social Psychology, 46,* 333-345.

Bartko, W. (1989, April). *Gender and contextual differences in correlates of children's household work.* Poster presented at the Biennial Meeting of the Society for Research in Child Development, Kansas City.

Baumrind, D. (1971). Current patterns of parental authority. *Developmental Psychology Monograph, 4,* (1, Pt. 2).

Crouter, A., & McHale, S. (1989, April). *Child-rearing in dual- and single-earner families: Implications for the well-being of school-aged children.* Paper presented at the Biennial Meeting of the Society for Research in Child Development, Kansas City.

Elder, G. (1974). *Children of the great depression.* Chicago: University of Chicago Press.

Elkind, D. (1981). *The hurried child.* Reading, PA: Addison-Wesley.

Goodnow, J. (1988). Children's household work: Its nature and functions. *Psychological Bulletin, 103,* 5-26.

Harris, D., Clark, K., Rose, A., & Valasek, F. (1963). The relationship of children's home duties to an attitude of responsibility. *Child Development, 25,* 29-33.

Hedges, J., & Barnett, J. (1972). Working women and the division of household tasks. *Monthly Labor Review, 95,* 9-14.

Hoffman, L. (1979). Maternal employment: 1979. *American Psychologist, 34,* 859-865.

Hoffman, L. (1989). Effects of maternal employment in the two-parent family. *American Psychologist, 44,* 283-292.

Huston, A. (1983). Sex-typing. In P. Mussen (Ed.), *Handbook of child psychology* (Vol. 4, pp. 387-467). New York: Wiley.

Kohlberg, L. (1964). Development of moral character and moral ideology. In L. Hoffman & M. Hoffman (Eds.), *Review of child development research* (Vol. 1, pp. 383-431). New York: Russell Sage.

McClelland, D. (1961). *The achieving society.* New York: Free Press.

McHale, S., Bartko, W., Crouter, A., & Perry-Jenkins, M. (in press). Children's housework and their psychosocial functioning: The mediating effects of parents' sex role behaviors and attitudes. *Child Development.*

Montemayor, R. (1983). Parents and adolescents in conflict: All families some of the time and some families all of the time. *Journal of Early Adolescence, 3,* 83-103.

Newson, J., & Newson, E. (1976). *Seven years old in the home environment.* London: Allen & Unwin.

Postman, N. (1982). *The disappearance of childhood.* New York: Laural Books.

Propper, A. (1972). The relationship of maternal employment to adolescent roles, activities, and parental relationships. *Journal of Marriage and the Family, 34,* 417-421.

Robinson, J. (1977). *How Americans use time: A social psychological analysis of everyday behavior.* New York: Praeger.

Smetana, J. (1988). Concepts of self and social convention: Adolescents' and parents' reasoning about hypothetical and actual family conflicts. In M. Gunnar & W. Collins (Eds.), *Development during the transition to adolescence: Minnesota symposium on child psychology* (Vol. 21, pp. 79-122). Hillsdale, NJ: Erlbaum.

Straus, M. (1962). Work roles and financial responsibility in the socialization of farm, fringe, and town boys. *Rural Sociology, 27,* 257-274.

White, L., & Brinkerhoff, D. (1981a). Children's work in the family: Its significance and meaning. *Journal of Marriage and the Family, 43,* 789-798.

White, L., & Brinkerhoff, D. (1981b). The sexual division of labor: Evidence from childhood. *Social Forces, 60,* 170-181.

Whiting, B., & Whiting, J. (1975). *Children of six cultures.* Cambridge, MA: Harvard University Press.

Winn, M. (1983). *Children without childhood.* New York: Pantheon.

Zill, N., & Peterson, J. (1982). Learning to do things without help. In L. M. Loasa & I. E. Sigel (Eds.), *Families as learning environments for children* (pp. 343-374). New York: Plenum.

Father's Employment:
A Neglected Influence on Children[1]

Julian Barling

...children can acquire occupational knowledge directly. As they listen to their parents talk about their jobs, as they see their parents come home tired after a hard day at work, as they spend time at parents' workplaces, they may develop feelings and ideas about work. (Piotrkowski & Stark, 1987, p. 3)

Standing in glaring contrast to the wealth of speculation, theorizing, and research on all aspects of mothers' employment, there is a dearth of empirical research on the effects of fathers' employment on father-child interactions and their children's behavior. The major reason for this is the ideological position that initially prompted research on maternal employment. Consistent with a "deprivation framework," it was assumed that absence caused by maternal employment would harm the child and the mother-child relationship. This "deprivation framework" also minimized the role of fathers in all aspects of child development compared to that of mothers, assuming that fathers were disinterested, or at least less interested in the parenting role. Hence, fathers' employment was presumed not to affect children (Booth & Edwards, 1980). This belief poses practical difficulties for research on the effects of fathers' employment on children. Very few fathers are voluntarily non-employed. Thus, while large groups of voluntarily non-employed mothers can be contrasted with voluntarily employed mothers, large groups of voluntarily non-employed fathers do not exist. Even if groups of voluntarily non-employed fathers could be assembled, socio-economic confounds would restrict the validity of any results obtained: Presumably, voluntarily nonemployed fathers would be either extremely wealthy or exceptionally poor.

---

[1]Preparation of this Chapter was supported by grants from the Social Sciences and Humanities Research Council of Canada (Grant #: 410-88-0891) and Imperial Oil. The author expresses considerable appreciation to Karyl E. MacEwen for her assistance throughout the writing of this Chapter.

181

This situation is now changing, and interest is being expressed about the effects of fathers' employment on children's behavior, and on father-child interactions. Several factors account for this change. First, interest in the role of the father in child development in general has increased tremendously (e.g., Booth & Edwards, 1980; Lamb, 1981; 1982). Second, the rising number of employed mothers has forced more fathers to become involved in the parenting role. Third, in considering the link between work and family, the emphasis is moving away from employment status toward a consideration of subjective employment experiences. A focus on fathers' employment experiences rather than their employment status makes it possible to investigate the effects of fathers' employment on children.

Several issues concerning fathers' employment and their children's behavior will be considered in this chapter. These include the effects on children of fathers' job-related absence, whether fathers influence their children's choice of occupation, the effects of fathers' subjective employment experiences, and fathers' unemployment. Lastly, concerns common to all these topics (e.g., the combined effects of mothers' and fathers' employment, the central role of the father-child relationship, causal inferences, and the severity of any effects on children) will be evaluated.

Job-related Father Absence

Concern is often raised about the effects of fathers' absence on children. For example, Hillenbrand (1976, p. 451) noted that "Among the many stresses which assault today's American family, father absence is an increasingly frequent phenomenon." Consequently, it should not be surprising that there is a large body of research investigating this issue. However, the majority of this research has investigated the consequences of nonjob-related fathers' absence, i.e., absence because of death, divorce, and desertion. Before analyzing the effects of job-related father absence, it is important to understand how different reasons for father absence (whether job-related or not) affect behavior.

Piotrkowski and Gornick (1987) proposed a framework for understanding the effects of two types of job-related father absence, namely ordinary and extraordinary absences. Ordinary job-related father absences are predictable and temporary; their stable departure and reunion rituals help children understand and cope with the absence. Thus, if a father consistently leaves for work and returns home at the same time each and every day, this will soon be viewed and accepted as part of the father's occupational role by other family members. On the contrary, the timing of separations (i.e., the pattern of days/nights spent at home and on the job), and the pattern of daily hours spent at home/work (i.e., at what time the father leaves and arrives home) in extraordinary job-related absence are unpredictable and unstable. Hence, for example, children may have difficulty adapting to fathers' rapidly rotating work schedules. Barling (1990b) suggests that ordinary and extraordinary absence also differ in terms of their duration. He classifies protracted absences, such as three month naval tours-of-duty (Marsella, Dubanoski & Mohs, 1974) or nine months at sea (Lynn & Sawrey, 1958) as extraordinary, regardless of whether they are regular and predictable. Another factor that discriminates between ordinary and extraordinary father absence is the emotional connotations associated with different types of father absence (Barling, 1990a). Intrafamily conflict is likely to be greater when fathers' absence is a function of desertion or divorce rather than job-related. When father absence is work-related, the grief and loss experienced would not even be comparable with that associated with father absence as a function of death or desertion. Thus, the subjective meaning of job-related father absence depends on the reasons for the absence and is more important than the objective occurrence of the absence (Pratt & Barling, 1988). Following Piotrkowski and Gornick (1987), therefore, it is likely that ordinary job-related father absence exerts no harmful effects on children, whereas extraordinary job-related absence might.

Ordinary Job-related Father Absence

There is little research on the effects of ordinary job-related father-absence on children. Several factors contribute to this situation. Unlike mothers, fathers are expected to be absent from the family because of employment; indeed, their daily *presence* in the home because of unemployment is sometimes assumed to be non-normative and detrimental. Also, there is little variability among fathers regarding the amount of ordinary job-related absence: Most fathers spend approximately the same number of hours working each day. For statistical reasons (range restriction), this would decrease the likelihood of uncovering statistically significant effects of father absence on children. In one study of a group of young fathers ($\underline{M}$ age = 22.9 years), McHale and Huston (1984) showed that the greater the number of hours devoted to their jobs each week, the less fathers interacted with their infants. The lower quantity of time spent with their infants is predictable given the finite number of hours per week. More important is the finding that the number of hours spent on the job each week by the fathers did not predict most aspects of the *quality* of the father-infant relationship. Thus, the data support Piotrkowski and Gornick's (1987) argument that fathers' ordinary work-related absences exert no detrimental effects on their child-rearing behaviors.

Extraordinary Job-related Father Absence

The effects of fathers' extraordinary job-related absence has been examined in studies investigating the link between fathers' shift work and their children and the effects of fathers' prolonged job absence on their children. Because shift work involves irregular, unpredictable patterns that might interfere with the fulfillment of family roles, it can be predicted that father absence due to shift work will interfere with the father-child relationship. In two separate studies, fathers who were involved in shift work and were absent from the family during the evenings (when family participation is critical) reported poorer father-child relationships than employed fathers who were present during these periods (Mott, Mann, McLoughlin & Warwick, 1965; Volger, Ernst, Nachreiner & Hanecke, 1988). Nonetheless, we cannot conclude from either of these two studies that fathers who work shifts actually functioned more poorly. They may have experienced higher levels of guilt regarding child-rearing because of their absence from the family at critical times, which led them to question their adequacy as parents. Supporting this idea, there are no data showing that fathers involved in shift work differ from those working regular shifts on objective indices (e.g., teacher reports, direct observations) of father-child interaction.

A number of studies have focused on protracted father absence, particularly in the military or merchant navy setting. These studies will be discussed according to whether they focus on the effects of extraordinary job-related father absence on mother-child interactions or on child behavior problems.

Mother-child Interactions. Marsella et al. (1974) proposed that job-related father absence affects children through its direct effects on mothers' child rearing attitudes and behaviors. They studied mothers whose husbands were nuclear submarine personnel and used a longitudinal design to assess mothers during alternating periods of husband presence and absence. They found that mothers showed significantly more maternal domination and control (e.g., strictness and intrusion) under conditions of father presence than father absence. One possible reason for this is that in their interactions with their children, fathers overcompensate their children for their absence. Realizing this, mothers might feel the need to retain some control. Hillenbrand (1976) found that mothers were more likely to be perceived as the dominant parent as the length of the husband absence increased, and Beckman, Marsella and Finney (1979) showed that mothers' depression was significantly associated with their husbands' job-related absence. Specifically, mothers were more depressed during periods of husbands' absence. One implication emerges from these studies. As Marsella et al. (1974) noted, when mothers' child rearing attitudes and behaviors change according to husbands' patterns of job-related presence and absence, their children will be faced with seemingly inconsistent maternal childrearing attitudes and behaviors. These inconsistencies may make it difficult for children to understand, predict and control mothers' responses. However, concerns exist about the generalizability of Marsella et al.'s (1974) findings. Generalizing to nonmilitary populations from military employees or their wives may be hazardous because of the unique chronic stresses they endure, especially given the peculiar fears that arise when one's spouse is on a nuclear submarine (Marsella et al., 1974).

Cotterell (1986) investigated the effects of fathers' prolonged job absence on wives' child-rearing attitudes among working class families in four small rural towns in inland Australia. Fathers were categorized as "absent" if participation in regular family activities and child rearing was restricted by job-related absences (e.g., shift work, or travelling sizable distances that kept them away from their families for days). They were contrasted with a separate group of fathers from the same geographical areas whose jobs did not require these absences. Like Marsella et al. (1974), Cotterell (1986) found that father absence was associated with mother-child interactions. In Cotterell's (1986) study, mothers whose husbands were frequently absent played with their children *less* and provided *less* cognitive stimulation than did mothers whose husbands were present. One plausible explanation for this finding is the greater number of household tasks assumed by mothers under conditions of father absence. These duties would leave mothers with less time to spend with their children. Also, mothers may not have felt it necessary to overcompensate for their spouses' job-related absence, because the absence under study was of shorter duration in Cotterell's (1986) study. Even though Cotterell (1986) notes some limits to the generalizability of the findings because of the attitudes in rural and mining towns in Australia, it would appear that extraordinary job-related father absence might exert some effect on mother-child interactions and/or child rearing attitudes. Both Marsella et al. (1974) and Cotterell (1986) showed that mothers' child rearing behaviors covary with job-related father absence and father presence.

Children's behavior. The question of whether prolonged job-related father absence affects children's social behavior has been examined. Hillenbrand (1976) investigated whether the amount of job-related father absence a child experienced was related to child's intelligence and social behavior. The length of father absence was significantly correlated with children's quantitative ability: The longer the father absence, the *greater* the child's quantitative ability. In this study, the average length of absence was 26 months. There was also a significant birth order effect, because first born children were most likely to manifest higher levels of quantitative ability. Hillenbrand (1976) also found that this general pattern of results was stronger for sons than for daughters. Hillenbrand's (1976) findings are the only ones pointing to a beneficial effect associated with extraordinary job-related father absence. However, because of the length of the father absence in this study, the findings may be more consistent with the "downward extension" hypothesis, which suggests that certain children (e.g., first born sons) subsequently will fare better following exposure to periods of hardship, because the additional duties and obligations they must bear prepares them for later responsibilities. This will be considered in more detail later in this chapter, together with findings on the effects of unemployment.

The second study to investigate the effects of job-related father absence on children's social behavior focused on the families of Norwegian sailors (Lynn & Sawrey, 1958). In that study, absentee fathers were merchant sailors or whalers who were away from home for at least nine consecutive months of each year and a maximum of 24 months. They were contrasted with fathers who were continuously present. All fathers held supervisory jobs. Significant differences existed between the children of these two groups. There was less secure identification with absentee fathers and greater immaturity and poorer social adjustment among their children. However, these two groups differed not only in terms of length of absence but also in terms of the type of job, position in the organizational hierarchy, and socioeconomic status, limiting the extent to which any differences between these two groups can be attributed solely to fathers' absence. Also, it is likely that a selection confound existed in Lynn and Sawrey's (1958) study (and others examining extraordinary job-related father absence). Individuals who are willing to accept job conditions that require such lengthy absences from the family may have specific personality traits and/or family circumstances and expectations. Together, these confounds limit the extent to which any negative effects that emerge in such studies can be attributed solely to job-related father absence.

With only one exception (Hillenbrand, 1976), the studies reviewed above suggest that some negative effects are associated with extraordinary job-related father absence (and the meaning of Hillenbrand's finding will be discussed later). Hence, it is possible that when job-related father absence is prolonged and extraordinary, negative effects accrue to the mother-child relationship, the mother's child rearing attitudes, and to children's behavior. In contrast, ordinary job-related father absence exerts no negative effects on children's behavior.

A more important issue centres on the conceptualization and operationalization of father absence. In all these studies, the meaning of the father's absence for the father, the mother and/or the child is ignored. Thus, current research on job-related father absence is based on a deficit-oriented deprivation model similar to that invoked when hypothesizing that maternal employment status is synonymous with maternal deprivation (Barling, 1990a). This model can only provide limited information as to why father absence exerts negative (or in some cases, positive) effects (Pederson, 1976). To obtain more comprehensive information, the subjective meaning of job-related father absences for children, for wives and for fathers themselves must be understood. It is possible that children feel the same emotions (e.g., pride, embarrassment) in their absentee fathers' jobs as other children do when their employed fathers are continuously present. This points to the need for further understanding and research on the subjective meaning of job-related father absence for the child, the father and the mother.

Intergenerational Occupational Choice: Like Father, Like Son?

The notion that sons come to resemble their fathers is not new. One question that has intrigued social scientists and the lay public is whether sons tend to choose the same occupation as their fathers. In evaluating whether fathers' choice of occupation influences children in general and sons in particular, two questions will be addressed: Does a link exist between fathers' and sons' occupational choice, and if so, how does it come about?

Similarities between Fathers' and Sons' Occupational Choice

Numerous studies have been conducted assessing whether children choose the same or similar occupations as their fathers. These studies show consistently that the prospect of sons pursuing the same occupation as their fathers is significantly greater than chance.

One of the earliest studies using a large sample of college students ($\underline{N}$ = 3,211; Nelson, 1939) demonstrated the trend for sons to enter the same occupations as their fathers. For example, Nelson (1939) noted that seven of 54 bankers' children themselves chose banking. Likewise, 124 children of the 570 fathers involved in commerce chose commerce for themselves. Both these statistics far exceed chance expectations given the extensive number of occupational choices open to the children. Nelson (1939) notes further that in male-dominated occupations (e.g., dentistry and the ministry), the probability that children follow in their fathers' footsteps would have been even greater had the sample excluded daughters.

Since then, several studies have replicated and extended Nelson's (1939) earlier findings. Jensen and Kirschner (1955) analyzed a representative sample of 8,000 heads of households in six cities across the United States. Where differences existed between fathers' and sons' occupations, they occurred because sons progressed further up the occupational hierarchy than their fathers. Aberle and Naegele (1952) found that when fathers were asked about their sons' future occupations, fathers first denied holding any specific aspirations for their children. However, it later became apparent that any occupation chosen by sons was acceptable to fathers as long as it was a middle-class, professional, or business occupation, and no father visualized downward mobility for his son. Lastly, in a sample of 70,015 males who had entered college in 1961, Werts' (1968) replicated earlier results that sons follow in their fathers' occupational footsteps. Werts (1968) also raised an issue that will be pursued further in this chapter: The data showing a link between fathers' and sons' occupations provides no information as to how such linkages emerge.

Reinhardt (1970) extended research on intergenerational occupational linkages by investigating whether sons who chose occupations similar to their fathers are more likely to be successful. Reinhardt (1970) studied 105 outstanding military jet pilots. Fathers of two-thirds of these superior jet pilots had served in the military, and 85 percent of them had been affiliated with the same division. Perhaps more importantly, Reinhardt (1970) investigated the occupations of 70 career failures, that is, jet pilots who were grounded because of unsatisfactory performance or voluntarily stopped flying. Only 3 percent of the fathers of the career failures were active or former military pilots. Because so many of the studies on the intergenerational transmission of occupation have focused on children regarded as successful (e.g., university students and graduates), Reinhardt's (1970) data on career failures are especially important.

Thus, Blaise Pascal's comment in 1656 that "The most important thing in life is the choice of a calling, but that is left to chance" (Jackman, 1984, p. 30) appears to be incorrect. Occupational choice by sons is not a random process. Instead, there is a substantial tendency for sons to follow in their fathers' occupational footsteps, and this tendency generalizes across cultures (Chopra, 1967). However, these studies raise one question that is at least as interesting and important as those that they answer. Specifically, given the existence of occupational intergenerational transmission, how this transmission occurs is a critical question that remains to be answered (Aldous, Hicks & Osmond, 1979).

Process of Influence of Fathers' Occupational Choice

The most direct way in which the intergenerational transmission of occupation might occur is via direct attempts by fathers to influence sons. It is possible that fathers engage in deliberate, conscious behaviors to bias their children's occupational choices. Breakwell, Fife-Schaw, and Devereux (1988) asked 3,160 teenagers in England two questions in this regard: Whether their parents had overtly attempted to influence their career choice, and if so, whether such attempts were successful. The teenagers reported that parents did indeed try to influence their choice of career directly, but they were not successful. Yet, these results may not capture the effects of deliberate attempts by fathers to influence their sons. First, the best way of assessing parents' influence on teenagers' choices may not be to ask teenage children. They might be most inclined to deny that their parents influence their behavior in any way. Second, Breakwell et al. (1988) did not separate their sample by gender of parent or child, even though data from different studies show that patterns of intergenerational occupational transmission differ for fathers and sons and fathers and daughters.

One alternative is that fathers indirectly influence their sons' choice of occupations. The research of Mortimer and her colleagues (e.g., Mortimer, 1974; 1976; Mortimer & Kumka, 1982; Mortimer, Lorence, & Kumka, 1986) clarifies this process. Mortimer's (1974) strategy of focusing on fathers' occupational values was motivated by Kohn's (1977) assumption that the occupational values a father espouses and requires for occupational success will influence his attitudes and behavior. Mortimer (1974) replicated previous findings showing that sons' occupational preferences matched their fathers' occupations. More importantly, she assessed the role of fathers' occupational values, functional similarity, and the father-son relationship in this process. Sons who did not follow their fathers' occupations exactly preferred occupations reflecting similar value structures to those inherent in their fathers' occupations. Functional similarity was important because sons of dentists and scientists who did not select their fathers' occupations expressed greater interest in medicine, and there was little movement away from the scientific/medical field. Similarly, sons of teachers overchose engineering, accounting, and scientific oriented professions, all of which require the interpretation of information as an integral part of the job. Mortimer (1976) replicated these results after controlling for the effects of fathers' and mothers' education, fathers' occupational status, and family income.

Mortimer's later analyses (Mortimer et al., 1986) extend these earlier findings. Mortimer and her colleagues controlled for children's grade point average (as an indicator of intelligence), isolated the role of the father-child relationship, and investigated different aspects of sons' career attainment ten years after the initial assessment. Essentially, Mortimer et al. (1986) showed that the closeness of the father-child relationship moderated the relationship between fathers' socioeconomic status and their children's work values: These occupational linkages were stronger under conditions of a close father-son relationship. In addition, specific values were associated with unique occupational outcomes. For example, intrinsic values were associated with autonomy, extrinsic values with income, and people-oriented values were linked with the social content of the job.

Thus, there is consistent support for a link between fathers' and sons' occupational choices, and some processes underlying this link have been isolated. Yet the range of moderating factors that have been investigated remains limited. Other factors such as paternal job dissatisfaction should now be investigated (Barling, 1986; Mortimer, 1976). The occupational linkage process may weaken when children with close relationships to their fathers realize that their fathers are dissatisfied with their jobs. Finally, most of the research has investigated occupational linkages between father and son. Although similar results do not emerge when mothers' occupations and daughters' occupational choices are considered (Mortimer et al., 1986), reasons for these differences are not well understood. Role modeling has been suggested as one possible process (see Mortimer et al., 1986). Another possibility is that the range of occupations held by employed mothers was restricted in previous generations, but this is no longer as true for daughters in each successive generation. The consequence of this would be that daughters now have a wider range of occupations from which to choose, and this would influence the magnitude of any correlation between mothers' and daughters' occupational choice.

Fathers' Subjective Job Experiences

There are several important reasons for studying fathers' subjective job experiences. First, as noted earlier, the meaning of fathers' job-related absence may be a more critical determinant of children's behavior than the absence itself. Second, it is not just fathers' occupations that influence sons' occupational choice but their occupational values. Third, Pratt and Barling (1988) have noted that the subjective meaning of job events is more important than the event itself. Consistent with this, research shows that the meaning of employment is a more important determinant of marital functioning than employment status (Barling, 1990b). Similarly, the meaning of employment to mothers is a more consistent predictor of children's behavior than mothers' employment status (e.g., Barling, Fullagar, & Marchl-Dingle, 1988).

Fathers' Job Dissatisfaction

Some research on fathers' subjective employment experiences has considered the role of fathers' job dissatisfaction in child-rearing and child development (Cochran & Bronfenbrenner, 1979). Honzik (1967) reported one of the first studies on the effects of fathers' job satisfaction on children's intelligence, tracking a representative sample of children born between 1928 and 1929 for 30 years. There was a correlation between paternal occupational satisfaction and sons' intelligence but not daughters', and this pattern of results remained consistent across each of the 16 occasions the sample was tested. Honzik's (1967) study, however, has some important limitations. Neither occupational success nor socioeconomic status were controlled; it remains unclear why children's intelligence should be associated with fathers' job satisfaction; and no information is provided on factors moderating the effects of fathers' job satisfaction on children.

Barling (1986) also investigated the effects of fathers' job dissatisfaction on children. He found that fathers' job dissatisfaction was associated with children's conduct problems and hyperactivity. Two aspects of this study are noteworthy, as they enhance its external validity. First, unlike Honzik (1967), Barling (1986) controlled statistically for fathers' level of education in an attempt to control the confounding effects of socioeconomic status. Second, teacher reports of children's behavior were obtained to eliminate biases (e.g., social desirability, autocorrelation) resulting from parents reporting both on their children and their own behavior. However, the issue of how job satisfaction affects specific behaviors remains unanswered.

One model that has been advanced to account for this link is that job dissatisfaction influences the way in which fathers interact with their children. In turn, it is the nature and quality of father-child (and, of course, mother-child) interactions that directly affect child behavior (cf. Barling et al., 1988; Lerner & Galambos, 1985; MacEwen & Barling, 1989). The rationale for this latter link is that the existence of a close father-child relationship enables children to appreciate their fathers' job dissatisfaction and to realize its negative effects on their fathers (Barling, 1986; Piotrkowski & Stark, 1987).

Two separate empirical questions are contained in this argument. First, do father-child interactions mediate the relationship between fathers' job dissatisfaction and child behavior? In other words, does a relationship exist between fathers' job dissatisfaction and father-child interactions, and do these father-child interactions in turn influence children's behavior? Grossman, Pollack, and Golding (1988) assessed the role of fathers' job satisfaction and job involvement in predicting different aspects of the father-son relationship among five-year old children. The only significant predictor of the amount of time fathers spent with their children during the week and on the weekend was their job satisfaction, and this effect was negative: The greater the job satisfaction, the less time the father spent playing with the child. These results partially replicated those of Feldman, Nash, and Aschenbrenner (1983), who found that job satisfaction and job salience predicted lower levels of playfulness between fathers and their infants aged 6-8 months.

Nonetheless, both the quantity *and* the quality of the father-son relationship must be considered before a comprehensive understanding of the effects of fathers' job satisfaction on sons' behaviors can be achieved. Results from studies investigating this show that fathers' job satisfaction is positively correlated with the quality of the father-son relationship. Data from McKinley's (1964) earlier study support the notion that fathers' job satisfaction is positively associated with qualitative aspects of the father-son relationship. Regardless of socioeconomic status, fathers who expressed job dissatisfaction were more hostile in their interactions with their children and used more severe disciplinary techniques. Kemper and Reichler (1976) found that fathers' job satisfaction predicted the extent to which they rewarded their children, while job dissatisfaction predicted the use of punishment. Most recently, Grossman et al. (1988) showed that fathers' job satisfaction was significantly and positively correlated with the extent to which they supported children's autonomy and affiliation. Thus, two distinct patterns exist. Fathers who are satisfied with their jobs spend less time with their children. However, fathers' job satisfaction is *positively* associated with the quality of father-child interactions. As noted elsewhere in this chapter, mothers' child-rearing behaviors (namely, punishment and rejection) that result from employment experiences (namely, interrole conflict and role satisfaction) influence children's problem behaviors (namely anxiety/withdrawal, conduct disorders and attention/immaturity).

Hence, the second empirical question emerges, i.e., does the father-child relationship moderate the link between fathers' job experiences and child behavior? In other words, irrespective of any effects of fathers' job satisfaction on the father-son relationship, is the relationship between fathers' job satisfaction and children's behavior dependent on the quality of the father-child relationship? One possibility is that it is through a close father-child relationship that children will understand the positive and negative conditions their fathers experience at work and the way in which these conditions influence their fathers (Piotrkowski & Stark, 1987) and thereby be negatively affected.

In an attempt to understand this, Barling (1986) drew a parallel with research on parents' marital satisfaction, parent-child interactions, and child behavior. He noted suggestions in the clinical psychological literature that the quality of the parent-child relationship buffers the negative effects of marital dissatisfaction on children (Emery, 1982). More recently, fathers' experiencing daily work stress reported less positive involvement with their children (Repetti, 1989). Barling (1986) tested 161 fathers who were employed full-time using a composite measure of the father-child relationship that reflected the extent to which the father played with or laughed with, read to, explained or taught things to, and hugged or held the child. After statistically controlling for the effects of socioeconomic status, fathers' job dissatisfaction was associated with higher levels of both hyperactivity and conduct problems when there was a close father-son relationship. When fathers reported job dissatisfaction but the father-child relationship was not as close, scores for hyperactivity and conduct problems were significantly lower. Thus, knowledge about fathers' job dissatisfaction may be transmitted to children through a close relationship with the parent in question, and Piotrkowski and Stark's (1987) hypothesis is supported. Several aspects of this study are noteworthy: First, these results extend previous findings on the effects of mothers' job dissatisfaction on their children (Barling & Van Bart, 1984), and recent research showing how mother-child interactions mediate this link (MacEwen & Barling, 1989). Second, consistent with MacEwen and Barling (1989), it remains for future research to isolate specific paternal job experiences that influence children's behavior: In Barling's (1986) study, only job dissatisfaction influenced children's behavior.   Neither job involvement nor perceptions of the organizational climate exerted similar effects.

A further explanation for the effects of fathers' job dissatisfaction on children emerges from Kemper and Reichler's (1976) finding that fathers who are dissatisfied with their jobs are more punitive. Under conditions of a close father-child relationship, children of dissatisfied fathers would be exposed to a more hostile and punitive child-rearing style, which itself is associated with children's externalizing problems such as conduct problems (e.g., Emery, 1982; MacEwen & Barling, 1989; Patterson, 1982).   It remains for future research to identify other mediating mechanisms. This is crucial not only for theoretical reasons but also from a pragmatic perspective. It is doubtful whether job dissatisfaction can be prevented.   To alleviate any negative outcomes of job dissatisfaction, therefore, it becomes crucial to isolate the processes through which fathers' job dissatisfaction (and, of course, employed mothers' job dissatisfaction) exerts negative influences on children.

Fathers' General Employment Experiences

In evaluating the effects of fathers' subjective employment experiences, most research has focused on their job satisfaction. There have also been some studies on the effects of other subjective employment experiences on children's behavior, all of which have focused on its effects on child rearing attitudes and behaviors or the father-child relationship. Coburn and Edwards' (1976) results from a large sample are consistent with Piotrkowski and Katz' (1982) findings on employed mothers. Coburn and Edwards (1976) found that fathers experiencing high job autonomy valued self-control and independence for their children more than fathers experiencing low levels of job autonomy.   In contrast, fathers experiencing little autonomy on the job were more likely to value obedience and good manners by their children than their counterparts high in job-related autonomy. Piotrkowski and Katz (1982) showed that mothers' autonomy on the job was negatively associated with children's voluntary attendance at school, whereas mothers' skill utilization was positively associated with their children's scholastic achievement. These studies support Kohn's (1977) hypothesis that job-related values are consistent with child-rearing values. However, the causal nature of the relationship is unclear. While it is possible that occupations mold values, it is equally possible--as Coburn and Edwards (1976) note--that individuals choose occupations that are consistent with their preexisting values.

Interrole conflict involves the experience of psychological stress and discomfort that arises when role demands from home or family inhibit or prevent successful role fulfillment in the other domain. The experience of interrole conflict for fathers and husbands and its consequences for children has received substantially less attention than mothers' interrole conflict or fathers' job satisfaction. In one study, Baruch and Barnett (1986) showed that fathers' family roles and employment roles interfered with each other. Their results demonstrated further that fathers' participation in typical child care tasks was significantly and negatively associated with fathers' feelings that they required more time for their careers. Given the degree to which fathers are now participating in both family and job-related responsibilities, future research might profitably focus more on fathers' interrole conflict.

Thus, there is consistency across studies focusing on the effects of fathers' subjective work experiences on their children. While fathers' job satisfaction is associated with less time devoted to children, both job satisfaction and general employment experiences positively influence the quality of father-child interactions. In turn, father-child interactions mediated the link between fathers' employment experiences and children's behavior.

Fathers' Job Loss

So far, the effects of different aspects of fathers' jobs on their children have been considered. It is also appropriate to consider what happens to children when fathers lose their jobs, as this highlights two issues that have already been raised. First, it is not fathers' employment *status* (whether they are employed or not) that affects children's behavior. Instead, it is fathers' subjective experience of unemployment (or employment) that affects children. Second, the father-child relationship plays a critical mediating link between fathers' unemployment and children's behavior (e.g., McLoyd, 1989).

Despite concern that fathers' unemployment directly affects children's behavior, there is not much research assessing this specific issue. What research has been conducted can be categorized according to whether children's social behaviors or children's perceptions of employment are affected. With respect to the latter, some research has shown that children whose fathers are unemployed have a greater understanding of unemployment than children whose fathers are employed (Radin & Greer, 1987). Likewise, children with some exposure to fathers' unemployment expressed greater concerns about family-economic issues (Pautler & Lewko, 1984). In contrast, children of employed and unemployed fathers do not differ consistently with respect to their social or scholastic behavior (e.g., Madge, 1983; Friedemann, 1986). These findings suggest that children learn about the occupational world through their parents' experiences (cf. Piotrkowski & Stark, 1987) but that these effects do not necessarily generalize to non-occupational domains. Thus, there are no consistent differences between the children of employed and unemployed fathers regarding social behavior. Two factors might account for the lack of differences between the social behavior of the two groups. First, an inappropriate model has been invoked when investigating this issue and, second, the relationship between fathers' unemployment and children's behavior is indirect.

In the same way that it is now argued that maternal employment experiences are more important than maternal employment status (e.g., Barling, 1990a; Bronfenbrenner & Crouter, 1982), fathers' experience of unemployment is a more important determinant of children's behavior than whether or not they are unemployed. This is an important distinction. Contrasting employed and unemployed fathers implies considerable variation between these two groups yet very little variation within each group. Investigating only unemployed fathers implies considerable systematic variation within their experience of unemployment. With respect to children's behavior, there is variation among children of unemployed fathers. For example, Friedemann (1986) found no differences in the peer relationships of children of employed and unemployed fathers, but there was a greater range of scores for children of unemployed fathers. Although not assessed, it is possible that this within-group variation is systematic and is associated with their fathers' experience of unemployment. Thus, focusing on fathers' *experience* of unemployment may be more appropriate than a focus on unemployment *status*.

The second factor accounting for no differences in social behavior between children of employed and unemployed fathers concerns the father-child relationship during periods of unemployment. On a quantitative level, data from both cross-sectional and longitudinal studies (Radin & Harold-Goldsmith, 1989; Ray & McLoyd, 1986; Shamir, 1986; Warr, 1984a; Warr & Payne, 1983) show that unemployed fathers interact more with their children. On regaining employment, there is a decrease in the amount of interaction between fathers and children (Shamir, 1986), suggesting that changes in employment status are responsible for changes in time spent with children. More importantly, on a qualitative level, the nature of the father-child relationship changes when fathers become unemployed, and specific parenting styles mediate the relationship between unemployment and child behavior problems. As McLoyd (1989) notes, unemployed fathers who become less nurturant, more punitive and more inconsistent in their interactions with their children tend to affect their children most. Boys in such situations develop more externalizing disorders, while adolescent girls feel more inadequate, are hypersensitive, and manifest lowered aspirations (Elder, Nguyen, & Caspi, 1985; McLoyd, 1989). Also, the likelihood of children being physically abused increases when fathers are unemployed (Barling, 1990a; McLoyd, 1989). This again is important. Clinical impressions and empirical research show that children who are physically abused perform poorly academically and manifest significant behavioral problems, including conduct problems, aggression, withdrawal, anxiety, and depression (Ammerman, Cassisi, Hersen, & Van Hasselt, 1986).

This raises the question of how to account for the fact that some unemployed fathers manifest poor parenting styles, while others do not. One possibility is that fathers' differential experience of unemployment predicts their parenting style. There is wide variation in the way fathers experience unemployment. For example, where job dissatisfaction existed prior to the layoff, the experience of unemployment may not be negative (O'Brien, 1985), and there are numerous demographic, personality, and social resource factors that reduce any negative effects of unemployment (Warr, 1984b). In contrast, fathers who suffer greatest income loss may be most inclined to experience unemployment as negative (McLoyd, 1989). This lends more support to the argument that it is not unemployment status that should be examined but rather the subjective perception or experience of that event (McLoyd, 1989; Pratt & Barling, 1988). In this respect, Jahoda's (1982) interpretation of the manifest and latent functions of employment provides a framework for conceptualizing the subjective experience of unemployment. Within this framework, it is predicted that there are differences among unemployed people in their loss of income, the extent to which they structure and use their time, the nature and number of their social contacts, their sense of purpose, and their personal identity and social status. Other factors not identified by Jahoda (1982) include the experience of bereavement associated with job loss (Archer & Rhodes, 1987), which is associated with psychological well-being (Barling, 1990a; Jahoda, 1982).

Elder's (1974) analyses of longitudinal data collected during the Great Depression cast further light on factors that moderate the effects of unemployment on children. For example, first born children, especially sons, are most likely to *benefit* from their fathers' job loss in the long term. They are more likely to do better at school, to enter college, and show greater satisfaction with their jobs, marriages, and lives. Elder and his colleagues (e.g., Moen, Cain, & Elder, 1983) have offered the "downward extension hypothesis" to account for this phenomenon. They argue that children who are exposed to paternal unemployment encounter new challenges and perform new tasks. In families where the breadwinner is unemployed, first born sons may well have additional responsibilities thrust upon them. During the Great Depression,

...older children were called upon for household activities as families shifted toward a more labor intensive economy.... Adult-like responsibilities became more a part of the lives of both boys and girls. Boys tended to seek gainful employment, while girls helped with domestic responsibilities, including child care, meal preparation, house cleaning, sewing and ironing. The involvement of boys in work roles accelerated their liberation from parental control. (Moen et al., 1983, pp. 231-232)

This explanation may also account for Hillenbrand's (1976) finding that exceptionally prolonged job related absence of the father ($\underline{M}$ length of absence = 26 months; range = 0-63 months) was associated with positive benefits, especially for first born children. When father absence is so prolonged, first born children may be required to assume some of the same family and income role responsibilities as do children of unemployed fathers. Future research might investigate whether this is indeed the case.

Thus, there is some consistency in the effects of fathers' employment and fathers' unemployment on children. Whether we consider employment or unemployment, fathers' subjective experiences are more influential in determining children's behavior than is their employment status. The direction of the relationship is also consistent: Fathers' experiences of employment or unemployment are associated with their child-rearing styles and children's behavior. Also, the way in which the father-child relationship is affected by fathers' employment or unemployment experiences is a critical determinant of children's behavior.

Fathers' Employment and Job Loss: Conclusion

In reevaluating the effects of fathers' employment on children, several topics emerge. These include a contrast of objective and subjective employment characteristics, the combined effects of mothers' and fathers' employment on children, the specific nature of the employment experience, the importance of the father-child relationship, and the need to identify causal paths in the relationship between fathers' employment experiences and their children's behavior.

In terms of the relative effects of fathers' objective and subjective job characteristics on their children, the data are clear. First, fathers' ordinary job-related absences exert no negative effects on mother-son interactions or on children's behavior. Fathers' extraordinary job-related absences may exert negative effects on children, although methodological questions (e.g., selection factors, noncomparability of control and experimental groups) need to be answered. Second, fathers' occupational choice influences sons' occupational preferences, and fathers' personal work values exert direct and indirect influences in the process of occupational linkages (Mortimer, 1974, 1976; Mortimer & Kumka, 1982; Mortimer et al., 1986). Third, the meaning of paternal unemployment or job-related absence to fathers, mothers, and children is likely to be a more significant determinant of parent-child interactions and children's behavior than is fathers' employment status or job-related absence.

The next issue that emerges is whether the effects of mothers' and fathers' employment experiences are additive. This question is especially important because of the large number of mothers who are now employed. Research should now focus on the combined effects of mothers' and fathers' employment experiences on their children. If mothers and fathers both experience their jobs positively, is the effect on their children greater than when only one parent is satisfied with his/her work? Alternatively, what are the effects on children if both parents are extremely dissatisfied with their jobs? Despite the importance of this question, there are still very few studies on mothers' *and* fathers' employment experiences (e.g., Greenberger & Goldberg, 1989).

Third, recent research suggests that it is critical to focus on specific employment experiences if we are to understand their effects on children's behavior. MacEwen and Barling (1989) showed that mothers' interrole conflict and employment role satisfaction exerted different effects on personal strain: Interrole conflict resulted in cognitive difficulties and negative mood, but maternal employment dissatisfaction only resulted in negative mood. In turn, these two indices differentially influenced mother-child interaction: Cognitive difficulties resulted in mothers' using more rejecting behaviors with their children, while negative mood led to an increase in the use of both rejecting and punishing behaviors by the mother. Finally, maternal rejection was associated with children's internalizing behaviors (namely, anxiety/withdrawal), whereas mothers' punishment was associated with children's externalizing behaviors (specifically, conduct disorders and inattention/immaturity). Future research should investigate whether similar differential effects are obtained with fathers.

Fourth, one critical variable identified in this chapter is the father-child relationship. Whether the intergenerational transmission of occupation, fathers' employment or unemployment experiences are considered, the father-child relationship serves a critical and consistent mediating function. It is through a close father-child relationship that children learn about their parents' occupational experiences, and it is this knowledge that influences their behavior. Future studies on the effects of fathers' (and mothers') employment experiences cannot afford to ignore this variable. Because of the importance of such research, it may be worthwhile to supplement self-report measures of parent-child interactions with observational data. This would add greater credibility to any such findings. Fifth, although research on parental employment and children typically takes account of the child's gender, the age of the child is invariably ignored. Future research and theorizing should explicitly consider the child's age, because specific parenting styles and child behaviors may be appropriate for children of different ages.

Sixth, in studying the effects of fathers' employment experiences, the question of causality must be confronted. The overwhelming assumption is that fathers' employment affects children, directly or indirectly. But other alternatives remain possible. For example, problem or sick children could detract from parents' attention, effort, and success on the job, making it is less likely that they will experience job satisfaction. Alternatively, in the same way that marital functioning prior to unemployment predicts marital functioning following unemployment (Komarovsky, 1940), preexisting problems in children may be uncovered or exacerbated in the presence of negative parental experiences. In addition, the relationship between fathers' employment experiences and children's behavior could be spurious, with variables such as negative affect influencing both (Brief, Burke, George, Robinson, & Webster, 1988). Yet with very few exceptions (e.g., Mortimer & Kumka, 1982; Mortimer et al., 1986), both the literatures on mothers' and fathers' employment experiences are characterized by cross-sectional research designs which do not allow causal inferences to be tested.

One final question concerns the interpretation of the relationships between fathers' employment and their children. Invariably, these statistical relationships are modest in magnitude. This implies that while these relationships are statistically significant and conceptually interesting, their clinical impact is questionable. However, there is one instance in which fathers' employment characteristics exert a clinical effect on children. Specifically, children whose fathers are unemployed are more at risk of suffering physical abuse. Yet some caution is appropriate in interpreting this as a causal relationship. It remains unclear whether unemployment triggers new instances of child abuse or uncovers preexisting problems. Also, the relevant research has not isolated whether it is necessarily the unemployed father who is the abuser (Barling, 1990a).

In conclusion, therefore, several consistent patterns emerge. Fathers' ordinary job-related absence exerts no harmful effects, whereas extraordinary job related absence is more likely to be associated with child behavior problems. Fathers' and sons' choice of careers are linked, and fathers' experience of their jobs influences their children. The father-child relationship plays an important role in linking fathers' work to children's behavior. Thus, Abraham Lincoln's admonishment in 1858 that "My father taught me to work; he did not teach me to love it" (Jackman, 1984, p. 224) should not be taken to mean that fathers *cannot* teach their children to love their work. Instead, through the father-child relationship, fathers influence their children's attitudes toward their work both directly and indirectly.

Annotated Bibliography

Barling, J. (1990). *Employment, unemployment, and family functioning.* Chichester: Wiley.

An in-depth and current discussion of the relationship between men's and women's employment and family functioning. Topics discussed include the effects of job absence, job mobility, shift work, job satisfaction, Type A behavior, acute and chronic work stressors, and employment role experiences on several aspects of marital functioning. The effects of mothers' and fathers' employment on children are dealt with, as are the effects of unemployment on marital functioning and children. The effects of family functioning on employment are also considered.

Cleary, B. (1977). *Ramona and her father.* NY: William Morrow.
There are numerous books targeted at children that are meant to explain stressors that children might be exposed to (e.g., divorce, death of parent). This particular book describes what happens to a family when the father loses his job, the changes all family members experience when he is unemployed, and what happens when he is re-employed. This book is highly recommended because the situations depicted faithfully reflect the "academic" literature on unemployment.

McLoyd, V. C. (1989). Socialization and development in a changing economy: The effects of paternal job and income loss on children. *American Psychologist, 44,* 293-302.
This is a very recent and comprehensive summary of the effects on children and on the father-child relationship of fathers' unemployment.

Mortimer, J. T., Lorence, J., & Kumka, D. S. (1988). *Work, family, and personality: Transition to adulthood.* Norwood, New Jersey: Ablex.
Arguably, Mortimer's research has contributed most to our understanding of the intergenerational transmission of occupations. This book sets out be describing the results of the earlier work in this area, and then presents in considerable detail the 10 year longitudinal study.

Voydanoff, P. (1987). *Work and family life.* Beverly Hills, CA: Sage.
This book presents an overview of the interdependence between work and family. All the major issues are covered, and this

book would serve most adequately as an introduction to the literature
on work and family.

Bibliography

Aberle, D. F., & Naegele, K. D. (1952). Middle-class fathers' occupational role and
    attitudes toward children. *American Journal of Orthopsychiatry, 22,* 366-378.
Aldous, J., Osmond, M. W., & Hicks, M. W. (1979). Men's work and men's families.
    In W. R. Burr et al. (Eds.), *Contemporary Theories About the Family, Vol.
    1: Research-Based Theories* (pp. 227-256). New York: Macmillan.
Ammerman, R. T., Cassisi, J. E., Hersen, M., & van Hasselt, V. B. (1986).
    Consequences of physical abuse and neglect in children. *Clinical
    Psychology Review, 6,* 291-310.
Archer, J., & Rhodes, V. (1987). Bereavement and reactions to job loss: A
    comparative review. *British Journal of Social Psychology, 26,* 211-224.
Barling, J. (1986). Fathers' work experiences, the father-child relationship and
    children's behaviour. *Journal of Occupational Behaviour, 7,* 61-66.
Barling, J. (1990a). *Employment, stress, and family functioning.* Chichester: Wiley.
Barling, J. (1990b). Employment and marital functioning. In F. D. Fincham, & T.
    Bradbury (Eds.), *The psychology of marriage: Conceptual, empirical, and
    applied perspectives* (pp. 201-225). New York: Praeger.
Barling, J., Fullagar, C., & Marchl-Dingle, J. (1987). Employment commitment as a
    moderator of the maternal employment status/child behavior relationship.
    Journal of Occupational Behavior, 9, 113-122.
Barling, J., & Van Bart, D. (1984). Mothers' subjective work experiences and the
    behaviour of their preschool children. *Journal of Occupational Behaviour,
    54,* 49-56.
Baruch, G. K., & Barnett, R. C. (1986). Consequences of fathers' participation in
    family work: Parents' role strain and well-being. *Journal of Personality and
    Social Psychology, 51,* 983-992.
Beckman, K., Marsella, A. J., & Finney, R. (1979). Depression in the wives of nuclear
    submarine personnel. *American Journal of Psychiatry, 136,* 524-526.
Booth, A. & Edwards, J. N. (1980). Fathers: The invisible parent. *Sex Roles, 6,* 445-
    456.
Breakwell, G. M., Fife-Schaw, C., & Devereux, J. (1988).Parental influence and
    teenagers' motivation to train for technological jobs. *Journal of
    Occupational Psychology, 61,* 79-88.
Brief, A. P., Burke, M. J., George, J. M., Robinson, B. S., & Webster, J. (1988).
    Should negative affectivity remain an unmeasured variable in the study of
    job stress? *Journal of Applied Psychology, 73,* 193-198.
Bronfenbrenner, U., & Crouter, A. C. (1982). Work and family through time and
    space. In S. B. Kamerman and C. D. Hayes (Eds.), *Families that work: in
    a changing world* (pp. 38-83). Washington, DC: National Academy Press.
Chopra, S. L. (1967). A comparative study of achieving and underachieving students
    of high intellectual ability. *Exceptional Children,* 631-634.

Cleary, B. (1977). *Ramona and her father.* New York: William Morrow.

Coburn, D., & Edwards, V. L. (1976). Job control and child rearing values. *Canadian Review of Sociology and Anthropology, 13,* 337-344.

Cochran, M. M., & Bronfenbrenner U. (1979). Child rearing, parenthood, and the world of work. In C. Kerr, & J. M. Rosow (Eds.), *Work in America* (pp. 138-154). New York: Van Nostrand.

Cotterell, J. L. (1986). Work and community influences on the quality of child rearing. *Child Development, 57,* 362-374.

Elder, G. H. (1974). *Children of the Great Depression.* Chicago: University of Chicago Press.

Elder, G. H., Nguyen, T. V., & Caspi, A. (1985). Linking family hardships to children's lives. *Child Development, 56,* 361-375.

Emery, R. E. (1982). Interparental conflict and the children of discord and divorce. *Psychological Bulletin, 92,* 310-330.

Feldman, S. S., Nash, S. C., & Aschenbrenner, B. G. (1983). Antecedents of fathering. *Child Development, 54,* 1628-1636.

Friedemann, M. L. (1986). Family economic stress and unemployment: Children's peer behavior and parents' depression. *Child Study Journal, 16(2),* 125-142.

Greenberger, E., & Goldberg, W. A. (1989). Work, parenting and the socialization of children. *Developmental Psychology, 25,* 22-35.

Grossman, F. K., Pollack, W. S., & Golding, E. (1988). Fathers and children: Predicting the quality and quantity of fathering. *Developmental Psychology, 24,* 82-91.

Hillenbrand, E. D. (1976). Father absence in military families. *The Family Coordinator,* 451-458.

Honzik, M. P. (1967). Environmental correlates of mental growth: Prediction from the family setting at 21 months. *Child Development, 38,* 337-364.

Jackman, M. (1984). *The Macmillan Book of Business and Economic Quotations.* New York: Collier Macmillan.

Jahoda, M. (1982). *Employment and unemployment: A social-psychological analysis.* New York: Cambridge University Press.

Jensen, P. G., & Kirschner, W. K. (1955). A national answer to the question, "Do sons follow their fathers' occupations?" *Journal of Applied Psychology, 39,* 419-421.

Kemper, T. D., & Reichler, M. L. (1976b). Father's work integration and types and frequencies of rewards and punishments administered by fathers and mothers to adolescent sons and daughters. *The Journal of Genetic Psychology, 129,* 207-219.

Kohn, M. L. (1977). *Class and conformity.* Chicago: University of Chicago Press.

Komarovsky, M. (1940). *The unemployed man and his family: The effect of unemployment upon the status of men in 59 families.* New York: Arno Press.

Lamb, M. E. (1981). *The role of the father in child development.* New York: Wiley.

Lamb, M. E. (1982). Parental influences on early socio-emotional development. *Journal of Child Psychology and Psychiatry, 23,* 185-190.

Lerner, J. V., & Galambos, N. L. (1985). Maternal role satisfaction, mother-child interaction and child temperament: A process model. *Developmental Psychology, 21,* 1157-1164.

Lynn, D. B., & Sawrey, W. L. (1959). The effects of father-absence on Norwegian boys and girls. *Journal of Abnormal and Social Psychology, 59,* 258-262.

MacEwen, K. E. & Barling, J. (1989). *Maternal employment experiences affect children's behavior via mood, cognitive difficulties, and parenting behavior.* Manuscript submitted for publication, Department of Psychology, Queen's University, Kingston, Ontario.

Madge, N. (1983). Unemployment and its effects on children. *Journal of Child Psychology and Psychiatry, 24,* 311-319.

Marsella, A. J., Dubanoski, R. A., & Mohs, K. (1974). The effects of father presence and absence upon maternal attitudes. *The Journal of Genetic Psychology, 125,* 257-263.

McHale, S. M., & Huston, T. L. (1984). Men and women as parents: Sex role orientations, employment, and parental roles with infants. *Child Development, 55,* 1349-1361.

McKinley, F. G. (1964). *Social class and family life.* New York: Free Press.

McLoyd, V. C. (1989). Socialization and development in a changing economy: The effects of paternal job and income loss on children. *American Psychologist, 44,* 293-302.

Moen, P., Kain, E. L., & Elder, G. H. (1983). Economic conditions and family life: Contemporary and historical perspectives. In R. R. Nelson & F. Skidmore (Eds.), *American families and the economy: The high costs of living* (pp. 213-259). Washington, DC: National Academy Press.

Mortimer, J. T. (1974). Patterns of intergenerational occupational movements: A smallest-space analysis. *The American Journal of Sociology, 79,* 1278-1299.

Mortimer, J. T. (1976). Social class, work and the family: Some implications of the father's occupation for familial relationships and sons' career decisions. *Journal of Marriage and the Family, 38,* 241-256.

Mortimer, J. T., & Kumka, D. (1982). A further examination of the "Occupational Linkage Hypothesis". *The Sociological Quarterly, 23,* 3-16.

Mortimer, J. T., Lorence, J., & Kumka, D. S. (1986). *Work, family, and personality: Transition to adulthood.* Norwood, NJ: Ablex.

Mott, P. E., Mann, F. C., McLoughlin, Q., & Warwick, D. P. (1965). *Shift work.* Ann Arbor: University of Michigan Press.

Nelson, E. (1939). Fathers' occupations and student vocational choices. *School and Society, 50,* 572-576.

O'Brien, G. E. (1985). Distortion in unemployment research: The early studies of Bakke and their implications for current research on employment and unemployment. *Human Relations, 38,* 877-894.

Patterson, G. R. (1982). *Coercive family processes: A social learning approach.* Eugene, OR: Castalia.

Pautler, K. J., & Lewko, J. H. (1984). Children's worries and exposure to unemployment: A preliminary investigation. *Canada's Mental Health,* 14-38.

Pederson, F. A. (1976). Does research on children reared in father-absent families yield information on father influences? *The Family Coordinator, 25,* 459-464.

Piotrkowski, C. S., & Gornick, L. K. (1987). Effects of work-related separations on children and families. In *The Psychology of Work and Loss* (pp. 267-299). CA: Jossey-Bass.

Piotrkowski, C. S., & Katz, M. H. (1982). Indirect socialization of children: The effects of mothers' jobs on academic behaviors. *Child Development, 53*, 1520-1529.

Piotrkowski, C. S., & Stark, E. (1987). Children and adolescents look at their parents' jobs. In J. H. Lewko (Ed.), *How children and adolescents view the world of work* (pp. 3-19). San Francisco, CA: Jossey-Bass.

Pratt, L. I., & Barling, J. (1988). Differentiating between daily events, acute and chronic stressors: A framework and its implications. In J. R. Hurrell, L. R. Murphy, S. L. Sauter, & C. L. Cooper (Eds.), *Occupational stress: Issues and developments in research* (pp. 41-53). London: Taylor and Francis.

Radin, N., & Greer, E. (1987, April). *Father unemployment and the young child.* Paper presented at the biennial meeting of the Society for Research in Child Development. Baltimore.

Radin, N., & Harold-Goldsmith, R. (1989). The involvement of selected unemployed and employed men with their children. *Child Development, 60*, 454-459.

Ray, S. A., & McLoyd, V. C. (1986). Fathers in hard times: The impact of unemployment and poverty on paternal and marital relations. In M. E. Lamb (Ed.), *The father's role: Applied perspectives* (pp. 339-383). New York: Wiley.

Reinhardt, R. F. (1970). The outstanding jet pilot. *American Journal of Psychiatry, 127(6)*, 32-36.

Repetti, R. L. (1989, April). *Daily job stress and father-child interaction.* Paper presented at the biennial meeting of the Society for Research in Child Development, Kansas City, Missouri.

Shamir, B. (1986). Unemployment and household division of labor. *Journal of Marriage and the Family, 48,* 195-206.

Volger, A., Ernst, G., Nachreiner, F., & Hanecke, K. (1988). Common free time of family members under different shift systems. *Applied Ergonomics, 19,* 213-218.

Voydanoff, P. (1987). *Work and family life.* Beverly Hills, CA: Sage.

Warr, P. (1984a). Reported behaviour changes after job loss. *British Journal of Social Psychology, 23,* 271-275.

Warr, P. (1984b). Work and employment. In P. J. Drenth, H. Thierry, P. J. Willems, & C. J. Wolff (Eds.), *Handbook of work and organizational psychology (Vol. 1,* pp. 413-443). New York: Wiley.

Warr, P., & Payne, R. (1983). Social class and reported changes in behavior after job loss. *Journal of Applied Social Psychology, 13,* 206-222.

Werts, G. E. (1968). Paternal influence on career choice. *Journal of Counseling Psychology, 15,* 48-52.

Without Map or Compass: Finding the Way in Contemporary Dual-Earner Marriages

Alan J. Hawkins
and Ann C. Crouter

Although contemporary men and women have more alternatives to marriage and are less constrained by social norms than were their parents and grandparents, the institution of marriage remains popular (Espenshade, 1985; Hoffman & Manis, 1978). Only a small proportion of adults never marry. Even experiencing an unsatisfactory marriage does not significantly dampen men's and women's feelings about the institution of marriage; most divorced men and women marry again (Espenshade, 1985).

This does not imply, however, that the institution of marriage is the same for contemporary couples as it was for their parents and grandparents. The most potent force modifying the institution of marriage over the past thirty years has been the steady but dramatic increase in the proportion of married mothers employed outside the home. In 1985, the number of married women in the labor force was almost 28 million, over 40 percent of the labor force (U.S. Bureau of the Census, 1986a). In addition, in the mid-1980s, the labor-force participation rate of married mothers with children under the age of one passed the 50 percent mark (Hayghe, 1986). For both economic and personal reasons, most married adults today juggle the roles of spouse, parent, and employee. This juggling act has transformed the gender role norms that shape the institution of marriage.

Married life is particularly challenging when many of the norms that shaped one's parents' marriage have changed so dramatically that they appear to be unworkable in one's own marriage. Many of the parents of contemporary young adults married and raised children in a historically unique period of time when economic and social conditions exempted most married women from contributing economically to the family (Cherlin, 1983). The predominant social norms after World War II dictated that employment and motherhood were incompatible (Stewart & Healy,

1989). Mothers in the 1950s may have communicated positive attitudes about vocational interests to their daughters, but they did not model how to manage the intersection of work outside the home and family demands in their own lives. Similarly, contemporary men are the sons of fathers who were, for the most part, successful sole providers who were comfortable with that division of labor. In short, recent marriage cohorts consist largely of men and women whose parents did not model for them ways to manage successfully the multiple roles of spouse, parent, and employee. Accordingly, men and women today are operating with only a crude social map and imperfect compass as they traverse the challenging terrain of contemporary marriage.

Professionals who work with and study the family have observed these pioneering efforts over the past thirty years. (Indeed, many of these professionals have been participant-observers.) Through their efforts, we now have the beginnings of a social map of contemporary dual-earner marriage that, although lacking detail, can provide needed guidance to married couples who are struggling to manage work and family roles. This chapter will attempt to highlight two of the most important features of that map: the allocation of domestic labor and the challenge of coordinating two jobs while finding the time for marital companionship. Before proceeding, however, we specify some of the themes that underlie our discussion.

Underlying Themes

Dual-Earner Marriage and Dual-Career Marriage

Much of the scholarly and popular literature that addresses the impact of wives' and mothers' employment on marriage focuses on contemporary couples in which both husband and wife are pursuing careers. Careers are different from jobs in that careers are challenging professions with the opportunity for continuous learning and development. Careers often involve a series of related jobs, usually with increasing responsibilities and rewards, as well as norms about success and timing of progression from one step to the next (Gilbert & Rachlin, 1987; Wilensky, 1960). In contrast, most people have jobs with short ladders of occupational advancement that do not involve personal growth. Couples in which both husband and wife are involved in careers are a distinct minority--less than 15 percent of all working couples. In nearly 60 percent of working couples, both husband and wife are non-professionals (Moen & Dempster-McClain, 1987).

Although dual-job and dual-career couples share some common challenges in managing the work-family interface, there are many differences as well. Men and women in dual-career families often are psychologically and temporally invested in their jobs. They frequently are absorbed in their work and may experience stress as a result of their desire to achieve. Dual-career couples also have greater resources to provide high-quality child care for their children and to buy household services that ease the domestic workload (Hertz, 1986). In contrast, dual-job couples may be less psychologically absorbed in their work and may experience less intrinsic satisfaction from their labor. The stress that accompanies their work comes from the routine of daily employment in an unfulfilling job (Rubin, 1976). Furthermore, their work often is less financially rewarding, and this may constrain their efforts to find high-quality child care and purchase labor-saving services for the home. In short, dual-career and dual-job couples often differ in their attitudes about work and family roles and in their resources for managing the challenges that arise. We must be sensitive to those differences and allow for multiple ways of managing the work-family interface. In this chapter, we use the term "dual-earner family" to refer to all families in which both husbands and wives work outside the home, be it in a career or in a job.

Strains and Gains

Men and women work outside the home because of the economic, social, and psychological benefits to them and their families. Inherent in the dual-earner life-style, however, are stresses and strains that cannot be entirely eliminated, only managed. Moreover, the strains and gains (Rapoport & Rapoport, 1971) usually are tightly yoked. Consider, for example, a mother who is involved in a fulfilling career as a management consultant. She gains great personal satisfaction from her work, which allows her family to enjoy an attractive home and a comfortable standard of living. At the same time, she experiences considerable stress, having too much to do and not enough time in which to do it. Her husband assumes a heavier load of household tasks and child care, but this puts a strain on his work as he must negotiate with his boss for a flexible schedule in order to be home when the children get home from school. While he gains a richer relationship with his children because he spends more time caring for them, he also resents the strain it places on his work and leisure time. As this example suggests, any discussion that provides prescriptions for the so-called problems inherent in dual-earner marriages obscures the underlying reality of trade-offs. While there are better and worse paths to achieving a rewarding marital relationship for dual-earner couples, there are few straightforward paths.

Life-Span Variations

Our mapmaking is made more complex by the dimension of time. A dual-earner family rearing children confronts issues related to the work-family balance from the time the wife becomes pregnant at least until the last child has left home. Even this endpoint is arbitrary because parenting is a lifelong role (Hagestad, 1987). Most scholarly research on maternal employment and professional advice to dual-earner couples has been directed to parents of infants and preschoolers (see Brazelton, 1982; Hoffman, 1989). This is understandable, given that the transition to parenthood is a critical time for the marriage relationship and requires important adjustments (Cox, 1985). In addition, the most dramatic increase over the past thirty years in women's labor-force participation has come from mothers of infants and preschoolers (U.S. Bureau of the Census, 1986a). The employment of mothers of very young children presents important challenges to parents and to society.

Families today, however, have fewer children and have them closer together in time than in the past (Teachman, Polonko, & Scanzoni, 1987). This means that mothers and fathers spend fewer years in the labor-intensive period of parenthood, caring for young children, than in the past. At the same time, strong forces in contemporary society make it challenging to rear older children.

Issues of adolescent and preadolescent peer pressure, substance use, and sexual activity, for example, are increasingly difficult for parents to deal with. The adolescent and preadolescent child-rearing years need careful attention, too. Accordingly, our map will attempt to chart how the intersection of two jobs and the marriage relationship evolve over the child-rearing years.

The Allocation of Household Labor

One of the primary tasks of couples is to allocate the work of maintaining the home and caring for the children. When mothers are employed part time rather than full time, issues surrounding the allocation of household labor and child care may not present as significant a challenge to the marriage relationship, because wives have more time in the home for domestic labor than their husbands who are likely employed full time. When mothers are employed full time, however, the allocation of household labor and child care may be a greater source of frustration, disagreement, and conflict, because there is less time for daily household tasks and for interaction with children. How dual-earner couples resolve the problem of decreased time available for domestic labor will substantially shape the quality of the marital relationship.

The obvious strategy for resolving this problem is for dual-earner husbands and wives to share domestic labor equitably. For many couples, however, this will not be an easy solution; husbands often resist sharing and, in some cases, so do their wives (Pleck, 1985). Recent research and opinion polls document that there is a substantial minority of dual-earner wives, perhaps 20 percent - 25 percent, who do not want their husbands to participate significantly in domestic labor (Genevie & Margolies, 1987). Similarly, several scholars have concluded that many wives do not want more participation than they already receive from their husbands (see Hochschild, 1989; Pleck, 1985). Family scholars have speculated that for many dual-earner wives, especially those who have jobs rather than careers, the role of homemaker remains a primary source of identity, self-esteem, and satisfaction (Pleck, 1983). Even when wives work full time, they do not necessarily take on the psychological responsibility for providing; nor do men necessarily relinquish their identities as main providers (Hood, 1986; Perry-Jenkins, 1988). For some women, the homemaker role may be the only role in which they are able to exercise the autonomy and power that is important to psychological well-being (Long, 1986). The increased participation of husbands in domestic work may be seen as an encroachment on wives' hegemony in the home. By taking on almost all of the burden of domestic work themselves, these wives reinforce their identities as the "good mother and wife" (Genevie & Margolies, 1987).

The temptation is strong to dismiss these dual-earner wives' attitudes as unenlightened and a prescription for role overload that eventually will produce serious psychological dysfunctions or strains in the marital relationship. The majority of dual-earner wives, however, are employed in low-prestige, service-sector jobs with little potential for growth and control. While these jobs may help satisfy the need for affiliation, the ability to meet needs for achievement and power is limited. The family remains the primary source of achievement and influence for many women.

At first, the notion that the family offers power and influence to women may appear to be a dubious claim. After all, most treatises on family power argue that men wield significantly greater power in domestic life than women (Kranichfeld, 1987). However, the dominant economic and sociological perspectives of family power may have exaggerated the amount of power husbands actually have in the family. These perspectives have focused on the relative inequity of men and women in the economic and political spheres and how that translates into a position of dominance and control for men in the domestic sphere. But like two-dimensional maps of the world that make the northern countries look disproportionately larger than equatorial countries, the macro-level perspectives of family power may have distorted our perceptions of the kinds of power that women may hold in the family. Kranichfeld (1987) argues that a micro-level analysis of family power suggests that wives, because of their roles as caretakers, nurturers, and kinkeepers, are "more deeply, extensively, and enduringly embedded" in the lives of family members than are husbands (p. 42). Wives exercise greater influence in the family than do their husbands because of their emotional connections to family members which stem from daily caretaking. Sharing domestic work with their husbands may be difficult for some wives because it involves sharing influence over familial relations and control of household affairs (Ferree, 1987; Pleck, 1985).

The majority of dual-earner wives, however, are more than willing to risk a reduction of domestic power in return for their husbands' greater participation in household tasks and child care (Genevie & Margolies, 1987). One sign of this is a willingness on the part of many dual-earner wives to lower their standards with regard to housework (Ferree, 1988; Hochschild, 1989). Husbands may not aspire to as high a standard of domestic work as their wives, but their involvement decreases the total workload for dual-earner wives which, in turn, reduces the strains of balancing work and family life for wives.

Just as important to the marital relationship is the perception of a more equitable distribution of labor that comes from husbands' participation in domestic work. Pleck (1985) reports that wives' sense of overload is not a result of their total workload (employment and family) but results when their husbands do little or no domestic labor. He concludes that a sense of equity may be the critical variable in this situation. Equity theory suggests that individuals compare cost/benefit ratios and make judgments about the fairness of their situations. Individuals in inequitable relationships will be dissatisfied. Strict equality is not essential; rather, a perceived sense of fairness is the critical issue. [Indeed, substituting a rigid egalitarian concept of strict equality of workload may be just as detrimental and unworkable as the rigidity of traditional gender-role stereotypes (Gilbert & Rachlin, 1987).] Marital satisfaction is enhanced when both partners perceive the division of household labor to be a fair one.

Unfortunately, husbands often resist sharing. Studies over the past twenty years have documented, that, in general dual-earner husbands' participation in domestic work has not increased commensurate with their wives' participation in the labor force (Rexroat & Shehan, 1987). Of course, there is substantial variation. Modest increases in participation have been observed in families with more than one young child in the household, no older children, and the wife employed full time (Hoffman, 1989). On average, however, husbands in dual-earner families and single-earner families spend nearly equivalent amounts of time in domestic labor except when children are infants and toddlers (Crouter, Perry-Jenkins, Huston, & McHale, 1987; Pleck, 1983, 1985). Many husbands appear to be doing more and may feel that they are doing more because they are doing a greater proportion of the domestic work. This is because dual-earner wives spend less time in domestic labor than wives who are not employed (Pleck, 1983). Consequently, dual-earner husbands appear to perform a proportionately larger share of domestic labor because the overall quantity of domestic labor has decreased, but they have not really increased the time they devote to domestic tasks.

There are numerous factors that influence dual-earner husbands' lack of involvement in domestic work. First, we need to understand better some of the structural features of dual-earner families. Dual-earner husbands, on average, work significantly longer hours than their wives, many of whom are employed part time and part year. It is estimated that only 27 percent of married mothers hold full time, full year jobs outside the home (Ferree, 1988). Many dual-earner wives structure their employment around the needs of the family. Thus, they often work fewer hours, are home about the time children get home from school, do not work during the summer when children are not supervised in school much of the day, interrupt employment altogether during children's early years, and generally have more discontinuous labor-force participation patterns than men (Bianchi & Spain, 1986; Stipp, 1988). As a result, dual-earner wives tend to be employed in less-prestigious work and contribute proportionately less to the total family income. In fact, the proportion of income wives contribute to the total family income has not changed much during this century. By producing household goods, taking in boarders, and in other ways, wives contributed about 25 percent of family income in 1900. Today, because of continued gender segregation of the labor market, wage inequality, discontinuous labor-force participation, and less temporal involvement in work compared to husbands, wives contribute about 30 percent, on average, to the family income (Ferree, 1988).

In part because dual-earner wives generally work fewer hours during the week, fewer weeks during the year, and earn fewer dollars for their work than their husbands, husbands continue to see themselves mainly as providers, with few domestic responsibilities, and many dual-earners wives, though enacting the breadwinner role, still see themselves as secondary providers (Hood, 1986). Thus, many dual-earner wives do not push for greater domestic involvement from their husbands.

Research has shown that wives' attitudes about sharing domestic labor are crucial. If they do not hold strong beliefs about the equitable distribution of labor, they are unlikely to get it. On the other hand, if they believe strongly that their husbands must carry a fair share of domestic work, their husbands are likely to respond (Ferree, 1988; Hardesty & Bokemeier, 1989). If wives contribute significantly to the family income, then they are more likely to insist on an equitable division of domestic labor. Husbands' beliefs, on the other hand, appear to be unrelated to their participation (Hardesty & Bokemeier, 1989). Even dual-earner husbands who hold egalitarian views about the role of women in society usually do not act on those beliefs by doing housework unless their wives insist (Ferree, 1988).

Some scholars suggest, then, that dual-earner wives who see employment as an important part of their identities and see their economic contributions to the family as necessary will increasingly request and receive a more equitable division of domestic responsibilities. If this hypothesis holds, then we should begin to see significant change, especially among younger dual-earner couples. Young women are investing more in higher education than ever before (U.S. Bureau of the Census, 1986a, 1986b), and wives' labor-force participation is becoming more continuous, especially for younger women (Moen, 1985). In addition, young men's attitudes about what constitutes appropriate behavior for fathers have changed to include greater participation in the home, although many remain ambivalent about those changes (LaRossa, 1988). As a result, younger cohorts of dual-earner wives may successfully encourage their husbands to participate more equitably in domestic work.

A structural analysis of men's and women's patterns of labor-force participation cannot completely account for men's lack of involvement in domestic labor. We cannot overlook the socialization of males in our society. Most dual-earner husbands today grew up in families where mothers performed most of the household labor and fathers were the recipient of this service. In addition, boys probably were not required or expected to perform many "feminine" tasks, nor were they likely to gain much experience caring for small children. Moreover, societal values reinforced the privileged status of males that boys experienced in the home. Given this early socialization process, it is not difficult to see how the idea of egalitarian relationships in the home, now desired by most dual-earner wives and ambivalently assented to by their husbands, would be hard to adjust to for many dual-earner husbands. Of course, socialization is never a simple, uniform process. Some men, for example, may become actively involved fathers as a reaction to their own fathers' *lack* of involvement with them (Barnett & Baruch, 1987; Hochschild, 1989). But it is probably safe to say that recent cohorts of men reached adulthood without clear ideas of how to achieve an egalitarian marital relationship, even if they accepted that ideal.

Given the circuitous route by which some men find themselves involved in housework and child care, it probably is not surprising that an egalitarian division of labor may involve some costs to the marital relationship. As mentioned previously, husbands usually are not eager participants; they may need to be pushed into forfeiting their perceived exemption from daily domestic chores. Some husbands may compare their lot to that of single-earner husbands, whose domestic labors are less frequent and more voluntary, and thus feel deprived (Stanley, Hunt, & Hunt, 1986). Men may feel unskilled at homemaking and child care tasks and resist participation for that reason (McHale & Huston, 1984). Moreover, if a wife is critical of her husband's efforts because they do not meet her standards, he may resist even more. In addition, as a husband becomes more enmeshed in daily domestic chores, he experiences more of the problems and stresses associated with this work, as well as its pleasures (Baruch & Barnett, 1986; Lamb, Pleck, & Levine, 1985).

Accordingly, dual-earner wives' pushes will be met with resistance by some husbands (Goode, 1982). This may be a fertile source of negative interactions among dual-earner couples (Crouter, Perry-Jenkins, McHale, & Huston, 1987; Russell & Radin, 1983). Indeed, many dual-earner wives' unwillingness to insist on an equitable division of domestic labor may be a conscious strategy to avoid conflict and minimize their husbands' negative reactions to their employment outside the home, a strategy poignantly chronicled by Hochschild (1989) in her book, *The Second Shift*. The overload that can result may be seen as less costly and more manageable than marital conflict or dissolution.

In the long run, however, wives' reticence to ask for "help" may be detrimental. Studies suggest that wives whose husbands participate more in daily domestic work are less likely to have thought seriously about divorce (Huber & Spitze, 1983). In addition, employed wives' psychological health improves when husbands participate more in child care (Hoffman, 1989; Kessler & McRae, 1982; Pleck, 1985). Ross, Mirowsky, and Huber's (1983) study of 680 couples showed that husbands' "help" with household tasks was associated with decreased depression among dual-earner wives as long as wives' employment status was consistent with both spouses' preferences. (When husbands preferred that wives not be employed, depression for both husbands and wives increased.) Also encouraging in these studies is the finding that wives' increased psychological health did not come at the cost of decreased well-being for their husbands, as long as husbands preferred their wives' employment. Indeed, participative husbands may gain important benefits from their greater involvement. Although at first husbands who participate in domestic work may feel uncomfortable and unskilled, eventually they may develop their skills and learn valuable lessons about the difficulties of maintaining a household from day to day, gaining a deeper appreciation for the domestic role (Beer, 1983; LaRossa, 1988). Early investments of time with young children are likely to yield high dividends in closer father-child relationships as children grow older. In short, when dealing with husbands' initial resistance to equitable household participation, persistence rather than retrenchment on the part of dual-earner wives may eventually yield important benefits for both that outweigh the short-term costs (Hawkins & Belsky, 1989).

Dealing with the conflict. The challenge for dual-earner couples, of course, is to learn how to deal with the short-term increase in marital conflict that is produced by pushes for equitable involvement. Here, communication skills are crucial. Effective communication about the division of domestic labor should be an integral part of the relationship from the beginning. However, before-marriage discussions about household labor may be naive, and effective premarital counseling on these issues may be needed. The transition to parenthood will require another period of intensive communication, as domestic work increases dramatically, child care is added to the workload, and attitudes about proper gender roles become more salient than ever before. Gilbert and Rachlin (1987) argue that the introduction of children alters the complexity and viability of the dual-earner life-style: ". . . the presence of children often brings to the surface spouses' unconscious or heretofore untested beliefs and values about mothering and makes apparent the norms of our patriarchal society as well as the structure of occupational work" (p. 20). Parent-preparation classes should focus on these complex issues as much as they do on the biological aspects of pregnancy, birth, and infancy. Throughout the child-rearing years, and especially at significant family transitions, couples need to establish a shared view of what needs to be done and who should be responsible for doing it. Needless to say, communication is the key factor in establishing that common view (Gramling & Forsyth, 1987).

While prescriptions for how to divide domestic labor must allow for wide variation, some general suggestions regarding the process of allocating work can be made. At least at first, clear delineation of who is responsible for what will help reduce potential conflicts. Indeed, the primary benefit of clearly defined responsibilities is that it minimizes the amount of potential disagreement over how things get done. Although a more flexible arrangement seems appealing, most couples will probably do well to postpone such an arrangement until they have arrived at a shared view of equitable participation. At all times, a framework of fairness rather than strict equality should guide couples' decision making regarding the division of domestic labor (Gilbert & Rachlin, 1987).

Some on-the-job training by wives may be necessary to help husbands feel comfortable performing their tasks. Initial reluctance to take on domestic chores may be the result of not knowing how to do them rather than unwillingness to do them (McHale & Huston, 1984). Also, once responsibilities have been decided, dual-earner wives must be willing to relinquish personal control of these tasks. This means that husbands should be free to decide when and how tasks are accomplished without criticism from wives.

Standards for neatness and cleanliness may need adjustment (Ferree, 1987). Attitudes about the way things should be done in the home can be very deeply ingrained, but they are almost always somewhat arbitrary. Accommodating individual preferences as much as possible regarding who does which tasks will help things to run more smoothly, diminish potential conflict, and enhance positive feelings about family life. Courtesy and frequent expressions of appreciation also will be helpful. At first, such expressions may seem annoyingly unidirectional, initiated by wives to thank husbands. But behavior often precedes attitudes. After experiencing the responsibility for domestic work, men may arrive at a new appreciation of their wives' unsung efforts. In the long run, it is hoped that what began as almost contractual agreements about who does what will evolve into mutual commitments to a structure of marriage that allows both wives and husbands to benefit from personal investment in both work and family.

Finding Time for Marital Companionship

Solving the problem of the division of domestic labor may be important to a healthy marriage relationship, but it only removes one potential barrier to satisfactory family life. The intricate, ongoing process of negotiating who does what is hardly the stuff of romance novels. Contemporary men and women desire intimacy and fulfilling companionship from marriage. Where once economic and institutional factors were the glue of marriage, they are now subordinate to the psychological needs that marriage is expected to meet (Burgess, Locke, & Thomes, 1963). Healthy doses of time together are required to meet the psychological needs of intimacy and companionship. How does the fact that both husband and wife are employed affect both the quality and quantity of companionate activity?

Quality of Time Together

Family scholars have hypothesized two contrasting processes in relation to work and the quality of family time. The first process assumes a zero-sum game of available energy such that investment in one role subtracts from investment in all others. Thus, significant involvement in work outside the home is thought to lead to role strain that negatively impacts one's performance in the role of spouse. While this kind of role strain exists, the second process recognizes that multiple roles for adults may increase psychological well-being, rather than jeopardize it (Marks, 1977; Thoits, 1987). Multiple roles present multiple opportunities for self-expression, social interaction, and achievement. Multiple roles also reduce vulnerability to disruption of any single role. Moreover, satisfying involvement in one role can energize an individual's performance in other roles. When people enjoy their employment, it may spill over into their family lives and increase their abilities to function well in their domestic roles (Crouter, 1984). For example, Crouter and her colleagues (Crouter, Perry-Jenkins, Huston, & Crawford, 1989) found that husbands who returned home from work feeling good participated more in housework and engaged in fewer negative interactions (quarrels, petty arguments, etc.) with their wives. Dual-earner men and women who enjoy their work may find the time they have together to be sufficient and satisfying because they bring a positive mood to the time they spend together.

Unfortunately, for many people, their jobs do not come with such fringe benefits. Negative emotional spillover from work to home also is common. Bolger, DeLongis, Kessler, and Wethington (1989), for example, found that spousal arguments were more likely to occur on a day when husbands or wives had had an argument with the boss at work. Those with unsatisfying jobs probably are at greater risk for this negative spillover, which undoubtedly decreases the quality of time together as a couple.

Quantity of Time Together

We also should be cautious about simplistic generalizations concerning the quantity of time dual-earner couples have to spend together. Although dual-earner couples live in comparatively time-poor environments, it is tempting to exaggerate the comparative lack of time they have for each other. If a couple's work schedule overlaps, then potential companionate time is reduced only by the amount of time needed to complete daily domestic tasks. In this situation, the actual amount of time together may not differ much from single-earner households. In our own study of 152 dual-earner and single-earner families in central Pennsylvania, we found that dual-earner and single-earner couples did not differ in their satisfaction with time together as a couple. It may be that the evening hours for these families are filled with the tasks of dinner preparation and getting children to bed for both kinds of couples. Although a couple's total work time (combined hours) reduces time together, the effects are quite modest (Kingston & Nock, 1987). Most dual-earner families claim to deal with work-schedule issues in a nondisruptive manner (Kingston & Nock, 1987).

Nevertheless, finding sufficient time for marital companionship may be a problem for many dual-earner couples, especially when schedules do not overlap. Nearly one-third of all dual-earner couples with wives employed full time and children under five years old have one spouse working a non-day or irregular schedule (Presser & Cain, 1983). Among young dual-earner couples (ages 19-26), the figures are even more striking: 45 percent of couples with wives employed full time and children under five years old were "shift-work" couples, and 57 percent of couples with wives employed part time had one spouse working a non-day or irregular work schedule (Presser, 1988). It is uncertain if the higher figures for younger couples are due to family lifestage effects, cohort effects, or an interaction of the two. Nevertheless, there is a large percentage of dual-earner couples with young children whose work schedules do not overlap much, and this undoubtedly limits the amount of time available for marital companionship. Moreover, there is reason to suspect that this percentage will continue to rise in the foreseeable future because the kinds of jobs that will grow the most in the next few years are in service-sector occupations that employ many non-day workers, and a large number of dual-earner wives are in these jobs (Presser, 1987).

, Therefore, the issues surrounding marital companionship for dual-earner couples will differ substantially depending on the pattern of spouses' work schedules. If work schedules overlap considerably, then finding time for companionship will be less challenging than when schedules do not overlap much (Kingston & Nock, 1987; Perry-Jenkins, 1986). Most dual-earner couples, however, will at one time or another probably spend time in each group. Although we are aware of no longitudinal studies that can answer the question how dual-earner spouses' work schedules overlap across time, it seems reasonable to assume, given the dynamic nature of work lives and careers, that many dual-earner couples will experience nonoverlapping schedules at some stage during the family life cycle.

Overlapping work schedules. For dual-earner couples with work schedules that overlap considerably, the challenge of finding enough time together is comparatively reduced. Still, there is less flexibility with which to manage non-work time, and if both spouses work long hours, time together and energy for worthwhile interaction suffer. When spouses arrive home, there may be a list of daily household chores to do, in addition to spending time with children. Given that daily tasks must be accomplished, it is important that both spouses are involved; otherwise, if only one spouse (presumably the wife) is doing the work, there will be little time left over for companionate activities. This highlights the importance of our previous discussion on the division of household labor and suggests the interconnection of problems of time for marital companionship and the division of domestic labor.

Nonoverlapping work schedules. When the hours that dual-earner spouses work do not overlap considerably, the problem of time for marital companionship becomes more acute. Staines and Pleck (1983) reported that spouses who work non-day or irregular work schedules report greater feelings of conflict between work and family life. Although the appropriate data do not yet exist to answer questions about the impact of this problem over time, the problem may be sufficiently challenging that most couples extract themselves from the situation as soon as they can. There is some evidence for this in cross-sectional research. Older dual-earner couples are significantly less likely to have minimally overlapping schedules than are younger couples (Presser, 1988), perhaps implying an avoidance of the situation. Younger couples may be unable to cope as well with diminished companionate time because they have had less time together to establish their relationship. Gramling and Forsyth (1987) hypothesize that when time together is significantly restricted due to work schedules, husbands and wives are hampered in their ability to construct a common view of their world, which enhances family relationships. Thus, they come to see their world in different ways that imbue the time they spend together with more potential for conflict. If this is true, then nonoverlapping work schedules may be most challenging precisely in those early years of marriage when they are most likely to exist.

The interaction of quality and quantity time together. While families generally are resilient and adaptive, a minimum quantity of time may be necessary to enjoy enough quality time together, and this threshold may not be met by many shift-work couples, especially younger couples with children. Also, nonoverlapping work schedules may restrict the benefits to be gained by involvement in other social networks and leisure, especially for spouses with non-day work schedules (Kingston & Nock, 1987). Even if one works during the day, with only one parent in the home at a time, it may be difficult to participate in revitalizing leisure activities outside the home. Thus, there are greater risks of becoming socially isolated, which can negatively affect psychological well-being.

Creating Time Together

Dual-earner couples, especially those with nonoverlapping schedules, must actively manage time to find enough of it for companionate activities. A casual, "laid-back" approach to managing companionate time is unlikely to overcome the obstacles of two work schedules, child care, and household tasks. Dual-earner couples should understand that continual effort to manage time may be as important to the quality of their relationship as their communication skills. Windows of time, when they exist, should be scheduled and jealously guarded.

Moreover, dual-earner couples need to create special times for companionate activity. Some of the added financial resources that result from two incomes should be reserved for these occasions. The anticipation of these special occasions can go a long way towards dissipating frustration at the lack of daily time spent together. It may be better to plan more frequent but less lengthy vacations, rather than a single two-week annual vacation.

In addition, dual-earner couples may need to become creative at turning daily chores and routines into brief opportunities for discussion. Rather than one parent washing dishes while the other bathes the children, these activities could be done together in about the same amount of time. Romance and intimacy may be absent from these shared daily tasks, but they provide an opportunity to "connect" and talk about the events of the day.

Conclusion

Contemporary adults in dual-earner marriages are social pioneers. Because their parents' experience of marriage is significantly different from their own, due in part to changing patterns of women's employment outside the home, dual-earner men and women today must discover new paths for successful marriages. Their efforts have produced a social map that, although lacking detail, will help those men and women who follow it to negotiate better the challenging terrain of dual-earner marriage.

We do not expect that the issues we have highlighted--the division of labor and marital companionship in dual-earner families--will be equally salient in all family contexts. Indeed, we should expect that couples will interpret and handle these issues somewhat differently depending, for example, on their social class and ethnic background. Indeed, Ferree (1988) argues that working class dual-earner couples may be inadvertent trailblazers in establishing more equitable patterns of household work. Ferree selects working-class couples for that role because employed wives in blue-collar families are likely to earn the proportion of income that would lead them to be seen and to see themselves as breadwinners. Similarly, scholars have noted differences in the extent to which working- and middle-class couples ascribe importance to marital companionship and shared leisure (Komarovsky, 1962; Rubin, 1976). Although this pattern seems to be changing somewhat, researchers have found higher levels of husband-wife leisure in middle-class than in working-class families.

Further complicating this discussion of dual-earner marriage is the fact that social expectations about roles are changing rapidly. For instance, in less than one generation cultural norms about what constitutes the "good father" have gone beyond provider and role model to involved caregiver and nurturer (LaRossa, 1988). Men have responded ambivalently to these changes. Thus, the social role of father is likely to undergo still further change. This implies that any map of contemporary dual-earner marriage may quickly become obsolete; it must evolve as contemporary men and women pass through the family life course and younger cohorts of men and women marry.

While the institution of marriage is as popular today as ever before, the demographics of divorce suggest that the survival of any given marriage is in greater doubt than in the recent past (Spanier, 1989). Given the value and importance placed on marriage and family life by nearly all adults (N.O.R.C. General Social Survey, 1982) and their desires for intimate and psychologically gratifying relationships (Bellah, Madsen, Sullivan, Swidler, & Tipton, 1985), achieving a successful marriage is likely to remain a high priority for contemporary and future men and women. Yet, as a society we make few efforts to help young people prepare for contemporary marriage. Perhaps we excuse ourselves because of deeply ingrained values that eschew public interference with family life or a hope that adequate preparation is obtained through parental instruction and observation. However, the pace of social change has been so rapid that even conscientious parents may not appreciate the unique challenges their children face in a marriage relationship today. While parental preparation will continue to be important, there is much we could be doing to supplement premarital training. Educational, religious, and community institutions should offer more extensive instruction to young adults concerning the challenges of contemporary marriage and teach them the communication and negotiation skills that will be needed to surmount successfully these challenges. Perhaps most importantly, these institutions can play a role in preparing couples to be flexible, to understand that as their relationship unfolds, societal definitions of and norms about marriage will be undergoing a continual process of change as well.

Sources of Help

Some couples experiencing some of the difficulties discussed in this chapter may benefit from marriage counseling. Therapists can be identified through local mental health associations, family physicians, and through the states' Psychological Association. Couples should be sure to specify an interest in finding someone with experience in working with dual-earner couples.

Another source of help can be the workplace itself. If a work organization has an Employee Assistance Program, it may offer workshops or programs in this area. Other work organizations have utilized outside consultants to conduct "work/family seminars" during the lunch hour. Businesses may be willing to sponsor such a program.

Annotated Bibliography

The following sources may provide dual-earner couples and professionals with further information and insights into the two major themes of this chapter: The division of domestic labor and finding time for marital companionship.

Crosby, Faye J. (1987). *Spouse, parent, worker: On gender and multiple roles.* New Haven, CT: Yale University Press.
    This edited volume contains several insightful essays on the effects of multiple roles on women and men in contemporary society.

Gerson, Kathleen (1985). *Hard choices: How women decide about work, career, and motherhood.* Berkeley, CA: University of California Press.

This study relied on intensive interviews with young women about the employment and family decisions they had made in their lives and the reasons underlying those decisions. It reveals the complexity behind the increase in employment for women and some of the personal, interpersonal, and societal factors that contribute to the roles women assume in young adulthood.

Hertz, Rosanna (1986). *More equal than others: Women and men in dual-earner marriages.* Berkeley, CA: University of California Press.

This book provides an intimate and often provocative perspective on the marital challenges faced by individuals involved in demanding careers.

Hochschild, Arlie (1989). *The second shift: Working parents and the revolution at home.* New York: Viking.

With both simple statistics and complex portraits of 50 Bay Area dual-earner couples, this book poignantly portrays the unequal distribution of domestic labor and its effects on men and women.

Pleck, Joseph H. *Working wives/working husbands.* Beverly Hills, CA: Sage, 1985.

This concise paperback provides one of the most readable and thorough summaries of the issues surrounding the division of domestic labor in dual-earner households.

Presser, Harriet B. (1987). Work shifts of full-time dual-earner couples: Patterns and contrasts by sex of spouse. *Demography, 24,* 95-112.

This article provides a closer look at the numbers that are making shift work a common and important feature of contemporary dual-earner marriage. For more information on work scheduling, see the other articles by Presser in the references to this chapter.

Rubin, Lillian B. (1976). *Worlds of pain: Life in working-class families.* New York: Basic.

This social-science classic provides a view of work-family conflict often missed by professionals as it portrays marital relationships in working-class families.

Bibliography

Barnett, R. C., & Baruch, G. K. (1987). Determinants of fathers' participation in family work. *Journal of Marriage and the Family, 49,* 29-40.

Baruch, G. K., & Barnett, R. C. (1986). Consequences of fathers' participation in family work: Parents' role strain and well-being. *Journal of Personality and Social Psychology, 51(5),* 983-992.

Beer, W. R. (1983). *Househusbands: Men and housework in American families.* New York: Praeger.

Bellah, R. N., Madsen, R., Sullivan, W. M., Swidler, A., & Tipton, S. (1985). *Habits of the heart: Individualism and commitment in American life.* Berkeley, CA: University of California Press.

Bianchi, S. M., & Spain, D. (1986). *American women in transition.* New York: Russell Sage Foundation.

Bolger, N., DeLongis, A., Kessler, R. C., & Wethington, E. (1989). The contagion of stress across multiple roles. *Journal of Marriage and the Family, 51(1),* 175-183.

Brazelton, T. B. (1982). Issues for working parents. *American Journal of Orthopsychiatry, 56(1),* 14-25.

Burgess, E. W., Locke, H. J., & Thomes, M. M. (1963). *The family: From institution to companionship* (3rd ed.). New York: American.

Cherlin, A. (1983). Changing family and household: Contemporary lessons from historical research. *Annual Review of Sociology, 9,* 51-66.

Cox, M. J. (1985). Progress and continued challenges in understanding the transition to parenthood. *Journal of Family Issues, 6(4),* 395-408.

Crouter, A. C. (1984). Participative work as an influence on human development. *Journal of Applied Developmental Psychology, 5,* 71-90.

Crouter, A. C., Perry-Jenkins, M., Huston, T. L., & Crawford, D. (1989). The influence of work-induced psychological states on behavior at home. *Basic and Applied Social Psychology, 10(3),* 273-292.

Crouter, A. C., Perry-Jenkins, M., Huston, T. L., & McHale, S. M. (1987). Processes underlying father involvement in dual- and single-earner families. *Developmental Psychology, 23(3),* 431-440.

Espenshade, T. (1985). Marriage trends in America: Estimates, implications, and underlying causes. *Population Development and Review, 11(2),* 193-245.

Ferree, M. M. (1987). Family and job for working-class women: Gender and class systems seen from below. In N. Gerstel & H. E. Gross (Eds.), *Families and work* (pp. 289-301). Philadelphia: Temple University Press.

Ferree, M. M. (1988, November). *Negotiating household roles and responsibilities: Resistance, conflict, and change.* Paper presented at the National Council on Family Relations Annual Meeting, Philadelphia.

Genevie, L., & Margolies, E. (1987). *The motherhood report*. New York: Macmillan.

Gilbert, L. A., & Rachlin, V. (1987). Mental health and psychological functioning of dual-career families. *The Counseling Psychologist, 15(1)*, 7-49.

Goode, W. J. (1982). Why men resist. In B. Thorne & M. Yalom (Eds.), *Rethinking the family* (pp. 210-218). New York: Longman.

Gramling, R., & Forsyth, C. (1987). Work scheduling and family interaction: A theoretical perspective. *Journal of Family Issues, 8(2)*, 163-175.

Hagestad, G. O. (1987). Parent-child relations in later life: Trends and gaps in past research. In J. B. Lancaster, J. Altmann, A. S. Rossi, & L. R. Sherrod (Eds.), *Parenting across the life span: Biosocial dimensions*. New York: Aldine.

Hardesty, C. & Bokemeier, J. (1989). Finding time and making do: Distribution of household labor in nonmetropolitan marriages. *Journal of Marriage and the Family, 51(1)*, 253-267.

Hawkins, A. J., & Belsky, J. (1989). The role of father involvement in personality change in men across the transition to parenthood. *Family Relations, 38*, 378-384.

Hayghe, H. (1986, February). Rise in mothers' labor force activity includes those with infants. *Monthly Labor Review*, 43-45.

Hertz, R. (1986). *More equal than others: Women and men in dual-career marriages*. Berkeley: University of California Press.

Hochschild, A. (1989). *The second shift: Working parents and the revolution at home*. New York: Viking.

Hoffman, L. W. (1989). Effects of maternal employment in the two-parent family. *American Psychologist, 44(2)*, 283-292.

Hoffman, L. W., & Manis, J. D. (1978). Influences of children on marital interaction and parental satisfactions and dissatisfactions. In R. M. Lerner & G. B. Spanier (Eds.), *Child influences on marital and family interaction: A life-span perspective* (pp. 165-213). New York: Academic.

Hood, J. C. (1986). The provider role: Its meaning and measurement. *Journal of Marriage and the Family, 48(2)*, 349-359.

Huber, J., & Spitze, G. (1983). *Sex stratification: Children, housework, and jobs*. New York: Academic Press.

Kessler, R. C., & McRae, J. A. (1982). The effect of wives' employment on the mental health of married men and women. *American Sociological Review, 47*, 216-227.

Kingston, P. W., & Nock, S. L. (1987). Time together among dual-earner couples. *American Sociological Review, 52*, 391-400.

Komarovsky, M. (1962). *Blue-collar marriages*. New York: Random House.

Kranichfeld, M. L. (1987). Rethinking family power. *Journal of Family Issues, 8(1)*, 42-56.

Lamb, M. E., Pleck, J. H., & Levine, J. A. (1985). The role of the father in child development: The effects of increased paternal involvement. In B. B. Lahey & A. E. Kazdin (Eds.), *Advances in child clinical psychology* (Vol. 8, pp. 229-266). New York: Plenum.

LaRossa, R. (1988). Fatherhood and social change. *Family Relations, 37(4)*, 451-457.

234   *Alan J. Hawkins and Ann C. Crouter*

Long, V. O. (1986). Relationship of masculinity to self-esteem and self-acceptance in female professionals, college students, clients, and victims of domestic violence. *Journal of Consulting and Clinical Psychology, 54(3),* 323-327.

Marks, S. R. (1977). Multiple roles and role strain: Some notes on human energy, time, and commitment. *American Sociological Review, 42(6),* 921-936.

McHale, S. M., & Huston, T. L. (1984). Men and women as parents: Sex role orientations, employment, and parental roles with infants. *Child Development, 55,* 1349-1361.

Moen, P. (1985). Continuities and discontinuities in women's labor force participation. In G. H. Elder (Ed.), *Life course dynamics* (pp. 113-155). Ithaca, NY: Cornell University Press.

Moen, P., & Dempster-McClain, D. I. (1987). Employed parents: Role strain, work time, and preferences for working less. *Journal of Marriage and the Family, 49,* 579-590.

N.O.R.C. General Social Survey. (1982). Chicago: National Opinion Research Center, The University of Chicago.

Perry-Jenkins, M. A. (1988). *The provider role: Implications of men's provider role attitudes for household work and marital satisfaction.* Unpublished Doctoral Dissertation, The Pennsylvania State University.

Perry-Jenkins, M. A. (1986). *The impact of the family work-week on marital companionship.* Unpublished Master's Thesis, The Pennsylvania State University.

Pleck, J. H. (1983). Husbands' paid work and family roles: Current research issues. In H. Z. Lopata & J. H. Pleck (Eds.), *Research in the interweave of social roles: Families and jobs.* (Vol. 3, pp. 251-333). Greenwich, CT: JAI.

Pleck, J. H. (1985). *Working wives/working husbands.* Beverly Hills, CA: Sage.

Presser, H.B. (1988). Shift work and child care among young American parents. *Journal of Marriage and the Family, 50,* 133-148.

Presser, H. B. (1987). Work shifts of full-time dual-earner couples: Patterns and contrasts by sex of spouse. *Demography, 24,* 99-112.

Presser, H. B., & Cain, V. (1983). Shift work among dual-earner couples with children. *Science, 19,* 876-879.

Rapoport, R., & Rapoport, R. N. (1971). *Dual-career families.* Harmondsworth, England: Penguin Books.

Rexroat, C., & Shehan, C. (1987). The family life cycle and spouses' time in housework. *Journal of Marriage and the Family, 49,* 737-750.

Ross, C. E., Mirowsky, J., & Huber, J. (1983). Dividing work, sharing work, and in-between: Marriage patterns and depression. *American Sociological Review, 48,* 809-823.

Rubin, L. B. (1976). *Worlds of pain: Life in working-class families.* New York: Basic.

Russell, G., & Radin, N. (1983). Increased paternal participation: The father's perspective. In M. E. Lamb & A. Sagi (Eds.), *Fatherhood and social policy* (pp. 139-165). Hillsdale, NJ: Erlbaum.

Spanier, G. B. (1989). Bequeathing family continuity. *Journal of Marriage and the Family, 51(1),* 3-13.

Staines, G. L., & Pleck, J. H. (1983). *The impact of work schedules on families.* Ann Arbor: Institute for Social Research.

Stanley, S. C., Hunt, J. G., & Hunt, L. L. (1986). The relative deprivation of husbands in dual-earner households. *Journal of Family Issues, 7,* 3-20.

Stewart, A. J., & Healy, J. M., Jr. (1989). Linking individual development and social changes. *American Psychologist, 44(1),* 30-42.

Stipp, H. H. (1988). What is a working woman? *American Demographics, 10(7),* 24-27, 59.

Teachman, J., Polonko, K., & Scanzoni, J. (1987). The demography of the family. In M. B. Sussman & S. K. Steinmetz (Eds.), *Handbook of marriage and the family.* New York: Plenum.

Thoits, P. A. (1987). Negotiating roles. In F. J. Crosby (Ed.), *Spouse, parent, worker: On gender and multiple roles* (pp. 11-22). New Haven, CT: Yale University Press.

U.S. Bureau of the Census. (1986a). *Current Population Reports,* Series P-23, No. 146, Women in the American economy, by C. M. Taeuber & V. Valdisera, U.S. Government Printing Office, Washington, DC.

U.S. Bureau of the Census. (1986b). *Current Population Reports,* Series P-20, No. 408, School enrollment—Social and economic characteristics of students: October 1982, by P. M. Siegel & R. R. Bruno, U.S. Government Printing Office, Washington DC.

Wilensky, H. L. (1960). Work, careers, and social integration. *International Social Science Journal, 12(4),* 543-560.

From Maternal Employment to Child Outcomes: Preexisting Group Differences and Moderating Variables[1]

Martha J. Zaslow,[2]
Beth A. Rabinovich,
and Joan T. D. Suwalsky

Introduction

As the rate of employment among mothers in the United States has increased, so has the sense of urgency about clarifying the implications of maternal employment for children. Now, with more than half of the mothers of young children in this country employed, and the pattern extending even to mothers of infants in the first year of life (Hofferth & Phillips, 1987; Statistical Abstract, 1988; U.S. Department of Labor, 1986), it has become a high priority to understand how a mother's employment status is related to her children's development.

Yet the findings of decades of research into the implications of maternal employment for children have not "cooperated" in yielding a clear and simple pattern of group differences. Indeed the findings range widely from those indicating that maternal employment benefits children, to those indicating no effects whatsoever, and to those showing problems for children when their mothers are in the labor force. It is impossible, given existing findings, to say that children consistently and unambiguously benefit from, or are harmed by, maternal employment.

---

[1]This chapter was initiated at the encouragement of Leon J. Yarrow, and we dedicate it to his memory.

[2]Martha Zaslow is a Senior Research Associate/Consultant with the Committee on Child Development Research and Public Policy of the National Research Council. This chapter reflects her own views and those of her coauthors, which are not necessarily those of the Committee or the National Research Council.

There appears to be a good reason, however, that the research on maternal employment escapes simple summary: The implications of maternal employment for children vary according to such factors as the child's sex, the family's socioeconomic status, and the mother's role satisfaction. That is, in order to understand the way in which maternal employment and child development are related, it is necessary to take into account a set of intermediate steps (Bronfenbrenner & Crouter, 1982; Etaugh, 1974; Hoffman, 1974b, c, 1979; Maccoby, 1958; Zambrana, 1979). Lois Hoffman stated the problem eloquently: "The distance between an antecedent condition like maternal employment and a child characteristic is too great to be covered in a single leap" (1974b, p. 128).

These intermediate steps involve "moderating variables" and "mediating variables." According to Richardson and colleagues (1989, p. 558), "moderating variables may affect the direction and/or strength of the relationship between the independent and dependent variables." Such variables, then, help to explain *under what circumstances* maternal employment is related to child outcomes. "Mediating variables," by contrast, address the question of *why* maternal employment comes to be associated with child outcomes. Again turning to Richardson and colleagues (1989, p. 558), "mediating variables describe the mechanism through which the independent variable influences the dependent variable." Thus, for example, socioeconomic status acts as a moderating variable in that maternal employment appears to have differing implications for children from middle class, working, or lower income families. To determine why this might be the case, we must turn to such possible mediating variables as strength of belief in traditional sex roles at different socioeconomic levels and differing patterns of family interaction at these socioeconomic levels.

The research on maternal employment, over a period of decades, has made substantial progress in identifying and documenting how a "list" of moderating variables influences the direction and strength of the relationship between maternal employment and child outcomes. Work at the level of mediating variables, focusing on processes underlying these linkages, is at a much more preliminary stage. Accordingly, this chapter reflects an attempt to "sort" the maternal employment findings according to the set of moderating variables that we and others have identified in the literature. Whenever the evidence permits, we will also point to discussions of underlying processes, or mediating variables, within the context of particular moderating variables.

On the one hand, such a sorting effort does, we believe, yield a clearer if more complex picture of the findings. On the other hand the large literature on maternal employment, when sorted according to moderating variables, inevitably appears much more limited and spotty. We cannot present a definitive statement for the role of each of the moderating variables. Rather, we can extract from the research either articulated hypotheses for the functioning of each moderating variable or tease out of the literature new hypotheses. We can also provide our evaluation of the strength of the evidence regarding each of the moderating variables, both with respect to sheer amount of data, and as to quality of data.

Our presentation will organize the moderating variables into three groupings: those pertaining to *characteristics of the child* (sex, age, temperament), *characteristics of the family* (socioeconomic status and culture, maternal role satisfaction, and father involvement), and variables that go *beyond the family* (mother's employment circumstances and quality of child care). Given limitations of space, we will identify the major hypothesis or hypotheses for each of the moderating variables, give examples of relevant studies, and provide our assessment of the strength of the evidence.

Instead of launching immediately into a discussion of the moderating variables, however, we will begin by questioning the conceptualization of maternal employment as a condition that in itself has *effects* on children (see especially Hock, DeMeis, & McBride, 1988). As findings have accumulated, it has become increasingly clear that families in which mothers are employed differ in a number of important ways from families in which the mother is a homemaker even prior to the resumption of employment. These preexisting group differences should caution us away from such terminology as "the *effects* of maternal employment" and towards a viewpoint that maternal employment carries with it *implications* for development or has correlates. These implications do not necessarily arise only from the fact of having a mother in the labor force. This caution pertains throughout our discussion of moderating variables: we are clarifying patterns in the data rather than confirming causal linkages. Indeed the conclusion to our chapter will focus on how an understanding of moderating variables can provide a framework within which to extend our understanding of the processes underlying the linkages between maternal employment and child development.

Preexisting Group Differences

There is widespread acknowledgment in the research on maternal employment that families with employed and homemaker mothers frequently differ on a number of socioeconomic and demographic factors. Variables like maternal education (often reported to be higher among employed mothers; see Hoffman, 1984; Zaslow, 1987 for reviews of the evidence) family income (consistently higher when the mother is employed; Kamerman & Hayes, 1982), and number of children in the family (fewer in families with employed mothers; Kamerman & Hayes, 1982), tend to be reported in sample descriptions, and group differences are often (though not always) controlled.

Whereas differences in family income and fertility may arise out of a mother's employment circumstances, educational differences are likely to antedate and contribute to differing employment paths. Indeed national data (U.S. Department of Labor, 1986; Zaslow, 1987) indicate labor force participation rates to be higher among mothers with more years of education. Thus, controlling for differences in mother's education reflects one attempt by researchers to take into account the possibility of factors that distinguish between employed and homemaker mothers originating prior to their differing work patterns.

This acknowledgment of group differences and even of preexisting group differences for socioeconomic and demographic variables *is not matched by widespread awareness of preexisting group differences on psychological variables*. Recent work should caution us that such differences do occur both in mothers who choose differing employment paths *and* in their children.

The work of Hock and her colleagues, for example, underscores the fact that a mother's employment status reflects not only an objective situation but is also a "psychological variable," reflecting her *attitudes* toward the maternal and job roles:

> Researchers must realize that any child "outcomes" that are found may be due to differences in parental   beliefs and attitudes.... Our belief is that the mothers who [choose] certain types of care are different to begin with. (Hock, DeMeis, & McBride, 1988, p. 225)

Hock and colleagues have reported, among other findings, important attitudinal differences in new mothers antedating their differential employment patterns. Thus, for example, Hock, Gnezda and McBride (1984) found that women expecting to stay home with their healthy firstborn infants differed from those expecting to resume employment. When questioned in the newborn period and at three months, mothers expecting to stay home expressed stronger home orientations and stronger beliefs in the importance for the baby of exclusive maternal care. In another study, Hock, Christman, and Hock (1980) were able to examine attitudinal differences among mothers of newborns, all of whom *planned* to stay home with their babies, but approximately one-third of whom actually resumed employment despite these plans. Interviews shortly after the birth revealed that the mothers who eventually resumed employment despite their plans to stay home were more career oriented. Three months after the birth these mothers expressed less positive attitudes about the maternal role, stronger aversion to baby fussiness, and described their babies as less strongly and positively attached to them.

Mothers who choose to stay home, then, as a group, may differ in terms of the importance they place on work in the home, the maternal role, and in their tolerance for the more frustrating aspects of parenting. Recent work by Galambos and Lerner suggests that paralleling such differences, there may also be preexisting differences in baby temperament and health; differences that make it more or less likely for a mother to resume employment.

Using data from the New York Longitudinal Study, these researchers (Galambos & Lerner, 1987) found that employed mothers of toddlers described their children as less difficult in temperament both in infancy and toddlerhood than homemaker mothers. In addition, the presence of more severe physical problems in the child made it less likely that the mother was employed at this early point in her child's development. According to Galambos and Lerner (1987) difficult temperament and physical problems in a child "may present too many demands on a mother who, under less stressful conditions, may pursue employment" (pp. 95-96).

It is important to note that each of the factors that we have identified as differentiating between employed and homemaker mothers *before* the actual work status difference occurs may contribute independently to children's development. For example, some studies have reported *maternal education* to be a better predictor of child social or academic development than is maternal employment status (see D'Amico and colleagues, 1983; DeSai et al., 1989). *Temperament* in itself is considered to contribute to both socioemotional and cognitive development (evidence summarized by Campos, Barrett, Lamb, Goldsmith & Stenberg, 1983). As will be documented later in this chapter, *maternal attitudes* and particularly the "goodness of fit" between attitudes and actual employment status (i.e., role satisfaction) are linked to a variety of child outcomes.

Thus, what the literature often calls "outcomes" for children of maternal employment may not derive from the fact of employment at all but rather originate partly also in the complex web of variables with which a mother's employment decision is correlated. Mothers who *choose* employment differ from mothers who choose the homemaker role prior to the moment of divergence in employment, and the factors on which they differ may be important in themselves to the child's development. Similarly, the children of employed and homemaker mothers may be different to begin with. With few studies attempting to document or account for preexisting group differences beyond the sociodemographic, we should use caution in both our terminology and our conceptualization regarding "effects" of maternal employment.

Child Characteristics as Moderating Variables

Keeping in mind this caveat concerning the *origins* of any differences found in children's development according to their mothers' employment status, we now turn to an examination of factors that help explain the differing correlates of maternal employment for differing subgroups of children. In this section we ask whether child characteristics, specifically child sex, child age, and child temperament help clarify the findings on maternal employment.

Child Sex

The possibility that maternal employment may have differing implications for boys and girls has been a recurrent theme in the research since the 1970s (Bronfenbrenner & Crouter, 1982; Etaugh, 1974; Gold & Andres, 1977, 1978a, 1978b, 1978c; Hoffman 1974b, 1979, 1980, 1984; Smith 1981; Stuckey, McGhee & Bell, 1982; Wallston, 1973). Perhaps the strongest articulation of a hypothesis concerning sex differences comes from Bronfenbrenner and Crouter (1982):

> If one wished to select only a single variable to demonstrate the different effects maternal work could have on children, it would probably be sex of the child. By 1980 there had accumulated an appreciable body of evidence indicating that the mother's working outside the home tends to have a salutary effect on girls, but may exert a negative influence on boys. (p. 51)

More specifically, researchers hypothesize that *maternal employment is associated with a broadening of sex role concepts and higher personal and occupational aspirations in daughters* (e.g., Almquist & Angrist, 1971; Bacon & Lerner, 1975; Baruch, 1972, 1974; Dellas, Gaier, & Emihovich, 1979; Gibbons & Kopelman, 1977; Jones & McBride, 1980; Marantz & Mansfield, 1977; Miller, 1975; Stein, 1973; Tangri, 1972). *The negative implications of maternal employment for sons are hypothesized to occur specifically in the areas of parent-child relations and cognitive development for young middle class boys* (Belsky & Rovine, 1988; Bronfenbrenner, Alvarez, & Henderson, 1984; Bronfenbrenner & Crouter, 1982; Chase-Lansdale & Owen, 1987; DeSai et al., 1989; Gold & Andres, 1978b, c; Moore, 1975; Stuckey, McGhee, & Bell, 1982; Zaslow, Pedersen, Suwalsky,

& Rabinovich, 1989) *and in the areas of parent-child relations and adjustment for somewhat older, working class boys* (Douvan & Adelson, 1966; Gold & Andres, 1978b; McCord, McCord, & Thurber, 1963; Propper, 1972).

This pattern of sex differences may be seen as congruent with sex differences reported in other research areas, notably children's response to divorce, to mental illness within the family, and to economic stress (Zaslow & Hayes, 1986). Indeed, there has been discussion of the possibility that across a variety of stressful circumstances, boys are more negatively affected. Further, the possible basis for a pattern of sex differences consistent across stressful circumstances has been debated (Rutter, 1970; Zaslow & Hayes, 1986).

The assertion by Bronfenbrenner and Crouter that the sex difference pattern is consistently supported by the accumulated evidence in the maternal employment research however, must be questioned on a number of grounds. First, much of the evidence, particularly regarding girls and sex roles, is based on studies involving girls only. The conclusion that girls (but not boys) benefit in terms of broader, more flexible views of gender roles is most solidly based on studies including *both* sons and daughters of employed and homemaker mothers.

Second, the quantitative evidence (looking only at studies that include both genders as well as two or more employment groups), when carefully scrutinized, is actually far less consistent overall than has been suggested. Zaslow (1987) in a detailed evaluation of the evidence, found that only about half of the studies that met these criteria showed support for the hypothesis of more negative outcomes in sons of employed mothers in at least one developmental domain (cognitive, adjustment, family relations, or sex role ideology). Very recent comprehensive and longitudinal studies, searching for the possibility of sex differences in analysis after analysis of different child outcome variables, similarly question the presence and strength of the pattern (see especially Gottfried, Gottfried, & Bathurst, 1988).

Acknowledging that there is substantial inconsistency in the data concerning maternal employment and sex differences, the possibility nevertheless remains that support for the hypothesis is found in studies of a particular kind or kinds but not others. In light of this possibility, the review carried out by Zaslow (1987) asked whether studies supporting the sex difference hypothesis differed from those failing to support the hypothesis in some consistent matter. The review concluded that sex difference findings are concentrated among the studies that *more carefully establish comparability* across the homemaker and employed mother groups regarding socioeconomic status, maternal education, and family intactness. Studies reporting the hypothesized sex differences in at least one developmental domain were also *more likely to focus on middle class families, and families undisrupted by parental separation or divorce. Finally, findings supporting the sex difference hypothesis were concentrated among the studies specifying full-time maternal employment.*

Failure to control for variables like socioeconomic status and maternal education in studies of maternal employment would tend to tip the balance in favor of children of employed mothers (because of the higher income and maternal years of education in such families) and thus obscure any negative implications or differential implications for the sexes that might occur were such background factors held constant. Similarly, any negative implications of maternal employment for sons or positive implications for daughters may appear only when the mother's extent of employment exceeds a certain threshold.

The sex difference pattern, then, is most likely to appear in studies in which the role of maternal employment is best disentangled from confounding factors and in which the mother's employment role is more clearly differentiated. Although much remains to be done to clarify the findings regarding sex differences, the evidence to date suggests that outcomes for sons are indeed more negative in association with the mother's employment.

Age of Child

Age of child, as a factor moderating the implications of maternal employment for children, has received far less scrutiny than has child sex. Rather than pointing to a boldly stated hypothesis as we could for child sex as a moderating variable, here we must search for one in the existing literature. We find scattered references in the literature (drawing particularly from the work of Berndt, 1983; Dellas & colleagues, 1979; Gold & Andres, 1977; Hoffman, 1974a, 1974b, 1979; and Montemayor, 1984) to the view that there are *fewer developmental differences between children of employed and homemaker mothers with increasing child age.*

This hypothesis is appealing in that underlying processes can readily be evoked to explain the pattern. For example, time use data indicate that as children get older, parents at all education levels spend decreasing amounts of time with them (Hill & Stafford, 1980). Berndt (1983) points out that as the total amount of time spent with each child diminishes (i.e., with age), so does the difference between employed and homemaker mothers in time spent with children. If an important underlying process in the development of children with employed as opposed to homemaker mothers is time spent in interaction with parents, then as differences between groups on this variable diminish, so would differences in relation to maternal employment.

Dellas and colleagues, and Hoffman, have proposed related concepts. Dellas et al. (1979) note that with age, children respond to a broader social milieu. The relative importance to the child of the mother's employment may thus diminish with age, as others (peers, teachers) begin to have more of an impact. Hoffman (1974a, b, 1979) has observed that a dual role for the mother creates circumstances that may be particularly appropriate for adolescents. Independence granting, which benefits the development of older children, is easier for the employed mother, who relies less on her children for her self-definition. Hoffman also notes that the strain of maintaining dual roles is easier for the mother of older than younger children. By implication, role strain may be involved in the impact of maternal employment on the younger child.

The best evidence to address a developmental hypothesis would be longitudinal: studies that track the development of children with employed and homemaker mothers over a period of years, taking into account when in the child's development the mother resumed employment. The "age hypothesis" proposes wide initial group differences that converge over time. Until very recently (Gottfried & Gottfried, 1988) however, such data have been virtually unavailable. Rather, our picture of the implications of maternal employment for children of differing ages has come from piecing together the evidence from studies carried out cross-sectionally or focusing on single age groups.

Several of the available cross-sectional studies do suggest a pattern of diminishing influence of maternal employment with increasing age. Gold and Andres (1977) examined differences between children of employed and nonemployed mothers in three areas: sex role concepts, cognitive development, and adjustment, juxtaposing findings from separate samples of four-, ten-, and fifteen-year olds with the aim of discerning changes across age. In the youngest age group, sex role concepts, intellectual, and adjustment scores were all significantly associated with the mother's employment status. At ten years, sex-role concepts and academic achievement scores were strongly associated with maternal employment but adjustment measures showed only a slight relationship. Finally, "the oldest group of children show the least influence of employment status, with adjustment scores moderately, and sex role concepts slightly associated with maternal employment" (p. 28).

In an interview study with preadolescent and adolescent samples, Dellas, Gaier and Emihovich (1979) found differences in one of the five areas of investigation (sex role ideology) in the younger sample but no differences in the older sample according to maternal employment. These researchers reach a similar conclusion: that the effects of maternal employment "tend to diminish along the developmental continuum" (p. 587).

Focusing on IQ, achievement, and aptitude tests in a sample of children in the school system of Princeton, New Jersey, Hutner (1972) concluded that:

> As far as age of student was concerned, this study observed that elementary school students performed significantly better in academic achievement tests when their mothers did not work. On the other hand, high school were usually unaffected by maternal employment, and occasionally they performed better when their mothers worked part-time. (p. 35)

Although cross-sectional studies thus give some support to a "developmental hypothesis," it must be noted that Gottfried and Gottfried (1988), in an overview and evaluation of the findings of a set of recent *longitudinal studies* of maternal employment in middle class families, concluded that there were no reliable long term relations of maternal employment and subsequent development across a range of developmental outcomes. Interestingly, however, Gottfried and Gottfried do conclude that maternal employment is related (above and beyond variables like social class and family intactness) to home and family environment variables like educational attitudes, father involvement, and variety of children's experiences (excellent candidates for consideration as mediating variables). These home environment variables, in turn, have been found to be important predictors of development. This raises the possibility that most of the studies in the Gottfried and Gottfried compendium may not have tracked development over a long enough period of years to discern important developmental patterns. Further, this volume is limited to the study of middle class families. This first set of longitudinal studies, then, represents only a beginning, albeit an important one, in the task of resolving the issue of maternal employment and developmental stages.

The issue of maternal employment and child age has also been addressed in recent years by intensive focus on one developmental period: infancy. In keeping with the hypothesis that maternal employment may have the most extensive implications in the earliest years, researchers have raised the possibility that the daily separations associated with maternal employment may have particular implications for the emergence of trust and relatedness between infant and mother in the first year of life.

The issue of infant attachment and maternal employment is discussed in detail elsewhere in the present volume (Thompson's chapter). Briefly, a single but well-replicated finding is the focus of heated debate at present. The finding of interest is that when mothers resume employment more than part-time, and within the infant's first year of life, these infants show higher rates of a pattern of attachment termed "anxious-avoidant" (Barglow, Vaughn & Molitor, 1987; Belsky, 1988; Belsky & Rovine, 1988; Schwartz, 1983). This attachment pattern involves favorable responses to a friendly female stranger in a lab setting rather than clearly preferential orienting to the mother, and initial avoidance of the mother, rather than greeting or seeking the mother out for comfort, after the stress of brief separations from the mother in the lab assessment.

Although there is agreement among researchers as to this pattern of findings, there is debate as to its meaning and implications. On the one hand, some researchers have argued that maternal employment may have disrupted the emergence of mutually responsive mother-infant communication and that the higher rates of insecure-avoidant attachment predict less optimal development in the children (e.g., Belsky, 1988). Others, however, question whether a laboratory assessment based on mother-child separation has the same meaning for children of employed and homemaker mothers. Perhaps children of employed mothers, for whom separations are familiar, are showing greater autonomy and maturity, rather than "anxious-avoidance" (Clarke-Stewart, 1989; Thompson, this volume).

The debate about maternal employment in the infancy period will only be resolved when the data base is broadened. That is, we need to move beyond the assessment of attachment alone and examine development in infancy and toddlerhood across a range of socioemotional indicators. Further, we need to ask directly whether higher rates of "anxious-avoidant" attachment in children of employed mothers indeed have ominous implications for development rather than infer such negative implications. Finally, given that the majority of infants of employed mothers continue to show secure patterns of attachment, we need to ask "who are the infants showing the anxious-avoidant pattern?" Can they be distinguished, for example, on the basis of the quality or stability of the substitute care they are receiving? Are differences rooted in the type of preexisting group factors (e.g., mother's tolerance for the difficult aspects of parenting) we discussed previously?

Overall, the possibility that maternal employment has differing implications at differing ages is an unresolved and poorly examined one. We can expect new developments regarding this hypothesis as more studies come to use longitudinal approaches and as the debate on infant day care broadens.

Temperament

As our discussion of preexisting group differences noted, child temperament had been found in some studies (Lerner & Galambos, 1986; though see also Gottfried, Gottfried, & Bathurst, 1988) to be a factor contributing to whether or not a mother resumes employment after the birth of a child. Other studies have used difficult temperament as a child outcome variable, (see discussion below on maternal role satisfaction).

While child temperament has thus been cast in terms of *preexisting group differences*, and in terms of *child outcomes*, is there reason to believe it also functions as a *moderating variable*? That is do children with certain temperamental characteristics, particularly "difficult temperament," respond differently to a mother's being employed than do children with other temperamental characteristics, notably "easy temperament?"

Children with "difficult temperament," as identified in the work of Thomas and Chess (1977) tend to manifest negative mood, a relative lack of rhythmicity in their bodily functions (e.g., sleeping), to be slow to adapt to new situations and to show high intensity of responding. Evidence suggests that such children may be more difficult to interact with (Crockenberg & Acredolo, 1983), and may receive caregiving that is less responsive (Lerner & Galambos, 1986).

Lerner and Galambos (1986), in their discussion of temperament and maternal employment, propose the hypothesis that maternal employment may exacerbate the demands of caring for a child with difficult temperament. The demands of difficult children

> ...may be complicated when the mother exists within an extrafamilial (employment) system which imposes its own demands, such as scheduled attendance, commitment, good performance, and efficiency. (p. 76)

Thus child temperament can be seen as a moderating variable in that *the subgroup of children of employed mothers who also show difficult temperament may be hypothesized to show poorer adaptation to the special daily routines associated with maternal employment than children of employed mothers with easier temperament.*

There have been no empirical examinations to date, looking at the response to similar maternal employment circumstances of children with differing temperamental characteristics. Lerner and Galambos (1985, 1986), did look, however, at mother's role satisfaction in light of early child difficulty. Their analysis found no simple relation between the two variables: early child (difficult) temperament did not predict employed mothers' role satisfaction. Clearly, work is needed looking *within* groups of employed mothers at the development of children rated early to be of difficult or easy temperament.

The consideration of child temperament as a moderating variable is clearly at the very earliest stages. Given the role child temperament appears to play as a contributor to mothers' employment decisions and given the evidence suggesting differing patterns of interaction with children of difficult temperament, it would appear important that further work consider child temperament as a factor helping to shape the implications for children of maternal employment.

The sequence in which we have examined child characteristics as moderating variables parallels the depth in which each has been examined. For child sex there is a clearly articulated hypothesis and the evidence has been examined in detail and found, with some qualifications, to support the hypothesis. For child age we can identify a hypothesis in the literature. The issue is being given focused attention in research, but we cannot yet state whether the hypothesis is well supported. For temperament, however, we have only a hypothesis and virtually no pertinent data as yet. The literature thus raises the possibilities that maternal employment has the most negative implications for certain subgroups of boys, for children of younger ages, and for children of difficult temperament. Yet, all three hypotheses, and particularly the latter two, require further scrutiny.

Family Characteristics as Moderating Variables

Socioeconomic Status and Culture

Does it appear that a mother's employment role has differing implications according to socioeconomic status? In an excellent discussion of this issue, DeSai, Chase-Lansdale and Michael (1989) propose that we think in terms of the "net of resources" available to the child at different SES levels. Maternal employment, they hypothesize, has implications for three sets of resources: (1) parental attention, (2) income and its reflection in material resources available to the child, and (3) the quality of substitute care relative to that of parental care.

In considering these resources at differing socioeconomic levels (SES), DeSai et al. hypothesize that "there may be a stronger negative net effect of maternal employment on the child in high SES families" (p.547). Regarding income, in lower SES families, the salary associated with maternal employment "may make the difference in escaping poverty" (p. 547). Regarding parental attention and quality of substitute care, whereas children at all SES levels lose time with the mother when she is employed, at lower SES levels the education level of parents and substitute caregivers is relatively close. The "net" of resources for the child, on balance, thus appears more positive in low SES families. By contrast, for children of higher SES levels, these researchers hypothesize that in addition to a loss in parental attention, the income provided by the employed mother does not involve "an equally proportionate increase in the material resources for the child" (p. 547). Further, the substitute care is likely to be provided by a less well-educated caregiver, hypothetically less stimulating than a well-educated mother. The "net" of resources thus appears more negative in higher SES families according to DeSai et al. While one can question the assumptions made by DeSai and colleagues (e.g., that highly educated mothers engage in more stimulating caregiver behaviors than their substitute caregivers), their discussion yields a clear prediction that maternal employment has differing implications at different socioeconomic levels.

The research on maternal employment focuses disproportionately on middle class families. Less work has been carried out concerning working class families, and surprisingly little work has been done concerning low income families. When one looks at the findings at the two ends of the SES continuum, that is, for upper or middle class families vs. low income families, the "net resources" perspective is supported. The findings for working class families, however, as we will see, force us to question whether only time and material resources are at stake.

Turning first to the findings on low income families, perhaps the best evidence comes from work by Cherry and Eaton (1977) that encompasses physical growth measures as well as measures of psychological development. That their study involved a sample of economically stressed families is indicated by the finding that the children (from low income black families), were significantly below national norms in height and weight, and that a greater than expected proportion of the sample had IQs below 90.

Within this sample, when background factors were held constant to detect differences according to the mother's employment status, the differences favored the children of employed mothers. For example, within the subgroup of families in which the father was present, maternal employment was associated with more optimal physical growth and better language development at eight years. Within the subgroup living in the most crowded living conditions, children of employed mothers had better language development. The construct of "net resources" is particularly supported by the finding that physical growth was most advanced in children of families with two employed parents present and most retarded in the dual parent families with mother a homemaker and father employed.

Woods (1972) also reports positive outcomes associated with full-time maternal employment in a sample of fifth graders from a North Philadelphia black ghetto. In this sample, full-time as opposed to less than full-time employment of the mother was associated with better school and social adjustment, higher IQ, and with a perception of the mother as more consistent in discipline. Other studies present a similar picture. Heyns (1982), reviewing the evidence in this area, concluded that "studies of maternal employment among poor and black families have consistently found that a working mother contributes positively to the achievement of her children" (p. 240).

At the other end of the continuum, studies carried out with middle class samples are by no means entirely consistent in reporting less optimal development among children with employed mothers, as the net resources perspective predicts (see, e.g., Gottfried & Gottfried's review of longitudinal research in middle class samples, 1988). Yet at this socioeconomic level there are recurrent reports of negative implications, especially for boys.

In the area of cognitive development, for example, Schachter (1981) found significantly better performance on the Stanford-Binet in a middle class sample of children with homemaker, as opposed to employed, mothers. Gold and Andres (1978b), studying Canadian English-speaking children, found that at ten years, middle class boys with employed mothers scored significantly lower in language achievement and tended to score lower in math achievement than boys with homemaker mothers. At four years, English-speaking Canadian sons of employed mothers (both middle and working class) were found to have lower full scale IQ scores. These findings are in keeping with Moore's report (1975) of better reading scores at seven years in "exclusively mothered" boys.

In the domain of parent-child relations, there are also reports that maternal employment has negative implications for sons in the middle class. For example, middle class sons of employed mothers have been found to receive less parental attention both in the infancy period (Zaslow, Pedersen, Suwalsky, & Rabinovich, 1989), and in the preschool period (Stuckey, McGhee, & Bell, 1982). At ten years Gold and Andres (1978b) report that middle class sons of employed mothers were reported to be the group most likely to be unsupervised during the day.

Although the "net resources" view fits well with these findings at the upper and lower ends of the socioeconomic continuum, it does not account well for findings pertaining to working-class children. Here, too, one might expect that the increment in income derived from maternal employment would be associated with a positive "net" of influences and have positive implications. Yet, a number of studies focusing on working class families have reported difficulties for sons. For example, Gold and Andres (1978b) found that ten year old sons of employed mothers in the working but not middle class were described more negatively by their fathers, were shy and nervous, had poorer school relations, disliked school more and reported lower grades. Other studies reporting adjustment or parent-child difficulties at this socioeconomic level include those of McCord, McCord, and Thurber (1963), Douvan and Adelson (1966), and Propper (1972).

The "net resources" construct, as presented by DeSai and colleagues, pertains to time and material resources. In accounting for the findings in working class samples, researchers have most often sought explanations in the dimensions of culture or belief systems. As discussed by Hock and colleagues (1988), there are important cross-cultural differences regarding beliefs about maternal-child separation for the purposes of employment and about appropriate roles for men and women. Regarding socioeconomic subgroups within the United States in particular, it is hypothesized that traditional beliefs about sex roles for men and women are most strongly adhered to in the working class. In this group, then, the employment of the mother may suggest to the father that he is not succeeding as a breadwinner. Such an implication may resonate in parent-child and especially father-son relations (Propper, 1972).

There is good evidence of a stronger adherence to traditional sex roles among members of working as opposed to middle class families. For example, in a study of southern black adolescents, children of fathers in blue-collar or unskilled occupations were significantly more likely to see employment of the wife as a threat to marriage than children with fathers in white-collar jobs (King et al., 1976). In the Gold and Andres studies, at ten years working class fathers of boys held the most traditional views of any group. In their study of adolescents, Gold and Andres found that working class fathers had significantly lower scores than did middle class fathers on a measure of egalitarianism. Further, working class mothers, relative to middle class mothers, perceived a significantly greater power differential between themselves and their husbands in family decision making.

The possible implications of belief systems regarding appropriate roles for men and women is well illustrated by Canadian research focusing on English-speaking (Anglophone) and French-speaking (Francophone) children with employed and homemaker mothers (Gold & Andres, 1980; Gold, Andres, & Glorieux, 1979). Across a range of child outcome measures the Francophone children manifested fewer group differences according to the mother's employment status. Most notably, there were no group differences on cognitive and academic measures in the Francophone sample paralleling those found in the Anglophone sample.

In keeping with the hypothesis for working class samples in the United States, the data collected from parents in the Gold and Andres research revealed greater similarity in maternal and paternal roles in the Francophone than Anglophone samples. At four years, regardless of the employment status of the mother, French-speaking parents reported more joint supervision of the children, and less sex-differentiated parental behavior. At ten years, Francophone mothers reported greater similarity in parental functioning on household tasks and childcare activities; fathers reported more involvement in family activities, more interaction with children, and more sharing of household tasks with wives.

Within a cultural context of acceptance of relatively small differences between maternal and paternal behavior, the assumption of an employment role by the mother may involve minimal conflict and be readily accepted by the family. Similarly, a high rate of father involvement with children in Francophone dual income families is in accord with behavior already approved of and accepted for men. Thus, maternal employment within this cultural context does not create discrepancies from approved roles. Rather, it further intensifies a behavior pattern that is already accepted. In working class samples in the United States, as in the English-speaking Canadian families, the employment of the mother may create dissonance with belief systems.

To summarize, maternal employment may have differing implications for children at differing socioeconomic levels, both because of the differing net time and material resources maternal employment yields for children at different SES levels, and because socioeconomic groups are also cultural subgroups, with differing beliefs about appropriate roles for men and women. Findings to date point to more positive implications of maternal employment for children when it involves clear improvements in material resources available to the child and when the mother's employment role is more in harmony with cultural beliefs about appropriate roles for men and women.

Maternal Role Satisfaction

There is substantial variation *within* groups of employed mothers, as there is *within* groups of homemaker mothers, on psychological attitudes about employment and mother-child separation. According to Hock and colleagues (Hock, DeMeis, & McBride, 1988) and Lamb (1982), the failure to find clear and interpretable developmental differences between children of employed and homemaker mothers is due, at least in part, to the critical importance of attitudinal variables: If women *within* employment groups differ as much or more on attitudinal factors as women *differing* on employment status and if such attitudes are linked to child outcomes, then we would not expect to find clear-cut differences between children of employed and homemaker mothers on child outcome variables when mothers' attitude about employment is not taken into account.

The literature on maternal employment suggests that a number of attitudinal variables may play a role in child outcomes.

Hoffman (1974b), for example, pointed to the possible importance of role satisfaction, guilt about employment, and role strain. Of these, however, only role satisfaction has been the focus of extensive investigation.

As for the hypothesis concerning child gender as a moderating variable, there is a clear and strongly articulated hypothesis regarding maternal role satisfaction, and a body of studies considering this as a moderating variable dating from the 1960s (Hoffman, 1963; Yarrow, Scott, DeLeeuw, & Heinig, 1962). This hypothesis proposes that when *a mother is satisfied with her employment role, whether she is employed or a homemaker, her children show more optimal development, whereas dissatisfaction with employment role is associated with negative outcomes.*

The evidence regarding role satisfaction as a moderating variable, although not completely consistent (see Gottfried, Gottfried, & Bathurst, 1988; Gibbons & Kopelman, 1977; Lerner, Hess, & Banarjee, 1986; Schubert, Bradley-Johnson, & Nuttal, 1980; Weinraub, Jaeger, & Hoffman, 1988) is nevertheless impressive. It cuts across socioeconomic groups as well as cultural groups and pertains to a range of child outcome measures and all developmental periods. Finally, the most recent work regarding role satisfaction has begun to address key methodological issues as well as issues about processes that may underlie the linkage between maternal role satisfaction and child outcomes.

Considering the findings on maternal role satisfaction according to age of child, DeMeis, Hock, and McBride (1986) and Hock, DeMeis, and McBride (1988) in separate studies found that a mother's beliefs about the effects of nonmaternal care and employment related separation on infants were more strongly related to the mother's employment preference than actual employment status. Farel (1980) examined the implications of maternal work-attitude congruence for the school performance of a kindergarten sample from diverse backgrounds. In this sample, mothers who were not employed but either felt they would like to work or felt that working would be good for their children had children who scored lower on measures of school adjustment and achievement. In an elementary-school age sample, Williamson (1970) found a high positive correlation between mothers' happiness with their employment status and their children's grade point average summed for grades 1 through 6, both in an employed mother sample and a nonemployed mother sample, as well as both groups combined. Gold and Andres (1978b) found that for English-speaking ten-year-old Canadian middle- and working-class children having an employed mother who was content with her role was associated with the most egalitarian sex-role concepts in the children. Woods (1972) found significant correlations between mothers' positive attitudes toward employment in a lower SES black sample in which all of the mothers were employed, and a number of personality and adjustment scores in their ten-year-old children. Attitude was related to sense of personal worth, feeling of belonging, personal adjustment, family relations and total adjustment score from the California Test of Personality.

Beyond early childhood, Pearlman (1981) found that an adolescent daughter's perceptions of her mother's satisfaction with her employed vs. nonemployed life style was significantly correlated with the daughter's career ambitions. Pasquali and Callegari (1978) found a significant relation between mother's role satisfaction and the sex role identification of adolescent daughters in a middle and upper middle class sample from Brazil. Daughters identified more strongly with satisfied mothers, whether they were employed or at home. In samples of American college women, Baruch (1972) found that a mother's attitude toward the dual role pattern and her success with respect to it were significantly related to the daughter's attitude toward a dual role pattern for herself; the same author in a 1974 study found that mothers who were dissatisfied with their role pattern were rarely chosen by daughters preferentially over their fathers as models for a life pattern. Furthermore, Altman and Grossman (1977) found that daughters' perceptions of their mothers' "goodness of mothering" was significantly positively related to the daughters' perception of the mothers' role satisfaction.

Researchers have reported with some frequency that maternal attitude was a stronger or more consistent predictor of child outcome than was mother's employment status. Hock (1980) summarizes her research with infants by stating that the "results of this study support the belief that work status per se is not significantly related to ...infant developmental level, or to the quality of the mother-infant relationship." However, "regardless of work status per se, mothers whose beliefs about exclusive maternal care conflicted with their work status had infants who tended to exhibit more frequent and intense negative reunion behavior" (p. 100) (behavior suggestive of ambivalence in the mother-infant relationship). Farel (1980) found only sparse and inconsistent relations between kindergarten children's school adjustment and achievement and eight measures of mothers' present and previous employment. The same child measures were found to be related to congruence between the mother's actual employment role and her beliefs about maternal employment. Similarly, Williamson (1970) found no differences by maternal employment status in elementary school children's grade point averages, reading achievement, I.Q., absenteeism, or conduct but rather a significant correlation of maternal attitude toward her employment status and grade point average. She concluded in a similar vein to Hock that "if children see their mothers as happy with their employment position they will respond in a positive manner and meet the scholastic challenges set before them" (p. 612). Pearlman (1981) reports that although mothers' employment status *was* related to adolescent daughters' career orientation, daughters' perception of maternal role satisfaction was a stronger predictor. In Pasquali and Callegari's Brazilian sample (1978), the mother's enjoyment of her employment role rather than her employment status was related to the adolescent daughter's sex role identification. Baruch (1972) failed to find a relation between mothers' employment and daughters' attitude to a dual role pattern but did find a relation between mothers' and daughters' attitudes to the dual role pattern. Finally, perceived goodness of mothering was not different for college-age daughters of employed and nonemployed mothers in the study by Altman and Grossman (1977), although it was related to maternal role satisfaction as perceived by the daughters.

The findings in this area often have the problem that a single informant is used to evaluate both maternal attitude and child outcome as, for example, when college daughters have reported on their perceptions of their mothers as well as indicated their own career plans. Findings from a single informant may simply reflect consistent response tendencies across domains. However, several studies (e.g., Hoffman, 1963, and the Gold & Andres work) have related data collected separately from parents and children. Even more important, there are now studies using direct observation of parent and child behavior that indicate a link between maternal attitude and parent or child behavior.

Observing the behavior of 12-month-old infants in response to brief separations from mother and encounters with a stranger in a lab setting, Hock (1980) found that when the mother's employment status was at variance with her belief about the need of the infant for exclusive maternal care (i.e., she was employed but believed that a baby should be cared for only by the mother or at home but did not believe that the baby should be cared for exclusively by the mother), the infant was less likely to maintain proximity to the mother throughout the somewhat stressful lab situation and more likely to show signs of conflict upon reunion with the mother. Stuckey, McGhee, and Bell (1982), focusing on parental rather than child variables, found significant differences in observations of parental interaction with preschoolers according to whether the mother's employment status matched the mother's and father's attitude toward dual roles for women. When the parent's attitudes were not congruent with the mother's employment status, the parents were significantly more likely to exhibit negative affect to their children.

Hoffman (1989) notes that a further methodological problem has also been addressed in recent work. Perhaps a mother expresses greater role satisfaction *because* her children are doing well. Hoffman notes that recent work (Guidubaldi & Nastasi, 1987) shows role satisfaction to predict independent measures of child adjustment in school-age children taken 2 years later.

Finally, recent research on maternal role satisfaction has taken the important step of examining possible mediating variables, i.e., the *processes* by which maternal role satisfaction and child outcomes are linked. Lerner and Galambos (1985; 1988) examined the possibility that some aspect of mother-child interaction was the basis for this linkage. Their examination of the data from the New

York Longitudinal Study found that greater role dissatisfaction, whether a mother was employed or a homemaker, was associated with greater maternal rejection of the child, while greater role satisfaction was associated with more warmth and acceptance. Maternal rejection of the child at age three was predictive, in turn, of difficult child temperament at age four. The association between maternal role satisfaction and a rejecting quality in interactions with the child has also emerged in the work of Stuckey et al. (1982), as noted, and in that of Crockenberg and Litman (1989), who found that employed mothers who were less satisfied with their roles used more negative control in their interactions with their two-year-olds.

In summary, the hypothesis that children's development reflects their mother's role satisfaction whether the mother is employed or a homemaker, receives good support in the literature. Recent work points to the quality of mother-child interaction as a possible mediating variable, underlying the linkage between role satisfaction and child outcomes. Other attitudinal factors, however, such as role strain and guilt, have not been carefully examined.

Father Involvement and Endorsement

The literature raises two possibilities for how paternal behavior and attitude may help explain the association between maternal employment and child outcomes; one concerning *paternal involvement* in child care and household tasks, and one concerning *paternal endorsement* of the wife's employment role. *Father involvement and endorsement are both hypothesized to differ according to the wife's employment status. Further, both father involvement and endorsement are hypothesized to play a role in the development of children with employed as opposed to homemaker mothers.*

In its present state of development, the literature has given greater attention to the possibility of *group differences* in father involvement and endorsement according to mothers' employment status than to the *functioning of these variables with respect to children's development.* That is, the research is at only a preliminary stage in actually documenting the functioning of paternal behavior and attitude as moderating variables. We turn first, then, to the more thoroughly examined issue of group differences.

Group Differences on Father Involvement and Endorsement. Do fathers in dual and single-earner families differ in their extent of involvement in child care and/or household tasks or in their feelings about their wife's employment role? At first glance, the answer to each question appears clear-cut. Yet upon further examination, there appears to be active debate and disagreement on each issue.

Regarding father involvement, for example, Hoffman (1989, p. 286), notes that "probably the most clearly demonstrated effect of maternal employment is a modest increase in the participation of fathers in household tasks and child care." When parents have been *asked* about their extent of involvement in "family work" (Crouter et al., 1987) numerous studies indicate that fathers in employed-mother families participate more (see Gottfried, Gottfried, & Bathurst, 1988 for recent evidence; Bahr, 1974; Crouter et al., 1987; Hoffman, 1974b, 1979, 1984, 1989; Zaslow, Pedersen, Suwlsky, Rabinovich, & Cain, 1986 for reviews of the evidence). While father endorsement has been less thoroughly researched, here, too, upon first examination, the results appear clear-cut: Fathers (as well as mothers) appear to be more satisfied with the wife's role when she is *employed* (Gold & Andres, 1978a, b, 1980; Gold, Andres, & Glorieux, 1979).

Yet closer examination reveals debate regarding both father involvement and endorsement. Pleck (1983) has argued that the picture of father involvement differs according to whether parents are asked to *summarize* their involvement or whether their involvement is *sampled* in some way, as for example through time diaries. Subject summaries (the self-report measures most commonly used) suggest greater involvement than do the more precise time diaries. Pleck's overview of the finer-grained time diary studies found little or no increase in hours of family work contributed by fathers in dual, relative to single, wage earner families.

In a similar vein, the fine-grained portrayals provided by home observation studies have reported either a pattern of no group differences in father involvement according to the mother's employment role (Stuckey et al., 1982), or that fathers in dual earner families interact somewhat less with their young children (in all instances in these studies, infants) (Pedersen, Cain, Zaslow, & Anderson, 1982; Zaslow, Pedersen, Suwalsky, Cain, & Fivel, 1985; Zaslow, Pedersen, Suwalsky, Rabinovich, & Cain, 1986).

Although we tend to assume that father involvement has entirely positive connotations, recent evidence also questions this assumption. Crouter et al. (1987) found greater father involvement in single earner families to arise in a context of the father's perceived skill in such activities. However in dual-earner (blue collar) families such involvement was related to marital conflict. The authors suggest a pattern in which wives in dual earner families push their husbands to become involved and that there may be negative spouse interactions surrounding this pressure.

Thus, there is questioning at present about the degree to which increased father-involvement in dual income families comes about voluntarily or under duress and about whether greater father involvement in dual income families is a subjective perception that cannot be validated with more fine-grained measures. We note that a subjective sense of greater involvement may have importance whether or not it is confirmed by other measures. Further work may yield a differentiated picture of father involvement according to specific type of task (leisure activities vs. caregiving) (Crouter et al., 1987; Zaslow et al., 1986) and according to age of child, with the infancy period much more likely to be seen as the special domain of mothers (Zaslow et al., 1986).

Upon closer examination, the data regarding father endorsement of maternal employment similarly yield a complex picture. In particular, there is substantial variation in fathers' feelings about their wives' employment among subgroups. Kaufman (1975) summarized findings indicating that husbands' acceptance of their wives' employment doubles from lowest to highest SES levels in the United States. In the Gold and Andres' studies, while fathers with employed wives were more positive overall about their wives' employment roles, at the same time there were significant interactions with socioeconomic status. For English-speaking children at both ten and fifteen years, middle class fathers with employed wives were most content. Children's perceptions of their father's feelings show a similar pattern of variation by SES (King et al., 1976).

Studies carried out during the infancy period also depart from the general pattern of greater paternal endorsement when the wife is employed. Zaslow et al. (1986) reported that fathers of one-year-olds in a middle class sample tended to report less satisfaction with their wives' caregiving/employment balance than fathers with homemaker wives. Thus, even in a highly educated sample (and thus the group most likely to endorse maternal employment) father endorsement may be lower when the child is still an infant. Further work on father endorsement of maternal employment will undoubtedly yield a picture differentiated by both SES and child age.

Father Involvement and Endorsement as Moderating Variables. Work that attempts to document the role of father involvement and endorsement with respect to child outcomes in dual- and single-earner families is sparse. The most informative work regarding father involvement is that of Gottfried, Gottfried, and Bathurst (1988). These researchers found father involvement to be higher in middle class dual-earner rather than single-earner families. Further, father involvement when the children in the sample were both six and seven-years-old contributed positively to children's development independent of the mother's employment status. Greater father involvement was associated with higher IQ and academic achievement scores as well as maturity in social development. The researchers suggest that there may thus be an indirect link between maternal employment and child outcomes through extent of father involvement.

Lerner and Galambos (1987) report a linkage between father endorsement (as perceived by the mother) and maternal behavior with children. Father's negative feelings about the mother's role were associated with more maternal rejection of the child and among employed mothers with more limit-setting as well. Rejecting maternal behavior has been implicated in the development of difficult temperament (Lerner & Galambos, 1987) as well as in the emergence of insecure-avoidant infant-mother attachment (Zaslow, Rabinovich, Suwalsky, & Klein, 1988). The work linking father involvement and endorsement with child outcomes is at a beginning stage yet promises to be important in clarifying the associations of maternal employment and child outcomes.

In summary, family members tend to report greater father involvement in household and child care tasks when the mother is employed, yet attempts to document this pattern through observations and time diaries do not confirm it. Although overall fathers report greater endorsement of the wife's role when she is employed, paternal endorsement of maternal employment clearly varies by age of child and socioeconomic status. Preliminary work on the possible implications for children of the father's attitudes and family participation in association with maternal employment signals the potential importance of these little-studied factors. The study of maternal employment reflects a form of sexism, giving stronger attention to the role of maternal than paternal factors.

Factors Going Beyond The Family

Characteristics of Mother's Employment

It is possible to conceive of a number of aspects of a mother's employment that might act as moderating variables. Etaugh (1974), for example, listed the following factors as of potential interest: full- vs. part-time employment, regular vs. sporadic employment, duration of continuous employment, particular hours the mother is away, and status of occupation.

The existing research reflects almost exclusively on the first and last of these factors. For extent of employment, the hypothesis presently being entertained in the literature is that *part-time employment of the mother is associated with more positive child outcomes.* For status of occupation, the hypothesis that emerges from the literature is that *higher maternal occupational status is associated with better outcomes in children.*

Both extent of maternal employment and maternal occupational status have important demographic correlates. These correlates should challenge our understanding of the nature and origin of the findings for these moderating variables, very much along the lines of our earlier discussion of preexisting group differences. Before turning to a summary of the evidence on these factors as moderating variables then, we will first present findings regarding their demographic correlates.

Demographic Correlates. Rubin (1983), for example, found that part-time employment was not evenly distributed across ethnic and income groups in a study of 20 neighborhoods in Oakland, California. Black women were more likely than other groups to be employed full-time when employed at all. Part-time employment was found predominantly among higher-income married white women. According to Rubin, "these patterns suggest that only the wealthiest strata of two-parent families exercised, or could afford to exercise, the option of part-time employment" (p. 110). Are so-called benefits of part-time maternal employment rooted in greater availability of the mother to her children (as the literature implies) or rather in the more optimal financial circumstances it is associated with, even *within* socioeconomic levels (like middle class)?

Similarly, for mother's occupational status, we must ask whether findings reflect *preexisting* group differences (e.g., mother's education associated with attaining differing occupational levels), with financial differences *deriving* from differing occupational levels (and resulting in the purchase perhaps of higher quality child care), or differences in *maternal behavior or socialization practices* growing out of the mother's job experiences.

There is some evidence that the specifics of the mother's job do influence behavior at home, and, thus, that correlates with mother's occupational status are not purely artifacts of income or education differences. Piotrkowski and Katz (1982, 1983) present evidence of "spillover" from what the mother experiences on her job to how she acts at home. For example, in their (1983) study of minority mothers employed in relatively low status occupations, the greater autonomy the mother reported on the job, the more positive mood she reported on the job. Mother's reports of positive mood on the job were significantly related to daughter's perceptions of their mother's mood and interpersonal availability at home.

Finally, Gottfried and Gottfried (1988) note that *extent* of employment and *occupational status* represent opposing factors that may well cancel each other out in terms of implications for children: higher occupational status (with hypothetically positive implications for children) is correlated with more hours of employment (hypothetically associated with less positive implications). While we will consider the evidence for each factor separately, it will be important to keep in mind the possibility of their joint influence.

Evidence Regarding Extent of Employment. One set of findings suggesting more negative correlates of full-time maternal employment comes from the debate on infant day care. It is noteworthy that the pattern of elevated rates of "insecure avoidant" attachment found for infants of employed mothers pertains only to mothers employed *full-time.* For example, Schwartz (1983) found no differences in reunion behavior during the "strange situation" (an assessment used to rate patterns of attachment) between 18-month-olds enrolled part time or not at all in day care, whereas toddlers enrolled full time more often showed avoidance behaviors with their mothers.

Findings reported by Owen and Cox (1988) similarly point to differences in mother-infant *interaction* according to hours of employment. In a middle class sample, mothers employed more than 40 hours each week were found to be more anxious. Their interactions with their infants were less sensitive and animated. Bronfenbrenner and colleagues have reported more positive descriptions of three-year-old sons by parents when the mother is employed part rather than full time, irrespective of whether mothers were more or less highly educated (Bronfenbrenner, Alvarez, & Henderson, 1984; Bronfenbrenner & Crouter, 1982).

Recent data on school-age children, as summarized by Hoffman (1989) also suggest that part-time maternal employment may have positive implications. Longer hours of maternal employment are associated with lower scores on indices of achievement (Gottfried, Gottfried, & Bathurst, 1988) and social adaptation (Guidubaldi & Nastasi, 1987). Rubin (1983) reported that sixth graders with part-time employed mothers were much less likely to return to an empty house after school and more likely to have a mother volunteering in their activities.

Part-time maternal employment has also been hypothesized to have positive implications for older children "by achieving an appropriate balance of parental availability for meeting the adolescent's simultaneous needs for dependence and independence" (Bronfenbrenner & Crouter, 1982, p. 57). Douvan and Adelson (1966) in a more clinical and descriptive study, reported positive correlates of part-time maternal employment, particularly in adolescent daughters. These girls were seen by the researchers as active and energetic, involved in household as well as a range of leisure activities, and showing a balance of personal autonomy and involvement with family. Hutner (1972) found that among high school students with highly educated mothers, part-time employment of the mother was associated with higher scores on aptitude and achievement tests than full-time maternal employment.

It should be noted that several further studies report that extent of employment had either no correlates (Stuckey et al., 1982; Burke & Weir, 1978), or that *full*-time maternal employment had more positive implications (Woods, 1972; Stein, 1973). The evidence regarding extent of employment may best be described as "promising" but incomplete. Further studies are needed carefully taking into account the circumstances in which part-time and full-time employment have come about in families, reflecting our concerns about the demographic correlates of extent of employment.

Evidence Regarding Occupational Status. Gottfried, Gottfried, and Bathurst (1988), simultaneously considering both extent of maternal employment and mother's occupational status, found the latter to have more implications for children's development. Occupational status was positively related to level of cognitive development in toddlerhood, in the preschool and early school years, as well as to measures of achievement and social maturity.

Other findings also show differences on measures of achievement according to mother's occupational status. Keidel (1970) found higher grade point averages among 9th graders whose mothers were employed at a professional as opposed to an nonprofessional level. Similarly, Frankel (1964) found that high and low achieving boys, matched on IQ and SES, could be differentiated on the basis of the mother's occupational level.

A set of findings relates mother's occupational status to expectations of self in daughters. (There are no parallel data for sons.) For example, Gibbons and Kopelman (1977) found that fear of success in high school girls tended to decrease as mother's level of occupation increased. Pearlman (1981) found that mother's high occupational status was an important predictor of girls career choices. Macke and Morgan (1978) found evidence of "negative role-modeling" among black adolescent girls. When their mothers were employed in blue collar jobs, usually involving domestic work, they tended not to plan to emulate their mothers' employment pattern and showed low levels of work orientation. "Apparently, the undesirable qualities of the mothers' jobs had a consistently negative effect regardless of the mother's other characteristics" (p. 197). While related quite specifically to expectations for self, mother's occupational status has shown little relation to daughters' sex role orientation more broadly defined (Baruch, 1972, 1974; Seegmiller, 1980; Meier, 1972).

Gottfried, Gottfried, and Bathurst (1988) report that higher maternal occupational status is positively associated with the family process variables of positive family involvement and educational attitudes. Taken together with Piotrkowski and Katz's findings (1982, 1983), these findings suggest that a mother's emphasis on achievement in her own life may come to have ramifications for her children's expectations of themselves.

In summary, evidence suggests that part-time maternal employment and higher occupational status are both associated with more optimal development in children. However, the research also indicates that part-time employment and employment in more rewarding and professional jobs arise in the context of such factors as higher maternal education and family socioeconomic status. Work to date has not definitively confirmed that developmental differences in children originate in the employment circumstances of the mother rather than in these correlated demographic circumstances.

Child Care Quality

Research on the impact on children of day care has undergone a major reorientation in recent years (Belsky, 1984). Whereas work in this area initially focused on high quality, university-based day care centers, there has been growing interest in examining the types of nonrelative care actually available to most families, i.e., family day care (care by a nonrelative in a home) and community based center care. In addition, there has been a transition from viewing child care as a "global undifferentiated construct" (Anderson, 1980) to understanding that child care encompasses a broad range in terms of quality.

The hypothesis presently being actively examined in the research is that *the implications of maternal employment are more positive for children when child care is of higher overall quality.* In addition, researchers are asking which particular quality features are most closely linked with child outcomes.

The evidence on child care quality has recently been reviewed by Phillips and Howes (1987) and by the Panel on Child Care Policy of the National Academy of Sciences (Hayes, Palmer, & Zaslow, 1990). Reviewers concur that overall child care quality has implications for children's cognitive as well as social development when both care quality and development are measured contemporaneously. In addition, there is now a small set of studies suggesting that quality of child care experienced in the preschool years may have implications lasting into the early school years. Findings pertain to both family and center day care.

To give several examples of the findings showing linkages between child care quality and child development, McCartney (1984) found overall day care center quality to have "a profound effect on language development" (p.251). Similarly, studying family day care, Goelman and Pence (1987) found care quality to be a "potent predictor" of language development. Concerning social development, Howes and Olenick (1986) found that children attending low quality center care were less compliant and more resistant. Clarke-Stewart (1987) similarly reports less optimal social development in children attending family day care settings with features suggesting lower overall quality (caregivers who less often touched children, engaged then in conversation, read to them or gave them directions).

In one of the small set of longitudinal studies, Howes (1988b) found quality of early child care (encompassing a wide range of center and family day care settings) to be related to school skills and behavior problems in both boys and girls when examined at the end of first grade: higher quality early care predicted better academic and social adaptation early in elementary school. Other findings pointing to persisting implications of early care include the studies of Vandell, Henderson, and Wilson (1988) and Howes (1988a).

What however, are the components of higher quality child care? While many of the available studies use global or summary measures (e.g., the Harms & Clifford scale, 1980) to portray child care quality, there are studies that attempt to examine "quality" in greater detail (see Hayes, Palmer, & Zaslow, 1990 for overview of this evidence). Findings suggest that from the point of view of children's development, the single most important quality feature is the nature of caregiver-child interaction. For example, in a study looking at a variety of quality dimensions, McCartney, Scarr, Phillips, Grajek, and Schwarz (1982) found caregiver speech to children to be the strongest predictor of development.

Caregiver-child interaction cannot, however, be regulated or mandated, and much of the available research has focused on dimensions of care quality that can be more readily addressed through policies. The evidence (summarized in Hayes, Palmer, &

Zaslow, 1990; Phillips, 1988; Phillips & Howes, 1987) suggests that "structural" features of care quality, like group size, ratio, and caregiver qualifications play a key role in making more likely the warm, supportive, and stimulating caregiver-child interactions that appear central to development.

Children appear to benefit particularly from smaller groups, from caregivers with training specifically in the area of child development, and (particularly as infants and toddlers) from better caregiver-child ratios. Other factors that appear to be important are a child's continuity with a particular caregiver or caregivers, a daily routine that shows a balance between structure and open-ended activities rather than being strictly custodial, and well-organized and child-designed space and equipment. For family day care in particular, the degree of isolation vs. support and contact with other adults experienced by the caregiver may also be an important feature of care quality.

The evidence is good then, that quality of child care, whether defined globally or in terms of specific structural features, has implications for the development of the children of employed mothers.

Conclusion

In developmental psychology it has often been the case that as research on a particular issue progresses, an early conceptualization is outgrown and shed, and a new one comes to guide the work. The earliest research on maternal deprivation, for example, started with the simplistic conceptualization that under all circumstances, prolonged mother-child separation was severely damaging. But as the evidence accumulated, this conceptualization proved simplistic. The impact of maternal deprivation was found to vary substantially by the family circumstances surrounding child institutionalization, the child's physical condition, and especially the particular features of residential care (Rutter, 1981; Yarrow, 1961). Such "conceptual evolution" has been characteristic also in research on parental divorce, and as we have noted, research on day care.

Conceptual evolution is very clear in the research that is the focus of this volume. The work on maternal employment was originally organized around the question of whether maternal employment was a form of maternal deprivation, and thus harmed children. However, the great complexity in the results has clearly indicated that a simple group comparison strategy does not suffice. Maternal employment has a range of developmental correlates. This range of implications begins to be interpretable when we shed the simple group comparison strategy and consider moderating variables.

There are now the first indications that the moderating variable approach is giving rise to a third stage in the conceptual evolution of the maternal employment research: one focusing on underlying processes (or mediating variables). Thus, Lerner and Galambos (1987) have asked *why* maternal role satisfaction is linked to child outcomes; Crouter and colleagues (1987) have addressed the *circumstances* in which greater father involvement comes about in employed and homemaker mother families; and Piotrkowski and Katz (1982, 1983) focus on the *processes* underlying the connections between a mother's job circumstances and child outcomes. Work on moderating variables is beginning to inform and provide the basis for research addressing underlying processes.

Yet, it is clear from the present chapter that the work at the moderating variables "stage" is far from complete. In each set of moderating variables we have examined (child characteristics, family characteristics, and factors outside the family), there was only one moderating variable for which the evidence was sufficient for a detailed examination and which led to a reasonably confident conclusion. Our review suggests that given the available evidence, differences in child outcomes associated with maternal employment are most closely linked with the child characteristic of sex, the family characteristic of maternal role satisfaction, and the external factor of quality of child care. Maternal employment is more likely to be associated with less optimal child development in boys, when the mother is dissatisfied with her employment role, and when care quality is poor. The continued accumulation of evidence may be expected to modify our sense of the relative importance of the moderating variables within each set of factors.

The sheer number of moderating variables (8 considered in the present chapter and other potential factors, like family marital status, not even addressed here) suggests the great complexity of understanding the implications of maternal employment for any one child or subgroup of children. Further, we do not as yet know the relative "weights" each of the moderating variables assumes in predicting child outcomes.

It may prove useful in future work to expand the idea of the "net" of positive and negative factors in the lives of children of employed and homemaker mothers proposed by DeSai, Chase-Lansdale, and Michael (1989). While they offer this construct in discussing time and material resources available to children, the impact on any one child of maternal employment may best be thought of as the net of the positive and negative "tugs" on development associated with the full range of preexisting and moderating factors.

Bibliography

Almquist, E. M., & Angrist, S. S. (1971). Role model influences on college women's career aspirations. *Merrill-Palmer Quarterly, 17,* 263-279.

Altman, S. L., & Grossman, F. K. (1977). Women's career plans and maternal employment. *Psychology of Women Quarterly, 1,* 365-376.

Anderson, C. W. (1980). Attachment in daily separations: Reconceptualizing day care and maternal employment issues. *Child Development, 51,* 242-245.

Bacon, C., & Lerner, R. M. (1975). Effects of maternal employment status on the development of vocational-role perception in females. *Journal of Genetic Psychology, 126,* 187-193.

Bahr, S. J. (1974). Effect on power and division of labor in the family. In L. W. Hoffman & F. I. Nye (Eds.), *Working mothers* (pp. 167-185). San Francisco: Jossey-Bass.

Barglow, P., Vaughn, B. E., & Molitor, N. (1987). Effects of maternal absence due to employment on the quality of infant-mother attachment in a low-risk sample. *Child Development, 58,* 945-954.

Baruch, G. K. (1972). Maternal influences upon college women's attitudes toward women and work. *Developmental Psychology, 6,* 32-37.

Baruch, G. K. (1974). Maternal career-orientation as related to parental identificantion in college women. *Journal of Vocational Behavior, 4,* 173-180.

Belsky, J. (1984). Two waves of day care research: Developmental effects and conditions of quality. In R. C. Ainslie (Ed.),   *The Child and the Day Care Setting* (pp. 1-34). New York: Praeger.

Belsky, J. (1988). The "effects" of infant day care reconsidered. *Early Childhood Research Quarterly, 3,* 235-272.

Belsky, J., & Rovine, M. (1988). Nonmaternal care in the first year of life and the security of infant-parent attachment. *Child Development, 59,* 157-167.

Berndt, T. J. (1983). Peer relations in children of working parents: A theoretical analysis and some conclusions. In C. D. Hayes & S. B. Kamerman (Eds.), *Children of working parents: Experiences and outcomes* (pp. 13-43). Washington, DC: National Academy Press.

Bronfenbrenner, U., Alvarez, W. F., & Henderson, C. R. (1984). Working and watching: Maternal employment status and parents' perceptions of their three-year-old children. *Child Development, 55,* 1362-1378.

Bronfenbrenner, U., & Crouter, A. C. (1982). Work and family through time and space. In S. B. Kamerman & C. D. Hayes (Eds.), *Families that work: Children in a changing world*(pp. 39-83). Washington, DC: National Academy Press.

Burke, R. J., & Weir, T. (1978). Maternal employment status, social support and adolescents' well-being. *Psychological Reports, 42,* 1159-1170.

Campos, J. J., Barrett, K. C., Lamb, M. E., Goldsmith, H. H., & Stenberg, C. (1983). Socioemotional development. In P. H. Mussen (Ed.), *Handbook of child psychology* (Vol. 2, pp. 783-915). New York: Wiley.

Chase-Lansdale, P. L., & Owen, M. T. (1987). Maternal employment in a family context: Effects on infant-mother and infant-father attachments. *Child Development, 58,* 1505-1512.

Cherry, F. F., & Eaton, E. L. (1977). Physical and cognitive development in children of low-income mothers working in the child's early years.   *Child Development, 48,* 158-166.

Clarke-Stewart, K. A. (1987). Predicting child development from child care forms and features: The Chicago study. In D. A. Phillips (Ed.), *Quality in child care: What does research tell us?* (pp. 21-42). Washington, DC: National Association for the Education of Young Children.

Clarke-Stewart, K. A. (1989). Infant day care: Maligned or malignant? *American Psychologist, 44,* 266-274.

Crockenberg, S., & Acredolo, C. (1983). Infant temperament ratings: A function of infants, or mothers, or both? *Infant Behavior and Development, 6,* 61-72.

Crockenberg, S., & Litman, C. (1989, April). *Effects of maternal employment on maternal and child behavior.* Paper presented at the Society For Research in Child Development, Kansas City.

Crouter, A. C., Perry-Jenkins, M., Huston, T. L., & McHale, S. M. (1987). Processes underlying father involvement in dual-earner and single-earner families. *Developmental Psychology, 23,* 431-440.

D'Amico, R. J., Haurin, R. J., & Mott, F. L. (1983). The effects of mothers' employment on adolescent and early adult outcomes of young men and women. In C. D. Hayes & S. B. Kamerman (Eds.), *Children of working parents: Experiences and outcomes* (pp. 130-219). Washington, DC: National Academy Press.

Dellas, M., Gaier, E. L., & Emihovich, C. A. (1979). Maternal employment and selected behaviors and attitudes of preadolescents and adolescents. *Adolescence, 14,* 579-589.

DeMeis, D. K., Hock, E., & McBride, S. L. (1986). The balance of employment and motherhood: Longitudinal study of mothers' feelings about separation from their first-born infants. *Developmental Psychology, 22,* 627-632.

DeSai, S., Chase-Lansdale, P. L., & Michael, R. T. (1989). Mother or market? Effects of maternal employment on the intellectual ability of four-year-old children. *Demography, 26,* 545-561.

Douvan, E., & Adelson, J. (1966). *The adolescent experience.* New York: Wiley.

Etaugh, C. (1974). Effects of maternal employment on children: A review of recent research. *Merrill-Palmer Quarterly, 20,* 71-98.

Farel, A. N. (1980). Effects of preferred maternal roles, maternal employment, and sociographic status on school adjustment and competence. *Child Development, 50,* 1179-1186.

Galambos, N. L., & Lerner, J. V. (1987). Child characteristics and the employment of mothers with young children: A longitudinal study. *Journal of Child Psychology and Psychiatry, 28,* 87-98.

Gibbons, P. A., & Kopelman, R. E. (1977). Maternal employment as a determinant of fear of success in females. *Psychological Reports, 40,* 1200-1202.

Goelman, H., & Pence, A. R. (1987). Effects of child care, family, and individual characteristics on children's language development: The Victoria Day Care Research Project. In D. Phillips (Ed.), *Quality in child care: What does research tell us?* (pp. 89-104). Washington, DC: National Association for the Education of Young Children.

Gold, D., & Andres, D. (1977). Maternal employment and child development at three age levels. *Journal of Research and Development in Education, 10,* 20-29.

Gold, D., & Andres, D. (1978a). Comparisons of adolescent children with employed and nonemployed mothers. *Merrill-Palmer Quarterly, 24,* 243-254.

Gold, D., & Andres, D. (1978b). Developmental comparisons between ten-year-old children with employed and nonemployed mothers. *Child Development, 49,* 75-84.

Gold, D., & Andres, D. (1978c). Relations between maternal employment and development of nursery school children. *Canadian Journal of Behavioral Science, 10,* 116-129.

Gold, D., & Andres, D. (1980). Maternal employment and development of ten-year-old Canadian francophone children. *Canadian Journal of Behavioral Science, 12,* 233-240.

Gold, D., Andres, D., & Glorieux, J. (1979). The development of francophone nursery school children with employed and nonemployed mothers. *Canadian Journal of Behavioral Science, 11,* 169-173.

Gottfried, A. E., & Gottfried, A. W. (Eds.). (1988). *Maternal employment and children's development: Longitudinal research.* New York: Plenum.

Gottfried, A. E., Gottfried, A. W., & Bathurst, K. (1988). Maternal employment, family environment, and children's development: Infancy through the school years. In A. E. Gottfried & A. W. Gottfried (Eds.), *Maternal employment and children's development: Longitudinal research* (pp. 11-58). New York: Plenum.

Guidubaldi, J., & Nastasi, B. K. (1987). *Home environment factors as predictors of child adjustment in mother-employed households: Results of a nationwide study.* Paper presented at the meeting of the Society for Research in Child Development, Baltimore, Maryland.

Harms, T., & Clifford, R. M. (1980). *Early childhood environment rating scale.* New York: Teachers College Press.

Hayes, C. D., Palmer, J. L., & Zaslow, M. J. (Eds.). (1990). *Who cares for America's children? Child care policy for the 1990's.* Panel on Child Care Policy, Committee on Child Development Research and Public Policy, National Academy of Sciences. Washington, DC: National Academy Press.

Heyns, B. (1982). The influence of parents' work on children's school achievement. In S. B. Kamerman & C. D. Hayes (Eds.), *Families that work: Children in a changing world* (pp.229-267). Washington, DC: National Academy Press.

Hill, C. R., & Stafford, F. P. (1980). Parental care of children: Time diary estimates of quantity, predictability, and variety. *The Journal of Human Resources, 15,* 219-239.

Hock, E. (1980). Working and nonworking mothers and their infants: A comparative study of maternal caregiving characteristics and infant social behavior. *Merrill-Palmer Quarterly, 26,* 79-101.

Hock, E., Christman, K., & Hock, M. (1980). Factors associated with decisions about return to work in mothers of infants. *Developmental Psychology, 16,* 535-536.

Hock, E., DeMeis, D., & McBride, S. (1988). Maternal separation anxiety: Its role in the balance of employment and motherhood in mothers of infants. In A. Gottfried & A. W. Gottfried (Eds.), *Maternal employment and children's development: Longitudinal research* (pp. 191-230). New York: Plenum.

Hock, E., Gnezda, M. T., & McBride, S. L. (1984). Mothers of infants: Attitudes toward employment and motherhood following birth of the first child. *Journal of Marriage and the Family, 46,* 425-431.

Hofferth, S. L., & Phillips, D. H. (1987). Child care in the United States, 1970 to 1995. *Journal of Marriage and the Family, 49,* 559-571.

Hoffman, L. W. (1963). Mother's enjoyment of work and effects on the child. In F. I. Nye & L. W. Hoffman (Eds.), *The employed mother in America* (pp. 95-105). Westport, CT: Greenwood Press.

Hoffman, L. W. (1974a). Effects of maternal employment on the child--A review of the research. *Developmental Psychology, 10,* 204-228.

Hoffman, L. W. (1974b). Effects on child. In L. W. Hoffman & F. I. Nye (Eds.), *Working mothers* (pp. 126-166). San Francisco: Jossey-Bass.

Hoffman, L. W. (1979). Maternal employment: 1979. *American Psychologist, 34,* 859-865.

Hoffman, L. W. (1980). The effects of maternal employment on the academic attitudes and performance of school-aged children. *School Psychology Review, 9,* 319-335.

Hoffman, L. W. (1984). Maternal employment and the young child. In M. Perlmutter (Ed.), *Minnesota symposium in child psychology* (Vol. 17, pp. 101-128). Hillsdale, NJ: Erlbaum.

Hoffman, L. W. (1989). Effects of maternal employment in the two-parent family. *American Psychologist, 44,* 283-292.

Howes, C. (1988a). *Can age of entry and the quality of infant child care predict behaviors in kindergarten?* Paper presented at the International Conference on Infant Studies, Washington, DC.

Howes, C. (1988b). Relations between early child care and schooling. *Developmental Psychology, 24,* 53-57.

Howes, C., & Olenick, M. (1986). Family and child influences on toddlers' compliance. *Child Development, 57,* 202-216.

Hutner, F. C. (1972). Mother's education and working: Effect on the school child. *Journal of Psychology, 82,* 27-37.

Jones, L. M., & McBride, J. L. (1980). Sex-role stereotyping in children as a function of maternal employment. *Journal of Social Psychology, 111,* 219-223.

Kamerman, S. B., & Hayes, C. D., (Eds.) (1982). *Families that work: Children in a changing world.* Washington, DC: National Academy Press.

Kaufman, E. B. (1975). *Should mothers work? The effects of maternal employment on children.* Unpublished thesis, Bank Street College of Education, New York.

Keidel, K. C. (1970). Maternal employment and ninth grade achievement in Bismark, North Dakota. *Family Coordinator, 19,* 95-97.

King, K., Abernathy, T. J., & Chapman, A. H. (1976). Black adolescents' view of maternal employment as a threat to the marital relationship: 1963-1973. *Journal of Marriage and the Family, 38,* 733-737.

Lamb, M. E. (1982). Maternal employment and child development: A review. In M. E. Lamb (Ed.), *Nontraditional families: Parenting and child development* (pp. 45-69). Hillsdale, NJ: Erlbaum.

Lerner, J. V., & Galambos, N. L. (1985). Maternal role satisfaction, mother-child interaction, and child temperament: A process model. *Developmental Psychology, 21,* 1157-1164.

Lerner, J. V., & Galambos, N. L. (1986). Temperament and maternal employment. In J. V. Lerner & R. M. Lerner (Eds.), *Temperament and social interaction during infancy and childhood: New directions for child development* (No. 31, pp. 75-88). San Francisco: Jossey-Bass.

Lerner, J. V., & Galambos, N. L. (1988). The influences of maternal employment across life: The New York Longitudinal Study. In A. E. Gottfried & A. Gottfried (Eds.), *Maternal employment and children's development* (pp. 59-83). New York: Plenum.

Lerner, J. V., Hess, L. E., & Banerjee, P. (1986). *Maternal employment, maternal role satisfaction, and early adolescent outcomes.* Paper presented at the first meeting of the Society for Research in Adolescence, Madison, Wisconsin.

McCartney, K. (1984). Effect of quality of day care environment on children's language development. *Developmental Psychology, 20,* 244-260.

McCartney, K., Scarr, S., Phillips, D., Grajek, S., & Schwarz, J. C. (1982). Environmental differences among day care centers and their effects on children's development. In E. F. Zigler & E. W. Gordon (Eds.), *Daycare: Scientific and social policy issues* (pp.126-151). Boston: Auburn House.

McCord, J., McCord, W., & Thurber, E. (1963). Effects of maternal employment on lower-class boys. *Journal of Abnormal and Social Psychology, 67,* 177-182.

Maccoby, E. (1958). Effects upon children of their mothers' outside employment. In *Work in the lives of married women* (proceedings of a conference, sponsored by the National Manpower Council). New York: Columbia University Press.

Macke, A. S., & Morgan, W. R. (1978). Maternal employment, race, and work orientation of high school girls. *Social Forces, 57,* 187-204.

Marantz, S. A., & Mansfield, A. F. (1977). Maternal employment and the development of sex-role stereotyping in five- to eleven-year-old girls. *Child Development, 48,* 668-673.

Meier, H. C. (1972). Mother-centeredness and college youths' attitudes toward social equality for women: Some empirical findings. *Journal of Marriage and the Family, 34,* 115-121.

Miller, S. M. (1975). Effects of maternal employment on sex-role perception, interests, and self-esteem in kindergarten girls. *Developmental Psychology, 11,* 405-406.

Montemayor, R. (1984). Maternal employment and adolescents' relations with parents, siblings, and peers. *Journal of Youth and Adolescence, 13,* 543-557.

Moore, T. W. (1975). Exclusive early mothering and its alternatives: The outcome to adolescence. *Scandinavian Journal of Psychology, 16,* 255-272.

Owen, M. T., & Cox, M. J. (1988). Maternal employment and the transition to parenthood. In A. E. Gottfried & A. W. Gottfried (Eds.), *Maternal employment and children's development: Longitudinal research* (pp. 85-119). New York: Plenum.

Pasquali, L., & Callegari, A. I. (1978). Working mothers and daughters' sex-role identification in Brazil. *Child Development, 49,* 902-905.

Pearlman, V. A. (1981). Influences of mothers' employment on career orientation and career choice of adolescent daughters. *Dissertation Abstracts International, 41,* (11-A) 4657-4658.

Pedersen, F. A., Cain, R. L., Zaslow, M. J., & Anderson, B. J. (1982). Variation in infant experience associated with alternative family roles. In L. Laosa & I. Sigel (Eds.), *Families as learning environments for children* (pp. 203-221). New York: Plenum.

Phillips, D. A. (1988). *Quality in child care: Definitions.* Paper presented at the A. L. Mailman Family Foundation, Inc., Symposium on dimensions of quality in programs for children, White Plains, NY.

Phillips, D. A., & Howes, C. (1987). Indicators of quality in child care: Review of research. In D. A. Phillips (Ed.), *Quality in child care: What does research tell us?* (pp. 1-20). Washington, DC: National Association for the Education of Young Children.

Piotrkowski, C., & Katz, M. (1982). Indirect socialization of children: The effects of mothers' jobs on academic behaviors. *Child Development, 53,* 1520-1529.

Piotrkowski, C., & Katz, M. (1983). Work experience and family relations among working-class and lower-middle class families. In H. Lopata, & J. Pleck, (Eds.), *Research in the interweave of social roles, Vol. 3: Jobs and Families* (pp. 187-200). Greenwich, CT: JAI Press.

Pleck, J. H. (1983). Husbands' paid work and family roles: Current research issues. In H. Lopata & J. Pleck (Eds.), *Research in the interweave of social roles, Vol. 3: Jobs and Families* (pp. 251-333). Greenwich, CT: JAI Press.

Propper, A. M. (1972). The relationship of maternal employment to adolescent roles, activities, and parental relationships. *Journal of Marriage and the Family, 34,* 417-421.

Richardson, J. L., Dwyer, K., McGuigan, K., Hanson, W. B., Dent, C., Johnson, C. A., Sussman, S. Y., Brannon, B., & Flay, B. (1989). Substance use among eighth-grade students who take care of themselves after school. *Pediatrics, 84,* 556-566.

Rubin, V. (1983). Family work patterns and community resources: An analysis of children's access to support and services outside school. In C. D. Hayes & S. B. Kamerman (Eds.), *Children of working parents: Experiences and outcomes* (pp. 100-129). Washington DC: National Academy Press.

Rutter, M. (1970). Sex differences in children's responses to family stress. In E. J. Anthony & C. Koupernik (Eds.), *The child in his family* (pp. 165-196). New York: Wiley-Interscience.

Rutter, M. (1981). Social-emotional consequences of day care for preschool children. *American Journal of Orthopsychiatry, 51,* 4-28.

Schachter, F. F. (1981). Toddlers with employed mothers. *Child Development, 52,* 958-964.

Schubert, J. B., Bradley-Johnson, S., & Nuttal, J. (1980). Mother-infant communication and maternal employment. *Child Development, 51,* 246-249.

Schwartz, P. (1983). Length of day care attendance and attachment behavior in eighteen-month-old infants. *Child Development, 54,* 1073-1078.

Seegmiller, B. R. (1980). Sex-role differentiation in preschoolers: Effects of maternal employment. *Journal of Psychology, 104,* 185-189.

Smith, E. J. (1981). The working mother: A critique of the research. *Journal of Vocational Behavior, 19,* 191-211.

Statistical Abstract of the United States: 1988. Washington, DC: U.S. Bureau of the Census.

Stein, A. H. (1973). The effects of maternal employment and educational attainment on the sex-typed attributes of college females. *Social Behavior and Personality, 1,* 111-114.

Stuckey, M. F., McGhee, P. E., & Bell, N. J. (1982). Parent-child interaction: The influence of maternal employment. *Developmental Psychology, 18,* 635-644.

Tangri, S. S. (1972). Determinants of occupational role innovation among college women. *Journal of Social Issues, 28,* 177-199.

Thomas, A., & Chess, S. (1977). *Temperament and development.* New York: Brunner/Mazel.

U.S. Department of Labor, Bureau of Labor Statistics. (1986). Half of mothers with children under 3 now in labor force. Press release, August 20.

Vandell, D. L., Henderson, V. K., & Wilson K. S. (1988). A longitudinal study of children with day care experiences of varying quality. *Child Development, 59,* 1286-1292.

Wallston, B. (1973). The effects of maternal employment on children. *Journal of Child Psychology and Psychiatry, 14,* 81-95.

Weinraub, M., Jaeger, E., & Hoffman, L. (1988). Predicting infant outcomes in families of employed and nonemployed mothers. *Early Childhood Research Quarterly, 3,* 361-378.

Williamson, S. Z. (1970). The effects of maternal employment on the scholastic performance of children. *Journal of Home Economics, 62,* 609-613.

Woods, M. B. (1972). The unsupervised child of the working mother. *Developmental Psychology, 6,* 14-25.

Yarrow, L. J. (1961). Maternal deprivation: Toward an empirical and conceptual re-evaluation. *Psychological Bulletin, 58,* 459-490.

Yarrow, M. R., Scott, P., DeLeeuw, L., & Heinig, C. (1962). Childrearing in families of working and nonworking mothers. *Sociometry, 25,* 122-140.

Zambrana, R. E., Hurst, M., & Hite, R. L. (1979). The working mother in contemporary perspective: A review of the literature. *Pediatrics, 64,* 862-870.

Zaslow, M. J. (1987). Sex differences in children's response to maternal employment. Official document, National Academy of Sciences, National Research Council, Committee on Child Development Research and Public Policy, Washington, DC.

Zaslow, M. J., & Hayes, C. (1986). Sex differences in children's response to psychosocial stress. In M. E. Lamb, A. Brown, & B. Rogoff (Eds.), *Advances in developmental psychology* (Vol. 4, pp. 285-337). Hillsdale, NJ: Erlbaum.

Zaslow, M., Pedersen, F. A., Suwalsky, J. T. D., Cain, R., & Fivel, M. (1985). The early resumption of employment by mothers: Implications for parent-infant interaction. *Journal of Applied Developmental Psychology, 6,* 1-16.

Zaslow, M. J., Pedersen, F. A., Suwalsky, J. T. D., & Rabinovich, B. A. (1989). Maternal employment and parent-infant interaction at one year. *Early Childhood Research Quarterly, 4,* 459-478.

Zaslow, M. J., Pedersen, F. A., Suwalsky, J. T. D., Rabinovich, B. A., & Cain, R. (1986). Fathering during the infancy period: Implications of the mother's employment role. *Infant Mental Health Journal, 7,* 225-234.

Zaslow, M. J., Rabinovich, B. A., Suwalsky, J. T. D., & Klein, R. (1988). The role of social context in the prediction of secure and insecure/avoidant infant-mother attachment. *Journal of Applied Developmental Psychology, 9,* 287-299.

Afterword

Lois Wladis Hoffman

Research on maternal employment has moved to a new era. This volume marks the shift. Every chapter in this book, in the literature reviews and the presentations of new findings, conceptualizes the mother's employment status as a meaningful but complex variable that influences children, not directly and out of context, but in interaction with other aspects of the situation, and through its effects on other variables that mediate its influence.

I will first discuss the contribution of this volume to our understanding of how the context or social setting influences the meaning and impact of maternal employment. Four setting variables will be considered: the historical setting, social class, the community and physical site, and the family structure or form. Then the two major units that mediate the effects of the mother's employment status will be considered: family interaction and nonparental care.

The Setting

It is clear from these chapters that the effects of maternal employment are different at different historical periods, for different socio-economic groups, in urban and non-urban settings, and for two-parent and one-parent families. For example, Richards and Duckett point out in Chapter 5 that findings from research obtained several decades ago cannot be generalized to the present situation because maternal employment has become more commonplace and accepted today. The selective factors that determined which mothers were in the labor force and the prevailing social climate have changed. There are other changes, such as decreased family size and increased efficiency in household operations that have lessened the demands of the homemaker role (Hoffman, 1979; Pleck, 1983); new values about what one should expect from life; and increased marital instability.

Some data typically included in drawing conclusions about the current effects of maternal employment were collected in an era very different from the present. The widely-cited national study by

Douvan and Adelson (1966), for example, was actually conducted in the 1950s. It cannot be assumed that comparable results would be obtained today.

Throughout the book, social class is examined as a factor that moderates the effects of maternal employment. For example, in both Chapters 3 and 10, the authors take up the question of why young children with employed mothers in the lower class do not show cognitive deficits and are often found to score higher on tests of cognitive performance, while in the middle class some studies have found the opposite pattern: the employed mothers' children, particularly sons, score lower on cognitive tests. At first, this might seem surprising since the quality of nonmaternal care is generally higher in the middle class. The authors point out, however, that the differences between "mother-care" and "other-care" may be greater in the middle class. The middle-class mother has been found to be a particularly effective agent for cognitive stimulation, and it may be that even alternative care of good quality does not match the stimulating environment she provides. In the lower class, however, the educational level of parents and substitute caregivers is relatively close and may even favor the latter. Thus, the mother's employment may be a net loss for middle-class children and a net gain for lower class children. In addition, the lower class mother's wages make a greater difference in the family's economic conditions, often lifting them from the level of poverty, and this also could enhance the child's cognitive performance. This argument is not new (Hoffman, 1979), but it is presented in a way that highlights the complexity of the interacting patterns that mediate employment effects.

The community setting as a moderator variable is taken up by Galambos and Maggs in Chapter 6. Whether children who are in self-care after school are likely to show adjustment problems depends on the area in which they live and the physical setting. Studies of children in suburban and rural areas do not reveal negative effects, while studies in metropolitan areas have shown such outcomes. Similarly, there is no evidence for adverse consequences if the unsupervised time is spent at home, but if the time is spent outside the home, there is an increased likelihood of misconduct.

The theme that the ecology or context affects the relationships among the variables is applied also to the family. Variations in the family structure and ideology influence the meaning of the mother's employment status for the child's socialization. For example, relationships between the mother's employment status and family roles or child outcomes may be different in one-parent than in two-parent families. Thus, data reported from a study by Richards and Duckett in Chapter 5 indicate that although mothers' work status was not related to the emotional well-being of adolescent children living in two parent families, full-time maternal employment was linked to children's enhanced daily affect and self-esteem in single-mother families. In addition, only in the single-mother families was it found that children with employed mothers indicated higher affect when with the mother and better relations with their fathers. These researchers suggest that it is the increased sense of well-being in the mother that is carrying this effect; psychological well-being is strongly associated with paid employment among single women.

The prevailing family ideology also moderates the influence of the mother's employment. Hawkins and Crouter note that when the family holds traditional views, there is less likely to be a shift in the division of labor between the mother and father as an accommodation to the mother's employment. This, in turn, is likely to increase the stress on the mother from dual roles and to deprive the child of the positive effects of the father's active involvement in child care. The traditional ideology might also lead to a strain in the relationship between the father and son when the mother is employed. As noted in Chapter 10, by Zaslow, Rabinovich, and Suwalsky, in the working class, maternal employment is sometimes associated with difficulties between the father and son. In particular, sons are less likely to name their father as someone they admire. The traditional sex-role ideology is very prevalent in blue-collar families and it has been proposed that because of this, the mother's employment is often interpreted as a sign of failure on the part of the father which weakens his attractiveness as a role model.

A particularly interesting framing of the idea that relationships between variables will be different within different family forms has emerged recently in the literature. This is the idea that the inter-relationships among variables may be different in families with employed mothers than in families with full-time homemaker mothers. For example, Weinraub, Jaeger, and Hoffman (1988) found that in employed-mother families, the security of the mother-infant attachment was related to independence in the child, but in families with mothers who were full-time homemakers, it was the dependent children who tended to be the more securely attached. An interpretation of this result was that dependency was valued by the mothers for whom parenting was their full-time job, but independence was more valued by the employed mothers. Thus, the more valued characteristics could elicit more warm responsivity on the part of the mother, facilitating secure attachment, and also could be more effectively reinforced in the context of a secure attachment.

Comparable analyses are described in this volume. In the chapter by Bartko and McHale, data are reported that reveal that the effects of household task performance by children are different in employed-mother families than in nonemployed-mother families. There are two groups of boys who seemed better adjusted as indicated by feeling more competent, positive about their relationship with their parents, and less stressed about their chores: boys in dual-wage families who had high task involvement and boys in single-wage families who had low task involvement. This was particularly true when the tasks included those traditionally considered as feminine chores. Because these patterns were heightened when the mother's employment status, the father's task involvement, and the father's ideology were all congruent with the boy's role in tasks, Bartko and McHale interpret these results in terms of the congruence between the boy's role and the family pattern. They also note, however, that the consequences of children's task involvement may vary depending on its instrumental value to the family. Because children's tasks are very important for family functioning when the mother is employed, they are more likely to be accepted by the child as a family contribution and to enhance the child's self-esteem.

These analyses go beyond looking at the family as the mediator of maternal employment effects. That is, this is not just seeing the mother's employment as influencing family interaction which, in turn, influences the child. The mother's employment status changes the family so that the same pattern of behavior may have a different outcome for the child in different parental employment settings. In these recent analyses, employment status operates as a moderator variable. The same child characteristic may elicit a different response; the same parent behavior may have a different outcome.

The distinction between mediators and moderators is described in Chapter 10. The setting variables I have described are moderators. We now turn to a consideration of the two major mediators, the family and nonparental care.

The Mediators

Four of the chapters in this volume, Chapters 4, 7, 8, and 9, focus on the family as the mediator of employment effects, while Chapter 5 deals with both the family and the nonfamily experiences. Gottfried, in Chapter 4, stresses the absence of direct relationships between the mother's employment status and child outcomes but notes several relationships to family variables which, in turn, impact on the child. Among these are the father's role in the family, the cognitive stimulation that is provided, educational attitudes, and the quality of parent-child interaction. In this study, maternal employment is directly related to increased father involvement and higher educational aspirations for children, both of which relate to children's higher cognitive performance. Most of the effects of maternal employment on the family, however, are themselves moderated by other variables.

The chapters by Hawkins and Crouter and by Bartko and McHale each focus on specific aspects of the family: the husband-wife relationship and the role of children in household tasks. One of the issues analyzed by Hawkins and Crouter is how the father's participation in household tasks and childcare is affected by the mother's employment status. They deal with how the parents' ideologies can moderate the tendency for maternal employment to increase father participation. They note that it is not simply the father's resistance to move into traditionally female spheres that may be involved but also preferences and behaviors of the mother. The issue is important because the father's participation has been shown to have positive effects for children in both employed- and nonemployed-mother families as noted in Chapter 4, and in the former is particularly valuable for alleviating maternal stress and compensating for maternal nonavailability. Yet father participation that is not positively reinforced and supported by the family ideology can have adverse consequences for the marriage relationship. The concentrated focus on these mediating variables is a valuable contribution of this book.

Bartko and McHale take up an issue that has long been neglected in studies of maternal employment. Although previous work has noted that children's roles in household tasks increase when the mother is employed, this chapter takes up questions of how the children evaluate this work and how it affects their development. As already noted, this is influenced by the family ideology and the utility of the child's contribution. The authors' analysis shows that the child's participation in tasks is a link between the mother's employment status and positive outcomes for children.

Richards and Duckett examine several family variables as mediators between maternal employment and outcomes for adolescents. They report that fifth- and sixth-grade children spend less time with employed mothers but they did not spend less time with a parent. Their fathers compensated for their mothers' lack of availability. For ninth-grade children, the pattern was different. Among these older adolescents, daughters spent more time with the mother when she was employed, but for sons of employed mothers, the time spent with a parent was diminished. This difference in interaction patterns for sons and daughters is important because it is another link in explaining the long-standing observation that maternal employment seems to be either a positive influence for girls or to have no observed effects, while for boys, some negative effects have been observed.

There are four excellent chapters dealing with nonmaternal care, two that focus on preschool children (Chapters 2 and 3) and two that focus on older children and adolescents (5 an 6). The Thompson chapter provides a well-articulated review of the research on infant day care while the chapter by Galambos and Maggs fills in a major gap by dispelling the myths about "latch-key" children. The latter chapter not only reviews the recent research on children who are in self-care and presents new data, but also provides helpful suggestions for parents and lists resources for after-school care arrangements. In fact, a particular value of this volume is that each chapter concludes with practical suggestions, draws policy implications, and lists annotated references.

The chapter by Barling, Chapter 8, is different from the others in that it focuses not on mothers' employment but on fathers'; it deals with how fathers' employment affects family interaction patterns and the child's development. As in the other chapters, the research is analyzed in terms of complex patterns of interacting influences. This is particularly apparent in the discussion of the links between the father's job satisfaction and child outcomes. Barling notes, for example, that the father's job satisfaction predicts to a higher quality of interaction with the child but to less time with the child. He also notes that the impact of the father's job satisfaction on the child's behavior varies depending on how close they are: fathers' job satisfaction was related to sons' conduct disorders only when there was a close father-son relationship. Further, he points out that it is important to distinguish intrinsic job satisfaction from role conflict. This discussion has significance for the work on maternal satisfaction. A prevailing idea in the literature is that maternal satisfaction will have positive outcomes for children, but this view has been modified recently by the work of Greenberger and Goldberg (1989) which suggests that the effects of a mother's job satisfaction need to be examined in combination with her commitment to parenting. Furthermore, Gottfried points out in Chapter 4 that excessive work hours, which often accompany the most satisfying professional positions for women, may lead to a diminishment in the educational stimulation of the home environment. While we would not expect the same patterns to prevail for mothers' employment as for fathers', many ideas emerge in this chapter for new approaches to the study of maternal employment.

This book provides a comprehensive review of the research in the field and a report of new data. The results are communicated with a minimum of jargon, but they have not been overly simplified. They are described with insight and sensitivity to the complex process involved in socialization patterns. The effects of maternal employment depend on the social context, the physical setting, family structure, the accompanying ideologies and interpretations. Effects will be different depending on the nature of the job and the time and commitment involved. Outcomes for children are mediated by intervening steps, particularly by the effects on family interaction patterns and on the child's experience in nonmaternal care and how this differs from what it would be otherwise. Effects will vary with the child's gender, age, and personal qualities. By highlighting these issues, the book makes a major advance in our understanding of the meaning and significance of maternal employment. It is rich with suggestions for future research, and it provides valuable insights about the advantages and potential pitfalls of this now prevailing pattern.

Bibliography

Douvan, E., & Adelson, J. (1966). *The adolescent experience.* New York: Wiley.

Greenberger, E., & Goldberg, W. A. (1989). Work, parenting, and the socialization of children. *Developmental Psychology, 25,* 22-35.

Hoffman, L. W. (1979). Maternal employment: 1979. *American Psychologist, 34,* 859-865.

Pleck, J. H. (1983). Husbands' paid work and family roles: Current research issues. In H. Z. Lopata & J. H. Pleck (Eds.), *Research in the interweave of social roles: Families and jobs* (pp. 251-333). Greenwich, CT: JAI press.

Weinraub, M., Jaeger, E., & Hoffman, L. W. (1988). Predicting infant outcomes in families of employed and non-employed mothers. *Early Childhood Research Quarterly, 3,* 361-378.

Subject Index